Let the Word of Christ Dwell in You

Weekday Reflections
for Liturgical Year 2017/2018

MARTIN HOGAN

First published 2017 by Messenger Publications

ISBN 978 1 910248 78 2

Designed by Messenger Publications Design Department
Typeset in Times New Roman & DIN Condensed
Printed by Johnswood Press Ltd

Messenger Publications,
37 Lower Leeson Street, Dublin 2
www.messenger.ie

INTRODUCTION

This book contains a short reflection on the gospel reading for each of the weekdays of the liturgical year which begins with the first Sunday of Advent, 2017, and concludes with the feast of Christ the King, 2018. On the weekdays of any Liturgical Year, we read from a large proportion of all four gospels, with the gospels of Matthew, Mark and Luke featuring especially in Ordinary Time and the Gospel of John featuring more prominently in the seasons of Christmas, Lent and Easter.

I have always been struck by the concluding sentence of the fourth gospel, 'There are also many other things that Jesus did: if every one of them were written down, I suppose that the world itself could not contain the books that would be written' (*Jn 21:25*). The evangelist may be indulging in some hyperbole here, but, nevertheless, he is articulating his conviction that the full mystery of Jesus' identity cannot be fully expressed in any one piece of literature, not even in a gospel that is rooted in eye-witness tradition, like his own. Even the four gospels taken together do not exhaust the mystery of Jesus. There is more to Jesus than all four evangelists together have managed to express. Each evangelist gives us an inspired portrait of Jesus. We are fortunate to have these four portraits of Jesus, even if no one of them and not even all four together, fully capture the mystery of Jesus, who was the fullest revelation of God possible in human form. Yet, the gospels reveal all we need to know about Jesus for our lives of faith. They give us the portrait of Jesus that the Holy Spirit wants us to have. The Holy Spirit, working through various human agents, has given us this wonderful gift of the four gospels. We give thanks to God for all four evangelists and for the priceless legacy they have left us, under the guidance and direction of the Holy Spirit.

Just as the gospels were written under the guidance of the Spirit, we need the Holy Spirit if we are to enter deeply into the gospel text, if the word of Christ is to dwell is us richly (*Col 3:16*). In his first letter to the Corinthians, Paul declares that, 'No one comprehends what is truly God's except the Spirit of God' (*1 Cor 2:11*). As we prayerfully place ourselves before the gospel text, we invite the Spirit of God to help us truly hear the words of the gospel which are 'spirit and life' (*Jn 6:63*). The short reflections in this book express how I have come to hear the word of God as I struggled to break it open for a parish congregation during weekday Mass. I hope that in some small way they may assist others to hear this Spirit-filled word.

There is much to hear in this word of the Lord, because it is inexhaustible. Saint Ephrem, the poet-theologian of fourth century Syriac-speaking Christianity, has expressed this quality of God's word in a memorable way, 'God has fashioned his word with many beautiful forms, so that each one who studies it may consider what they like. He has hidden in his word all kinds of treasures so that each one of us, wherever we meditate, may be enriched by it. His utterance is a tree of life, which offers you blessed fruit from every side. It is like that rock which burst forth in the desert, becoming spiritual drink to everyone from all places.'

4 December, Monday, First Week of Advent

Matthew 8:5-11

The words of the centurion in today's gospel reading have made their way into our Mass in a slightly altered version, 'Sir I am not worthy to have you under my roof; just give the word and my servant will be healed'. It is strange that the words of a pagan, a representative of the occupying power in Israel at the time of Jesus, should come to be on the lips of believers during our most important liturgical gathering, the Eucharist. This centurion was no ordinary pagan. Jesus identifies him as having a faith greater than anything he had come across anywhere in Israel. What distinguishes this man's faith was his tremendous trust in Jesus' word, 'Say but the word...'. He didn't need to meet Jesus face-to-face; he didn't require Jesus to come to his house. It was enough for Jesus to speak at a distance, and he believed that his servant's situation would change for the better. In that sense, this centurion is a good Advent figure. Advent is a time when we try to attend to the Lord's word more fully, allowing it to enter our hearts and release its life-giving power there. During this season, we are invited to entrust ourselves to the Lord's word, like the centurion in today's gospel reading. In the words of Saint Paul, it is a time when we allow the Lord's word to dwell in us richly.

5 December, Tuesday, First Week of Advent

Luke 10:21-24

In the gospel reading, Jesus makes a distinction between 'the learned and the clever' and 'mere children'. It is children, those considered uneducated, who are open to Jesus' revelation of the unique relationship between himself and God the Father, whereas the learned and clever are closed to it. Most of Jesus' disciples would not have been regarded as among the learned and the clever, and yet, Jesus says to them, 'happy the eyes that see what you see'. They have come to see what Jesus came to show us; they have come to recognise the intimate relationship of knowledge and love between Jesus and God his Father. It does not mean that learning and study are always a barrier to a relationship with God. Faith will always seek understanding; it will always question and even doubt. Yet, in the end, faith needs to go beyond understanding into a realm where understanding falters and where we need to surrender to the mystery of God in Jesus. Jesus is suggesting that such a surrender often comes easier to children than to the learned and the clever. This links with another saying of Jesus in the gospels, 'Unless you become like little children, you will not enter the kingdom of God'. When it comes to God and the things of God, our intellect and our learning can only bring us so far. There comes a point when we need to allow ourselves to be drawn into the deeper mystery of God, by the Holy Spirit, the Spirit of wisdom and insight spoken of in the first reading.

6 December, Wednesday, First Week of Advent
Matthew 15:29-37

There are two questions asked in today's gospel reading. One is asked by the disciples and the other is asked by Jesus. The question that the disciples ask – 'Where could we get enough bread in this deserted place to feed such a crowd?' – is a somewhat despairing question, or, at least, a defeatist question. It is a question that does not really have any hope of an answer. The question that Jesus asks – 'How many loaves have you?' – is a much more focused question. It is a question that already points people in the direction of a solution to the problem they were facing, the problem of how to feed a large crowd in a deserted place. Jesus' question called forth those seemingly insignificant human resources among the crowd, seven loaves and a few fish, that he could nevertheless work with in a very powerful way. Today's gospel assures us that Jesus can work powerfully through the little that we possess. If he is to do that, however, we may need to ask the right kinds of questions, not the kinds of questions that leave people feeling that nothing can be done, which was the kind of question the disciples asked. We need to ask hopeful questions, of the kind Jesus asked, questions that encourage us to look at what we actually have been given, and to trust that the Lord can accomplish far more with those resources that we might imagine.

7 December, Thursday, First Week of Advent
Matthew 7:21, 24-27

The weather is a great topic of conversation in Ireland. Maybe that is because it changes so frequently. There is always something to say about it. We are very familiar with the weather referred to in today's gospel reading: rain, floods and gales. Such weather was less common in Palestine, the land of Jesus. Yet, occasionally in the winter months people had to contend with rain, floods and gales. It was probably tempting for builders in that climate just to build for the better weather that was the norm. However, the really wise builder built with a view to the worst case scenario, even though it may not arise very often. That meant paying more attention to the foundations of a house than might have seemed necessary. Jesus draws a lesson from this scenario for our own lives. Our lives can be going along fine for a period of time and then some severe storm hits us unexpectedly. We find ourselves in a kind of a whirlwind that throws everything out of kilter. Jesus is saying in the gospel reading that we need to prepare for that scenario. Our lives need the kind of foundation that will enable us to survive such traumatic experiences. Jesus offers himself as that foundation. If we listen to his words and try to live them every day of our lives, we will be putting down a foundation that will stand to us when the storms come. We don't wait for the storm to come to start looking for a foundation. The laying of a foundation that gives us something of God's own strength is something we do every day, little by little, by opening our lives to the Lord's word and allowing it to shape who we are and all that we say and do.

8 December, Friday, Solemnity of the Immaculate Conception

Luke 1:26-38

Gerard Manley Hopkins, in his poem, 'The Blessed Virgin compared to the Air we Breathe', concludes with a prayer to Mary, 'Be thou then, O thou dear | Mother, my atmosphere; | My happier world, wherein | To wend and meet no sin'. Today's feast celebrates Mary as that happier world wherein we meet no sin. She was untouched by that sin of Adam referred to at the beginning of today's first reading. Since Adam rebelled against God's will for his life, he was uncomfortable in God's presence. He hid from God and God had to call out to him, 'Where are you?' Mary had no reason to hide from God because she was always open to doing God's will. She lived her life in the light of God's presence. She was, in that sense, full of God. It was because Mary was so full of God from the first moment of her conception that she could respond to God's call to her through the angel Gabriel with the words, 'Let what you have said be done to me'.

We don't often speak of Mary as Saint Mary. We have other ways of referring to her. Yet, today's feast celebrates Mary's sainthood, her sanctity. We consider her the greatest of all the saints because we believe that she was holy from the first moment of her conception. No more than any of the other saints, Mary was not removed from the struggles and sufferings of the human condition. Something of her struggle comes through in today's gospel reading. She was initially deeply disturbed by the words of the angel Gabriel. She was full of questions in response to Gabriel's good news, 'How can this come about?' Luke goes on to tell us in his gospel that Simeon announced to her that a sword would pierce her soul. She stood at the foot of the cross suffering the agony of watching her only Son die a slow and painful death. It was in the midst of all the struggles and pains of life that she lived out her 'yes' to God's will for her life. Mary's holiness from her conception does not remove her from us. She is our companion on our pilgrim journey. She is given to us as a perpetual help. That is why we ask her to pray for us 'sinners' now and at the hour of our death.

9 December, Saturday, First Week of Advent

Matthew 9:35-10.1, 6-8

Today's gospel reading refers to those who are 'harassed and dejected' and 'lost'. Jesus noticed that the crowds were 'harassed and dejected, like sheep without a shepherd', and he sends his disciples to bring his compassionate presence to the 'lost sheep of the House of Israel'. Jesus had a special sensitivity to those who were spiritually dejected and lost. He wanted them to have an experience of God as a caring, compassionate shepherd. This was at the heart of Jesus' proclaiming the good news that the kingdom of heaven is close at hand. Jesus was announcing, and he wanted his disciples to announce in his name, that God was present in a strikingly new way as the compassionate Shepherd to all who were in need of his life-giving presence. This is also the message of today's first reading. Isaiah declares that God 'will be gracious to you when he hears your cry'. We can all count ourselves among the harassed, dejected and lost from time to time. The days and weeks leading up to Christmas can leave some people feeling more harassed and dejected than usual. Advent is a time when we are invited to prayerfully open ourselves to the daily coming of the Lord as compassionate shepherd. The Lord wants to give to us without any charge. In the words of the gospel reading, 'You received without charge'. As we receive from the Lord, we are then sent out, like the twelve, to give without charge, to be channels of the Lord's compassionate presence to all those we encounter in these Advent days.

11 December, Monday, Second Week of Advent

Luke 5:17-26

Jesus exercised a unique authority during his public ministry. One expression of that authority was when he cleansed the Temple of those who sold animals for sacrifice and exchanged coins for the Temple currency, all within the Temple precinct. Another expression of his unique authority is found in today's gospel reading. When he is brought face-to-face with a paralysed man, Jesus speaks as the Son of Man who has authority on earth to forgive sins. This was a very striking claim because it was understood that only God could forgive sins and there were various Temple rituals and sacrifices to gain God's forgiveness for the sins of the people. It is not surprising that it scandalised the religious experts of the day, the Pharisees. 'Why is this man talking blasphemy?' they asked. Yet, as Pope Francis never tires of saying, Jesus is the face of God's mercy. The now glorious Son of Man, the Risen Lord, continues to make present God's mercy to all who seek it in faith. It is striking that nothing is said of the paralytic's faith in the gospel reading. It was the faith of his friends that Jesus saw - 'seeing *their* faith'. It was the faith of the little group around the paralytic that opened him up to an experience of God's healing and merciful love in Jesus. Our own faith can continue to do the same for others today. By each of us seeking the Lord in faith we can lead others to encounter the face of God's mercy in Jesus.

12 December, Tuesday, Second Week of Advent
Matthew 18:12-14

The same parable can serve different purposes in different gospels. In Luke's gospel the parable of the lost sheep is joined to the parable of the lost coin and the lost son or sons. The image of the searching shepherd, the searching woman and searching father reveal the searching heart of Jesus' own ministry. He came to seek out and to save the lost. He thereby revealed God's searching love which seeks out those who have strayed. The parable of the lost sheep we have just heard is taken from Matthew's gospel. In Matthew, the parable is part of a long discourse of Jesus on life in the community of the church. In that chapter, there is an emphasis on the community's responsibility to care for 'the little ones'. The reference here may be to those whose faith is weak or vulnerable, or to those who are not highly regarded by the standards of the age. Immediately before the parable of the lost sheep in Matthew, Jesus issues a strong warning to those who would put a stumbling block before these little ones, who would scandalise them. The parable of the lost sheep, in contrast, calls on the members of the community to seek out the little ones, as a shepherd seeks for his one lost sheep out of a flock of one hundred. In that context, the parable of the lost sheep can be heard as a call to take seriously our responsibility to bring each other to the Lord. We can undermine the faith of others, becoming a stumbling block to them. We can also restore or nurture the faith of others, becoming a devoted shepherd to them. Indeed, this role is an important dimension of our baptismal calling.

13 December, Wednesday, Second Week of Advent
Matthew 11:28-30
The first reading declares that 'young men may grow tired and weary'. We know from experience that it is not only young men who can grow tired and weary. We can all grow tired and weary. Tiredness and weariness comes to us all from time to time. Indeed, in the words of the gospel reading, we can find ourselves labouring and feeling overburdened. The run-up to Christmas can have that effect on people. Other, more traumatic experiences in life can leave us feeling tired and weary, labouring and overburdened. That first reading also declares that the Lord 'does not grow tired or weary'. Because he does not grow tired or weary, he calls out to those who are tired and weary, inviting them to come to him, and promising them rest. The Lord can be our strength when we are weak, our rest when we are tired, our support when we are burdened. The great Advent prayer is our invitation, 'Come, Lord, Jesus'. However, in the gospel reading, it is the Lord who invites us to come. His call to us is prior to our

prayer to him. When in responding to that call of the Lord we experience him as our strength, our rest, our support, we, in turn, can be a source of strength, rest and support to each other. The strength we receive from the Lord is for others as well as for ourselves.

14 December, Thursday, Second Week of Advent
Matthew 11:11-15

John the Baptist is a great Advent saint. He features more prominently in Advent than in any other season of the church's year. In today's gospel reading Jesus speaks about John in glowing terms. A greater than John the Baptist has never been born; it is towards him that all the prophecies were leading; he is the prophet Elijah whose return was expected ahead of the coming of the Messiah. Yet, in that same gospel reading, Jesus makes the extraordinary statement that the least in the kingdom of heaven is greater than John the Baptist. John announced the coming of Jesus, but he didn't live to see the death and resurrection of Jesus, the coming of the Holy Spirit, the birth of the church. To that extent we are all more blessed than John the Baptist was. We have tasted the good fruit of Jesus' death and resurrection. The Holy Spirit has been poured into our hearts. Through our baptism, we are members of Christ's body, the church. We are greater than John, not because we have done more than John or are living better lives than he lived, but because we have been more greatly blessed than John. As Jesus says elsewhere in the gospels, 'Blessed are the eyes that see what you see and the ears that hear what you hear'. With that greater blessing goes a great calling. We can never take for granted the ways we have been blessed. We need to keep growing in our appreciation of what we have been given and to keep responding to the call to give generously to others out of what we have received from the Lord.

15 December, Friday, Second Week of Advent

Matthew 11:16-19

Weddings and funerals are very much part of what goes on in every church. There is obviously a great difference between the mood of a wedding and the mood of a funeral. In today's gospel reading, Jesus associates the mood of John the Baptist's ministry with that of a funeral and the mood of his own ministry with that of a wedding. He criticises his contemporaries for rejecting both the ministry of John the Baptist and that of Jesus. They reject John the Baptist as being too sorrowful and severe, 'He is possessed'. They reject Jesus as being too joyful and lax, 'Look, a glutton and a drunkard, a friend of tax collectors and sinners'. Jesus compares his contemporaries to truculent children in the market place who refuse to join in other children's games, whether it is the game of funerals or the game of weddings. These children, like Jesus' contemporaries, will neither dance or be mourners. It is striking that Jesus identifies his ministry with the joy of a wedding feast and with the dance that is inspired by the playing of flutes. Jesus' ministry was good news; it celebrated the presence of the compassionate mercy of God. This was certainly good news for 'tax collectors and sinners', and for all who felt that God had cast them aside. Jesus' ministry remains good news for us today. He continues to make present to us the compassionate mercy of God. He calls us to join in this celebration of God's merciful love for sinners, to dance with joy to the music of the kingdom of God.

16 December, Saturday, Second Week of Advent

Matthew 17:10-13

In the weeks prior to the feast of Christmas John the Baptist features prominently. In today's gospel reading, Jesus refers to John the Baptist without mentioning him by name. The disciples ask Jesus about the Jewish tradition that the prophet Elijah will come before the coming of God's anointed one. This tradition is based on a text in the prophet Malachi, 'I am sending my messenger to prepare the way before me… I will send you the prophet Elijah before the great and terrible day of the Lord comes'. In the gospel reading Jesus declares that Elijah has already come and they treated him as they pleased, which is a clear reference to the recent execution of John the Baptist. Jesus sees in what happened to John a sign of what will happen to him, 'the Son of Man will suffer similarly at their hands'. We are about to celebrate the birth of Jesus and prior to that we will read the gospel about the birth of John the Baptist. However, today's gospel reading refers to the death of both John the Baptist and Jesus. We are being reminded that we cannot separate the birth of John and Jesus from their death. The cross casts its shadow over the crib of Bethlehem. When we look at the baby in the crib, we cannot but call to mind the good shepherd who laid down his life for his flock, the Son of Man who came not to be served but to serve and to give his life for all. It is that same self-giving love of Jesus that we celebrate at every Eucharist. As Paul reminds us, as often as we eat this bread and drink this cup we proclaim the Lord's death. We are sent from the Eucharist to live what we have proclaimed, to give what we have received.

18 December, Monday, Third Week of Advent

Matthew 1:18-24

In today's gospel reading we find Joseph struggling to do the right thing, what he believed God wanted of him. Mary's unexplained pregnancy left him in a very difficult situation. Presuming that her pregnancy indicated she had been unfaithful to him, Joseph found himself torn between what he understood God's law required him to do, viz. divorce Mary, and his own affectionate feelings for her. In this confusing situation, the gospel reading tells us that Joseph received guidance from the Lord, which he promptly followed. The complex situation in which Joseph found himself is not unlike the kind of situations in which many of us find ourselves from time to time. In so many of life's situations the best way forward is not always immediately clear. Like Joseph in the gospel reading, we can find ourselves torn between what our head is telling us and what our heart is saying to us. The gospel reading today invites us to have something of the openness of Joseph to the Lord's guidance. Joseph received the Lord's guidance through an angel. The Lord's guidance will often come to us through more ordinary means, such as through those in whom we confide. Their perspective on the situation we are struggling with can often bring a new and a fresh light. We can also experience the Lord's guidance through prayer. In prayer we allow the Lord to enlighten our minds and hearts so that we can move forward in the light that he provides.

19 December, Tuesday, Third Week of Advent

Luke 1:5-25

In today's gospel reading, Zechariah hears good news from the God's messenger, the angel Gabriel. His prayers of many years have been heard. His wife Elizabeth is to bear him a son, who will be named John. Yet, Zechariah cannot bring himself to believe this good news. 'How can I be sure of this?' he asks disbelievingly. As a result of his failure to hear the good news that God proclaimed to him, he was struck dumb. Perhaps we are being reminded that there is often a relationship between how well we hear and how well we speak. Zechariah's failure to really listen to what Gabriel was saying to him impacted on his ability to communicate with others. In our own interaction with each other, we often need to listen attentively before we speak. Good speaking often requires good listening. If someone has something to say to us, something they want to share with us, we need to listen carefully to what is being said, if the words we speak in response are to be helpful to that person. Today's gospel suggests that listening to the Lord is even more important than listening to each other. We need to listen especially to the Lord's good news, to the gospel of God's gracious love for us, God's great favour towards us. This was the message Zechariah failed to hear. If we really listen to the gospel, and allow the Lord's good news to enter us, our speaking will be somehow shaped by that good news. Our words, indeed our presence, will be good news for others.

20 December, Wednesday, Third Week of Advent

Luke 1:26-38

We can all find ourselves in situations that can seem beyond us. We wonder how we will be able to rise to what is being asked of us. We sense our own helplessness before the situation that is unfolding before us. We find something similar happening in Luke's depiction of Mary in today's gospel reading. The angel Gabriel had brought extraordinary news to this young woman of Nazareth, 'You are to conceive and bear a son, and you must name him Jesus'. Overwhelmed by the enormity of this announcement she asks, 'But how can this come about, since I am a virgin?' In response to her question, Gabriel assures her that this conception will be the work of the Holy Spirit, 'the Holy Spirit will come upon you and the power of the Most High will cover you with its shadow'. What seemed impossible to her is possible to God. It was in response to that reassurance that Mary surrendered to God's purpose for her life, 'Let what you have said be done to me'. The same Holy Spirit that came upon Mary has come upon us all. The Spirit is given to us all to help us in our weakness. When the call of life seems too much for us, the Spirit is our resource to help us to keep going. What seems impossible to us left to our own devices can become possible with the help of the Holy Spirit, 'for nothing is impossible to God'. The Lord can work powerfully in and through us with the help which he alone can give us.

21 December, Thursday, Third Week of Advent

Luke 1:39-45

In today's gospel reading we hear of the meeting between two women, Mary and Elizabeth. It is also the meeting between two infants, Jesus and John the Baptist, whom Mary and Elizabeth were carrying in their wombs. The child in Elizabeth's womb is described as leaping for joy at the greeting of Mary, because in some mysterious way, John, although still unborn, sensed the presence of Jesus in the womb of Mary. We are given a picture of John the Baptist as someone who is extremely sensitive to the presence of Jesus even as both John and Jesus were still in their mother's wombs. John the Baptist has something to teach us about the art of being sensitive to the presence of the Lord. Like the two disciples on the road to Emmaus we can often fail to recognise the Lord even though he is close to us. We can be so absorbed in our own experience, as those two disciples were, that we fail to see the Lord, fail to notice his presence. As we become more sensitive to the Lord's presence to us, we can help others to notice what we have noticed. In the gospel reading, the reaction of Elizabeth's child in her womb enabled Elizabeth to recognise Mary as 'the mother of my Lord'. Through her unborn child, Elizabeth came to see that Mary's visit was also the visit of the Lord. Advent and Christmas is a time when we help each other to become more aware of and alert to the presence of the Lord among us, especially in and through each other.

22 December, Friday, Third Week of Advent

Luke 1:46-56

Today's gospel reading consists of one of the great prayers of the gospels. It has been prayed by believers since Luke's gospel was written towards the end of the first century. It is an integral part of the evening prayer of the church, which is prayed every evening throughout the universal church. Yet, this prayer is a very Jewish prayer. The first reading today is the story of Hannah who brought her new born child Samuel to the Temple to present him to the Lord. The prayer she went on to pray to God points ahead in many ways to the prayer of Mary. Both women praise God for the birth of their child and recognise in what has happened to them a pattern to which God has always worked. Hannah sings of a God who raises up the poor from the dust and lifts the needy from the ash heap, just as Mary sings of a God who has exalted the lowly and filled the hungry with good things. Hannah saw herself as one of the poor and needy whom God raises up and Mary saw herself as one of those lowly and hungry whom God has filled. Both women have a rich insight into the God of Israel as one whose power is made perfect in weakness, in the words of Saint Paul. The God of whom they sing has been fully revealed in Jesus, Immanuel, God with us. He announced that he was sent to bring good news to the poor and to bring release to captives. The God of whom Mary sings and who comes to us through Mary's child invites us to approach him in our poverty, aware of our hunger for him, conscious of the ways we are captive and stand in need of his release.

23 December, Saturday, Third Week of Advent

Luke 1:57-66

Two days before we celebrate the birth of Jesus to Mary and Joseph, we read the gospel of the birth of John the Baptist to Elizabeth and Zechariah. Just as eight days after his birth Jesus was circumcised and formally named in accordance with the Jewish Law, so too John the Baptist was circumcised and formally named eight days after his birth. There was an element of controversy around the naming of Elizabeth and Zechariah's child, according to our gospel reading. The relatives and neighbours wanted convention to be followed by having the child named after his father, Zechariah. Elizabeth had a struggle on her hands to break with this strong convention, knowing that God wanted her child to be called John. It was Zechariah who decided the issue, by writing out the name John on a writing-tablet. This was a moment when convention had to give way to something new. God was ushering in a new age. With the birth of Jesus, and of John his precursor, it could no longer be business as usual. New wine would call for new wineskins. The Risen Lord's way of working among us often requires us to have the freedom to break with hallowed conventions. What Saint Paul calls the glorious freedom of the children of God is the freedom to go where the Lord seems to be leading us, even when that means heading into somewhat unfamiliar territory.

26 December, Tuesday, Saint Stephen

Matthew 10:17-22

In day to day living birth and death often occur side by side. The liturgy of the church reflects that reality. Yesterday we celebrated a birth, the birth of Jesus. Today, we celebrate a death, the death of Stephen, the first Christian martyr. It comes natural to us to celebrate the birth of new life, but we might ask, 'Why celebrate a death?' In celebrating someone's death, we are celebrating their life. Many of the funerals in our church are celebrations of life, celebrations of the person's earthly life and of the new life that awaits them beyond death. In celebrating Stephen's death, we are celebrating his life, the kind of person he was. The first reading makes reference to his wisdom and to his being filled with the Holy Spirit. The way Stephen died was in keeping with how he lived; in death he revealed the kind of person he was. He died full of faith and full of love. He was full of faith in the Risen Lord as revealed in his prayer, 'Lord Jesus, receive my spirit'. He was full of love, even towards his enemies, as shown by his second prayer, 'Lord, do not hold this sin against them'. Those words show Stephen to be a merciful person. He forgave his enemies and asked the Lord to forgive them. He models for us that generosity of heart which stands ready to forgive even those who do us harm. There is another character in that reading, Saul of Tarsus. It is said that those who witnessed

Stephen's stoning placed their clothes at Saul's feet and that Saul entirely approved of Stephen's killing. Saul, it seems, showed no mercy to Stephen. Yet, Saul or Paul went on to receive mercy from God. On his way from Jerusalem to Damascus, God revealed his Son to him. Paul understood this experience as a moment of extraordinary grace. As a result of this grace the zealous Pharisee and persecutor of the church became the great apostle of the Risen Lord to the Gentiles. He would go on to say in one of his letters, God's 'grace towards me has not been in vain'. If Stephen inspires us to be merciful, as Jesus was, r Paul encourages us to be open to receive the Lord's mercy. Paul's story reminds us that the wrong we have done is never a block to the Lord's gift of mercy, if only we are open to receive it.

27 December, Wednesday, Saint John, Apostle and Evangelist
John 20:2-8
Within the Christian tradition, we have always valued the four gospels above all other Christian literature. That is why we stand for the gospel reading, why we introduce it with the singing of the Alleluia, and why, during solemn Masses, we incense the Lectionary or Book of the Gospels. We sense that the Lord is present to us in a privileged way in and through the four gospels. Today we celebrate the feast of the writer of the last gospel to be written, the fourth gospel. This fourth evangelist has been traditionally identified with John, one of the Lord's closest disciples. There is a glorious quality to the portrait of Jesus in this gospel. It is as if he is transfigured on every page of this gospel, and not just in one scene as in the other three gospels. It is appropriate then that the gospel reading for the feast of this evangelist is an Easter gospel. It refers to three disciples, Mary of Magdala, Peter, and the disciple Jesus loved. This last disciple is not named but he has been identified with the disciple John in the Christian tradition. At the very end of the gospel reading, it is said of him that 'he saw and believed'. He alone believed that Jesus had risen, simply on the

evidence of the empty tomb. He saw more deeply than the other disciples. The fourth gospel that he inspired helps us to see more deeply too. In the opening chapter of his gospel, this evangelist wrote, 'the Word became flesh and dwelt among us'. He encourages us to see beneath the surface of things, to recognise the presence of the Word in the flesh of life. His gospel teaches us that the fabric of life can speak to us of the Lord. Light, water, bread, vines, gates, shepherds, paths, and so much else, can be a revelation of God if we can see them with the eyes of faith and love, with the eyes of the beloved disciple.

28 December, Thursday, Feast of the Holy Innocents

Matthew 2:13-18

There is a strong contrast in the gospel reading between God's efforts to preserve the life of Joseph and Mary's child and Herod's efforts to kill their child. The angel of the Lord prompts Mary and Joseph to flee into Egypt for their child's protection. Herod orders all the male children under two to be killed in the Bethlehem area to ensure the death of Joseph and Mary's child. God is always at work in our world to preserve and enhance life in its various forms, especially life at its most vulnerable. We tend to be at our most vulnerable at the beginning of our lives, in our mother's womb and in the first months of life, and also at the end of our lives when we often have to deal with sickness in one shape or form. The gospel reading today suggests that there are other forces in our world that, like Herod, work to eliminate life, especially when it is at its most vulnerable. Our calling from God, our mission in life, is to keep aligning ourselves with God's life giving work. The feast of the Holy Innocents reminds us that far too many innocent lives have been and, indeed, are being slaughtered. The sobbing and loud lamenting at the loss of innocent life that is referred to at the end of the gospel reading is all too familiar to our ears today. Yet the forces for life that have been released into the world through the life, death and resurrection of Jesus remain stronger than the forces of death. As baptised believers, we can each make those forces for life, that Spirit of life, tangible and visible in the way we live and relate to others.

29 December, Friday, Fifth Day in the Octave of Christmas
Luke 2:22-35

The prayer of Simeon in today's gospel reading has become part of the night prayer of the church, 'Now, Master, you can let your servant go in peace…'. It is the prayer of a man of faith who is ready to leave this world because his deepest longing has been fulfilled. He has finally set his eyes on the one for whom he had been waiting, the one whom God in the Jewish Scriptures promised to send as the light of the nations and the glory of Israel. It is the prayer of a truly contented person. This level of contentment is one that we might tend to associate with the life of heaven. We look forward to that eternal moment when we will see God face-to-face and all our deepest longings are satisfied. Today's gospel reading suggests that Simeon anticipated this heavenly quality of contentment in the Temple of Jerusalem as he held the child Jesus in his arms. 'My eyes have seen your salvation'. Here was a seeing that came close to that seeing of God face-to-face which awaits us in eternity. We will never have the opportunity of holding the child Jesus in our arms, but on our journey of faith there can be moments when we too see the Lord clearly with the eyes of faith. At such moments, fleeting as they may be, we sense that the deepest hunger and thirst of our heart is being satisfied. We cannot produce these moments. They come to us as a gift from the Lord. It is said of Simeon in that gospel reading that he came to the Temple at the prompting of the Spirit. The Spirit will lead us too to such moments of grace if we are as open to the prompting of the Holy Spirit as Simeon was.

30 December, Saturday, Sixth Day in the Octave of Christmas
Luke 2:36-40

According to Luke's gospel, when Mary and Joseph brought Jesus to the Temple in Jerusalem to present him to God, there were two people there who were advanced in years, a man and a woman, Simeon and Anna. It is Anna who features in today's gospel reading. She was eighty four years old and had been a widow most of her life, as she was only seven years married when her husband died. It is said of her that 'she never left the Temple, serving God night and day with fasting and prayer'. The house of God was her home; she seems to have lived there. Our parish church is our spiritual home; it is a place where we can spend time with the Lord, where we can be at home with the Lord and with each other, where we can linger in the Lord's presence. I am struck by the phrase that Anna was serving God night and day with fasting and prayer. When we think of serving God, some form of active service tends to come to mind first. We serve God by serving each other, especially the most vulnerable among us. Yet, Anna served God in another way, by fasting and prayer. We may not always think of prayer as a service of God. Yet, we are serving God when we pray. In prayer we give ourselves to God, our time, our attention, our heart and mind. We are serving God when we pray, and the fasting that is mentioned in connection with Anna can help us to enter more deeply into prayer. Anna's service of God in prayer did not remove her from others. On the contrary, the gospel reading tells us that she spoke of the child, Jesus, to all who looked forward to the deliverance of Jerusalem. Her prayer enabled her to recognise the child of Mary and Joseph as the one Israel had been waiting for, and her prayer inspired her to tell others about this child. For us too, whenever we serve God in genuine prayer, it will always flow over into the service of others, the service of God in others.

1 January, Monday, Mary, the Holy Mother of God

Luke 2:16-21

We have been celebrating the feast of Christmas and our focus has been on the child Jesus. Today's feast places the focus on the mother of the child, Mary. We celebrate Mary as the Mother of God because we believe that her child, Jesus, was God in human form. The title 'Mother of God' affirms something very important about Mary's child. This was, indeed, a fully human child in every sense, with all the same needs and vulnerability as any child. Yet, this particular child revealed God to us in a way no other child before or since has done. In looking upon the face of this child, we are looking upon the face of God. There is a mystery here which is not possible to fully fathom with the use of human reason alone. There is a great deal to be reflected upon here and, ultimately, surrendered to. Today's gospel reading presents Mary as doing just that. In response to the story that the shepherds had to tell, we are told that Mary 'treasured all these things and pondered them in her heart'. She treasured and pondered the announcement of the angels to the shepherds, 'to you is born this day, in the city of David, a Saviour who is Christ, the Lord'. 'Saviour', 'Christ', 'Lord' – these are very striking titles for her new-born child. There is indeed a great deal here to be treasured and pondered, not just for Mary but for all of us, because Mary's child was born 'to you', to each one of us. Our faith, and the content of our faith, is ultimately a gift from God, but it is a gift to be treasured and pondered. We spend our lives treasuring and plumbing the depths of God's gift of his Son to us and of God's relationship with us through his Son, in the Spirit. Mary's contemplative attitude before God's mysterious gift is a model for us all. As we begin this new year today, we pray that during the coming twelve months we might grow in our appreciation of the way God 'has blessed us in Christ with every spiritual blessing', in the words of Paul's letter to the Ephesians.

2 January, Tuesday before Epiphany

John 1:19-28

In today's gospel reading, John the Baptist is asked one of the really important questions of life, 'Who are you?' We can spend most of our lives trying to answer the question, 'Who am I?' It is not a question that lends itself to a quick and easy answer, because it is a probing question that enquires after what our values are, what is really important to us, what shapes how we live, what are gifts and limitations are. There is a sense in which we never fully answer the question, 'Who are you?' An important step in knowing ourselves is knowing who we are not, so that we don't try to be someone we are not. John the Baptist comes across in the gospel reading today as knowing who he is not. He is not the Messiah, he is not Elijah, and he is not the prophet. He might have liked to be all of these people, but he knew in his heart of hearts he wasn't. He does not claim to be someone he is not. He not only knows who he is not, he knows who he is. He is the voice crying in the wilderness calling on people to make a way for the Lord's coming. He is the witness, the person who points to Jesus and leads others to him. In a very real sense, he is what we are all called to be. John the Baptist embodies our baptismal identity. Even though we might have difficulty fully answering the question, 'Who am I?', as followers of Jesus, we can all give the answer, 'I am a witness'. That is our calling, to be the voice that leads others to the Word who became flesh and lives among us.

3 January, Wednesday before Epiphany

John 1:29-34

A section of today's first reading is often read at a funeral Mass. It contains one of the many different ways that the New Testament speaks about eternal life, 'we shall be like him (God) because we shall see him as he really is'. This verse speaks of a vision of God which is truly transformative, changing us more fully into the image of God, 'we shall be like him'. Elsewhere in this letter, the author says 'God is love'. The letter as a whole suggests that to see God as he really is amounts to seeing God as Love, and this seeing, this experience of God as Love, makes us more like God, more loving. Our ultimate destiny is to become the image of God who is Love. We cannot see God as he really is in this earthly life. Yet, God has sent us his Son as the fullest expression of his love in human form. We can look upon God's Son with the eyes of faith in this life. Yet we need people to reveal Jesus to us if we are to look upon him. That was the role of John the Baptist. He says in the gospel reading that it was to reveal him to Israel that he came baptizing with water. He witnessed to Jesus as the Chosen One of God. We continue to need John the Baptist figures today, people who can reveal Jesus to us, who can witness to him for us, so that we can look upon Jesus, the Risen Lord with the eyes of faith. The Lord needs each one of us to be a John the Baptist for each other, so that we can all see the Lord as God's love made flesh, and, thereby, anticipate that final and full seeing of God who is Love in eternity.

4 January, Thursday before Epiphany
John 1:35-42

We might be able to think of people in our lives who pointed us in a direction that proved to be very significant for us. At a certain moment in our lives they spoke a word to us or opened up some avenue for us that had an enormous impact for good on us. We may even have been that person for others, without our always being aware of it. Sometimes we only discover much later that something we said or did made a huge difference for the better to someone. Today's gospel reading suggests that John the Baptist was that kind of significant person for others. John the Baptist was so striking a person that other people came to him and some became his followers. Yet, in today's gospel reading we find John directing his own followers towards Jesus. The words he spoke to them, 'Look, there is the Lamb of God' would have a profound impact on their lives. Because of what John said, some of his own disciples became disciples of Jesus and their lives would be changed forever because of this. There was a great generosity of spirit in John. He didn't try to hold on to his followers; he was prepared to direct them towards someone greater than himself. He is a wonderful example of a non-possessive, self-emptying love for others. It is the kind of love we are all called to, a love that works for the good of the other, a love that is ready to point others in a direction that is good for them, even when that entails a painful loss for ourselves.

5 January, Friday before Epiphany

John 1:43-51

Nathanael is one of those intriguing characters in the gospels. He only appears in the gospel of John. When Philip bears witness to Jesus of Nazareth before Nathanael, he dismisses Philip's witness, 'Can anything good come from that place?' In the last chapter of John's gospel, we are told that Nathanael was from Cana, which wasn't very far from Nazareth. Perhaps people in Cana had a rather dusty opinion of people from Nazareth. Nathanael's starting point with regard to Jesus was one of extreme scepticism. Some of us may have found ourselves in that sceptical place on our faith journey, at least for a time. Like Nathanael, we were inclined to pour cold water on other people's faith. Yet, Nathanael did not stay in that place; he moved on from there. It was Philip who helped him to move on. Philip wasn't put off by Nathanael's initial scepticism; he stood his ground and called out to Nathanael, 'Come and see'. We are living in a sceptical age and the scepticism of others can be a real test of our own faith. Like Philip, we need to stand our ground so that our lives of faith become an invitation to others, 'Come and see'. The Lord did not think any the less of Nathanael because of his initial sceptical attitude. When he saw Nathanael coming to him he said, 'Here is an Israelite who deserves the name incapable of deceit'. The Lord saw the good in Nathanael, the openness in him to faith. The Lord is not put off by our own slowness to respond to his call. He continues to work in our lives, very often through others. Nathanael went on to justify Jesus' belief in him by making a great confession of faith, 'Rabbi, you are the Son of God, you are the King of Israel'. Scepticism can be the prelude to deep faith. Indeed, Jesus told Nathanael that he would come to see even greater things; he would grow even further in his faith. No matter where we are on our faith journey, there is always room for growth, there is always more to see, more the Lord wants to show us.

6 January, Saturday, The Epiphany of the Lord
Matthew 2:1-12
The wise men are depicted in the gospel of Matthew as seekers. Even though they were not Jewish, they set out on a search for the infant king of the Jews in response to the movement of a star in the heavens. The wise men speak to the searcher, the seeker, within each one of us. The adult Jesus would go on to say, 'Seek and you will find'. Although we have encountered the Lord for ourselves, we are all seeking him nonetheless. We remain seekers until the day comes when we will see the Lord face-to-face in eternity. In our search for him, the Lord will find ways of drawing us to himself, just as the three wise men were drawn to the child Jesus by a star. The Lord draws us to himself through his Word, through the Sacraments, especially the Eucharist, through each other, and through the natural world in all its wonder and beauty. We are not alone in our search; we are searching with others and the Lord himself is searching for us and drawing us to himself.

According to the gospel reading, when the wise men found the child for whom they had been seeking, the first thing they did was to worship him. We gather today on the feast of the Epiphany to worship the

Risen Lord. Our seeking the Lord will always be punctuated by times of worship, whether it is the church's official worship, like the Eucharist, or our own personal worship, our own moments of prayer. It is in times of worship that we seek the Lord most intently. In worship our focus is on the Lord; we surrender ourselves to him and acknowledge him as Lord of our lives. Having worshipped the child Jesus, the wise men offered him their gifts. We too offer the Lord our gifts and the most precious gift we can offer him is the gift of our lives. Saint Paul in his letter to the Romans calls on the church in Rome to 'present your bodies as a living sacrifice, holy and acceptable to God, which is your spiritual worship'. The offering of our lives to God ensures that our whole lives are, in a sense, an act of worship. We offer ourselves to the Lord, by placing ourselves, our gifts, at his disposal, by leaving ourselves open to whatever the Lord may be asking of us.

The gospel reading declares that after the wise men had offered the child Jesus their worship and their gifts they returned to their own country by a different way. As we seek the Lord, as we worship him and offer him our lives, the Lord will often prompt us to go on by a different way. Our own way never fully corresponds to the Lord's way. Throughout our lives, we hear the call to take a different way, a way that conforms more fully to the Lord's way. This is the call to a continuing turning towards the Lord and his way. The more we seek the Lord, the more we worship him and offer him our lives, the more we will hear that call of the Lord to take a different way.

8 January, Monday, First Week in Ordinary Time

Mark 1:14-20

The Lord's call most often comes to us in the context of our daily lives. That was certainly the case for Simon, Andrew, James and John in today's gospel reading. They were engaged in their daily tasks as fishermen when Jesus called them to follow him. Simon and Andrew were casting a net in the sea of Galilee. James and John were in their boat, mending their nets. This was the stuff of their daily lives. When the Lord's call came to them in the midst of their daily tasks, it resulted in their taking a completely new direction. They left the business of catching and selling fish and became fishers of people. Jesus would henceforth work through them to gather people into the nets of God's kingdom. When the Lord's call comes to us in and through our daily lives, it won't normally have such a life changing impact. The Lord won't necessarily call us to do something completely different. However, he will always call us to do what we are doing in a way that conforms more fully to his way. His call will always be a call to become more loving, more generous, less self-centred and self-regarding. This is the Lord's basic call to all of us. This is the call we find there in the gospel reading before the very particular call to the four fishermen, 'Repent and believe the Good News'. It is a call to keep turning more fully towards the Lord so that he becomes a more alive presence in our lives, shaping what we do and how we do it.

9 January, Tuesday, First Week in Ordinary Time
Mark 1:21-28
In today's gospel reading we find two very contrasting responses to Jesus. The man possessed by an unclean spirit reacted to him in a very hostile way, 'What do you want with us, Jesus of Nazareth? Have you come to destroy us?' Of course, Jesus had come to destroy the evil spirits, the powerful forces that held people captive and prevented them from living their lives as God intended. In contrast, we have the very positive response to Jesus of the people of Capernaum. His teaching made a deep impression on them. They were astonished at his actions, declaring, 'here is a teaching that is new, and with authority behind it'. We need to keep recovering something of that response of the people of Capernaum. Because we have heard the story of Jesus' words and deeds so many times before, we can easily cease to be astonished and deeply impressed. We can lose that sense of the

newness and liberating power of Jesus' message and life. We need to keep asking for fresh eyes and ears every time we approach the gospel story so that we can continue to be energised by the new wine of Jesus' words and deeds. That story is a living word for us now, the word of the Lord, and it retains the power to astonish and impress us if we allow it.

10 January, Wednesday, First Week in Ordinary Time
Mark 1:29-39

In the first part of the gospel reading today, people bring Jesus to Simon Peter's mother-in-law who was in bed with a fever, in Capernaum. In the second part of the gospel people bring all who were sick in Capernaum to Jesus. In both cases people mediated between Jesus and those who needed him. We can see in that an image of our own calling to bring Jesus to others and to bring others to Jesus. The Lord looks to all of us to mediate between himself and others. If the Lord is to get his work done, he needs all of us. In the third part of the gospel reading, Jesus' disciples try to bring Jesus back to Capernaum. 'Everyone is looking for you', they said. Yet, on this occasion, Jesus refused to go with them, because he had other places to visit, 'Let us go elsewhere', he said. Yes, people could bring Jesus to others and bring others to Jesus, but they were not in control of him. Jesus was subject only to his heavenly Father, and his disciples had to learn to submit to him, to go after him, rather than insisting that he go after them. That too is an important part of our calling. We need to yield to what the Lord wants to do and is doing; we are not in control or in charge of the Lord's work. Rather we try to allow the Lord to do his work in and through us. It remains his work rather than ours. It is above all in prayer that we attend to the Lord of the work, so that we can do the work of the Lord.

11 January, Thursday, First Week in Ordinary Time

Mark 1:40-45

The gospel reading today reveals the power of Jesus and, at the same time, his powerlessness. His power was displayed in his healing of the leper. This was a power that was rooted in his compassion and that did not hesitate to break one of the great taboos of the ancient world, touching a leper. This was a life-giving power that was ready to disregard the most hallowed of traditions in order to heal the broken and include the excluded. Whenever we find that kind of life-giving power at work in our world today, there the Risen Lord is to be found. Yet, Jesus who was so powerful in healing the man's leprosy was immediately shown to be powerless. He asked the healed man to be silent about what happened to him. Instead the man went away and started talking about it freely and telling the story everywhere and there was nothing that Jesus could do about it. Indeed, because of the excitement the man stirred up by his story, Jesus could not go openly into any town but had to stay outside in places where nobody lived, which is what the leper had to do before his healing. The man's refusal to do what Jesus asked had serious consequences for Jesus' work. There is a sense in which the Lord remains powerless today before our refusal to do what he asks of us. The mystery of human freedom can continue to render Jesus powerless. He needs us to respond with a ready and open heart to his call and his will for our lives. Only then will his life-giving work continue to be done in today's world.

12 January, Friday, First Week in Ordinary Time

Mark 2:1-12

In today's gospel reading it may seem strange to us that when the paralytic was brought before Jesus the first thing he said to him was, 'Your sins are forgiven'. It was only after making this statement that Jesus went on to say, 'Get up pick up your stretcher and walk'. The friends of the paralysed man would probably have expected Jesus to say, 'Get up, pick up your stretcher and walk' immediately. They had brought their friend to Jesus for physical healing. However, Jesus perceived that this man was in need of a deeper form of healing – a spiritual healing. He had a spiritual wound which needed healing before his physical disability could be addressed. Jesus came to heal the whole person, body and soul. In declaring himself before all to be the Son of Man who had authority on earth to forgive sins Jesus was stating that the primary focus of his ministry was the healing of our relationship with God. As Paul would go on to say, 'In Christ God was reconciling the world to himself'. Regardless of our physical well-being, we all stand in need of that deeper healing; we all need to hear the Lord speak those words to each of us personally that he spoke to the paralytic, 'My child, your sins are forgiven'.

13 January, Saturday, First Week in Ordinary Time
Mark 2:13-17

Pope Francis wrote a book entitled *The Name of God is Mercy*. It takes the form of an interview with Pope Francis by an Italian journalist. In the course of that lengthy interview, Pope Francis says that God's logic is a logic of love that scandalises the doctors of the Law. I was reminded of what the Pope said there by today's gospel reading. Jesus scandalises the doctors of the Law, the scribes of the Pharisees, by sharing table with people who were considered sinners by the same doctors of the Law. Pope Francis has spoken of Jesus as the human face of God's mercy. God's logic of love is reflected in everything Jesus says and does. Jesus reveals a God who doesn't wait for us to be perfect or blameless before engaging with us. Jesus engaged with people as they were, in all their frailty and weakness. That is how the Lord engages with each one of us. In the gospel reading we have just heard, Jesus calls Levi (or Matthew, as he is named in one of the other gospels) to become one of his disciples. Levi was a tax collector. The doctors of the Law would have considered such people to be beyond redemption because they kept breaking the Law. However, that was not Jesus' logic; it is not God's logic of love. Jesus called Levi out of love, just as he calls each one of us out of love. Jesus went on to share table with Levi's friends, other tax collectors and sinners. To share table with people in that culture was to enter into real communion with them. In sharing table with tax collectors and sinners Jesus was showing that God wants to be in communion with us just as we are. It is that experience of God's loving communion with us that will empower us to become the person God wants us to be and to live the life God calls us to live.

15 January, Monday, Second Week in Ordinary Time
Mark 2:18-22

It is clear from today's gospel reading that people saw a difference between the ministry of John the Baptist and the ministry of Jesus. Whereas John and his disciples were recognised as people who fasted a lot, Jesus and his disciples were not known for fasting. As a Jew, Jesus would have fasted. Prayer, fasting and almsgiving were three of the central Jewish practices that Jesus lived by and valued. Yet, the gospels suggest that sharing table was more important to Jesus than fasting. It was at table that he revealed the hospitality of God for all, especially for those who had been made to feel beyond God's favour. Jesus proclaimed a gracious God who wanted to enter into communion with us and wanted us to enter into communion with him and with each other. There was something new about Jesus' ministry in that sense. The God he revealed was not one who promoted laws and regulations but who called on people to care and provide for each other in response to God's caring and providing for them. This was the 'new wine' that Jesus refers to in the gospel reading that was ill suited to the old wineskins that the Pharisees were so protective of, such as the elaborate regulations about fasting. The image of Jesus as the bridegroom and the image of his ministry as new wine, suggests joy and celebration; it speaks of good news. It is vital that Jesus and his message would always remain good news for us, the good news of a gracious God who is constantly at work in a life-giving way in all of our lives.

16 January, Tuesday, Second Week in Ordinary Time
Mark 2:23-28
The issue of what is allowed and what is not allowed is always with us, whether in the secular or religious sphere. In the gospel reading there is a clash between Jesus and the Pharisees as to what is and isn't allowed under the Jewish Law. The Pharisees considered that the disciples action in providing for their hunger by picking ears of corn in the fields was not allowed on the Sabbath; it was understood by them to be a form of reaping which the Law forbids on the Sabbath. Jesus saw no problem with allowing his disciples to provide for them-selves in this way on the Sabbath. He quotes an incident in Scripture in support of his view. David allowed his followers to satisfy their hunger with the bread of the presence in the Temple, which strictly speaking, only the priests were allowed to eat. Jesus was clear that the need to satisfy one's hunger took precedence over the keeping of the particular interpretation of the Sabbath held by the Pharisees. Jews had the wisdom to discern when religious law was at the service of human well-being and when it was not. He had God's perspective on what is important and what is not. He then had the freedom to act accordingly. Such wisdom and freedom flowed from his intimate relationship with God. We all need something of that same wisdom and freedom. By watching what Jesus does and listening to what he says in the gospels we can begin to imbibe something of his wisdom and freedom.

17 January, Wednesday, Second Week in Ordinary Time
Mark 3:1-6

The clash between David and Goliath in the first reading is the quintessential conflict between weakness and power, with the weaker one triumphing over the more powerful one. We see a similar clash in today's gospel reading. The Pharisees and the Herodians, who had great political power in that culture, begin to discuss how to destroy Jesus, who had no such power. Even though they went on to put Jesus to death, it was Jesus, the powerless one, who triumphed over his powerful opponents, because God raised him from the dead and sent his Spirit upon his followers. David said before his conflict with Goliath, 'The Lord will rescue me', and it was the Lord who rescued Jesus from his enemies. Both readings remind us that when we find ourselves up against impossible odds, the Lord is our greatest resource. Writing from prison with the possibility of execution facing him, Paul could say, nevertheless, 'I can do all things through him who strengthens me'. In our own lives, when our resources seem no match for the challenge, we too can experience the Lord as 'my stronghold, my saviour', in the words of today's responsorial psalm. A little later in Mark's gospel, Jesus will say to his disciples, 'for God, all things are possible'.

18 January, Thursday, Second Week in Ordinary Time
Mark 3:7-12

In today's gospel reading, Mark gives us a very vivid picture of the popularity of Jesus during the early stages of his Galilean ministry. Great crowds from a very large area came to him, from as far north as Tyre and Sidon in modern day Lebanon, and as far east as Transjordania, modern day Jordan. They came to him in their need. In the words of the gospel reading, they were 'afflicted', and they recognised in Jesus one who could heal their affliction. It is often the way that we seek out the Lord with greatest passion and energy when we or someone we love is afflicted. Our vulnerability, whether it is physical, emotional or mental, opens us up to the Lord's presence. When all is well with us, we can go along without too much reference to the Lord. Our relationship with the Lord can deepen in times of personal crisis. It is not that our need of the Lord is any greater at such times, it is just that we become more aware of our need of the Lord when the sense of our own self-sufficiency is undermined. Those experiences of brokenness, which we might lament because of the pain they cause us, can be surprising moments of grace. Saint Paul made this discovery for himself. He came to recognise that what he termed the 'thorn in the flesh' he so desperately wanted to be rid of created an opening for the Lord to work powerfully in and through him, as he heard the Lord say to him, 'My power is made perfect in weakness'.

19 January, Friday, Second Week in Ordinary Time
Mark 3:13-19
In today's gospel reading we are told that Jesus appointed twelve 'to be his companions and to be sent out'. There seems a certain tension between both of those roles, companioning Jesus and being sent out from him. To companion Jesus is to be in his company; to be sent out is to be away from him. Yet, this was a creative tension. Spending time in Jesus' company prepared the disciples to be sent out by Jesus. They could only be sent out after they had spent time with Jesus. They needed to receive from him before they could give to others. They needed to observe him, to listen to him, before they could speak and act in his name. This creative tension is at the heart of all our lives as disciples of Jesus. We spend time in his company in prayer, and we go out from our prayer as his representatives before others. This is the two-fold movement of the Christian life – neither one can be dispensed with! The Christian life in its fullness has both a contemplative and an active dimension. The gospel reading hints that the contemplative dimension is the foundation of the active dimension.

The twelve needed to allow themselves to be companioned by Jesus before they could be sent out. We need to spend time with the Lord in prayer if we are to share in his work today.

20 January, Saturday, Second Week in Ordinary Time

Mark 3:20-21

This very short gospel reading from Mark gives us a little glimpse of how Jesus was misunderstood within his own family. Jesus is busily engaged in his ministry and his family come down from Nazareth to Capernaum to take charge of him because they believe he is out of his mind. A few chapters later in Mark's gospel Jesus is rejected in his home town of Nazareth and in response to that experience Jesus says, 'Prophets are not without honour, except in their hometown, and among their own kin, and in their own house'. Jesus was taking a path in life of which his family did not approve. Tension within families is something we have all experienced at some time or other. This was a dimension of human living that Jesus also experienced. He entered fully into the human condition, knowing from within its struggles, its tensions, its misunderstandings and the resulting pain for all concerned. He can walk compassionately with us through those experiences because he has been there himself. Jesus did not always go where his family wanted him to go because he was subject to a greater authority in his life, and that was God's authority. God's purpose drove him and he was faithful to that purpose even when it brought him into conflict with those for whom he had the strongest feelings of natural affection. We, his followers, are called to remain true to the Lord's direction, his guidance, his vision and values, even if that means for us what it meant for him, finding ourselves at odds with those who are nearest and dearest to us.

22 January, Monday, Third Week in Ordinary Time

Mark 3:22-30

We can all find ourselves being misunderstood or misjudged. We do something and it is interpreted in a way that is completely different to what we intended. We say something and it is heard in a very different way to what we wanted to say. It can be very upsetting when we are misjudged and misinterpreted in this way. The gospel reading suggests that Jesus was misinterpreted in the greatest way imaginable. Jesus was doing the work of God, healing the sick and releasing people from their demons. The Holy Spirit who came down upon him at this baptism was powerfully at work in all he said and did. However, some of the religious experts of the time held the view that the spirit at work in Jesus was an evil spirit, not the Holy Spirit. 'It is through the price of devils that he casts devils out'. It is hard to imagine a more serious misjudgement of others than to confuse the work of the Holy Spirit in their lives with the work of an evil spirit. It is what Jesus calls blasphemy against the Holy Spirit in the gospel reading, these religious experts were completely blind to the presence of the Holy Spirit in the life of Jesus. We might be tempted to think that we could not be so blind. Yet, we too can fail to recognise the presence and working of the Holy Spirit in the lives of others. We can be so focused on what we perceive to be their failings that we fail to see the presence of the Holy Spirit in them. The gospel reading calls on us to be alert to the signs of the Holy Spirit in each other, even when those signs are not always glaringly obvious.

23 January, Tuesday, Third Week in Ordinary Time

Mark 3:31-35

Today's gospel reading is the only passage in the gospel of Mark where the mother of Jesus appears. If we only had Mark's gospel this would be the only gospel portrait of Mary we would have. She is standing with other members of Jesus' family outside a house where

Jesus is teaching surrounded by his disciples. A few verses earlier Mark had told us why Jesus' mother and other members of his family were there. They had come to restrain him, to seize him, because people were saying that he had gone out of his mind. Here he was, upsetting all sorts of influential and powerful people, making deadly enemies for himself. Somebody needed to talk sense to him and who better than his mother. However, the plans of Jesus' mother and family for Jesus did not come to pass. When Jesus was informed that his mother and family members were outside waiting to see him, he pointed to the disciples seated around him and said, 'Here are my mother and brothers'. 'This is now my family', he was saying. Jesus had moved on from his blood family and was forming a new family of disciples, the nucleus of the Church. It cannot have been easy for Mary to come to terms with losing her son in this way. He was taking a path she did not always approve of and she did not understand. She was struggling to come to terms with the mystery of her son's identity. So often those close to us don't take a path we expect them to take, or want them to take. Like Mary, we struggle to come to terms with the mystery of the other's identity. Like her, we sometimes have to learn to let go and to let be, trusting that in the end God's purpose will prevail in the lives of those we love.

24 January, Wednesday, Third Week in Ordinary Time
Mark 4:1-20

The parable of the sower was probably spoken by Jesus as an encouraging word to his disciples. As Mark has been telling the story of Jesus' public ministry prior to Jesus speaking this parable, Jesus and his disciples have been encountering many difficulties and obstacles. The religious leaders have accused Jesus and his disciples of breaking the Sabbath; they have claimed that Jesus heals by the power of Satan. Jesus' own relatives have tried to take him in hand because of the general impression that he had lost the run of himself. In that context

Jesus draws the attention of the disciples to the farmer sowing seed in Galilee. The farmer has to deal with all kinds of obstacles, with the result that much of the seed that he sows never takes root, or if it does it never reaches maturity. Yet, in spite of obstacles and setbacks, the harvest is great. Jesus is saying, look beyond the obstacles, the setbacks, the disappointments; God is at work in my ministry and the harvest will be great in the end. We can all become absorbed by what is not going well, by the failures, the losses all around us. The parable encourages us to keep hopeful in the midst of loss and failure that our good efforts seem to yield, because the Lord is always at work in a life-giving way even when failure and loss seem to dominate the landscape.

25 January, Thursday, Conversion of Saint Paul
Mark 16:15-18

The conversion of Paul was one of the momentous events of the early years of the Church, perhaps the most momentous event after the death and resurrection of Jesus and the coming of the Holy Spirit. In his own words Paul went from 'violently persecuting the church of God' to becoming the Church's great apostle to the Gentiles. Paul went on to establish churches throughout modern day Turkey and Greece. Looking back on this transformation in his life, he always attributed it to God's grace. 'By the grace of God, I am what I am', he says in his first letter to the Corinthians, 'and his grace towards me has not been in vain'. Pope Francis seems to have undergone something of a conversion in his own life. Looking back over his time as provincial of the Jesuits in Argentina, he openly acknowledges that he made many mistakes. Some of those mistakes had serious consequences for others, particularly two Jesuits. He clearly has great remorse for those failures. Yet, it is clear from what he has said since becoming Pope that he has an even more powerful sense of God's mercy. He knows himself to be a forgiven sinner and that gives him a great joy and a great freedom, and a great understanding for the failings of other people. He seems like a man who never judges people. The story of Paul and of Pope Francis reminds us that God's mercy is available to all of us if only we keep asking for it. We are all forgiven sinners and, as forgiven sinners, the Lord can work powerfully through all our lives, as powerfully as he worked through the life of Paul, and as powerfully as he is now working through the life of Pope Francis.

26 January, Friday, Memorial of Saints Timothy and Titus
Luke 10:1-9

Today we celebrate the memorial of two of Saint Paul's closest associates, Timothy and Titus. In today's first reading, Paul addresses Timothy as a third-generation believer. He refers to the faith that came first to live in his grandmother Lois, and then in his mother Eunice, and then in Timothy himself. It seems that Timothy caught the faith in his home. The same is true for many of us. Our own faith owes a great deal to the faith of our parents and grandparents. The same could not be said of Paul. His parents and grandparents were Jewish. It was his life changing encounter with the Risen Lord that brought him to faith in Jesus, probably leaving him at odds with his parents and grandparents. Both Timothy's and Paul's experience reminds us that the Lord can touch the lives of people through the faith of family members, but he can also touch their lives in other, less conventional, ways. The Lord is always reaching out to us in one way or another. In the gospel reading, he reached out to the people of his time by sending out a very large group of seventy-two disciples with the message, 'The kingdom of God is very near to you'. Jesus' words to the seventy-two suggest that he was aware that this attempt on his part to touch the lives of a bigger number would not always be successful, 'I am sending you out like lambs among wolves'. Yet, the Lord was never put off by people's resistance. Whether people accepted or rejected him, it remained the case that 'the kingdom of God is very near to you'. The Lord is always near to us, and never tires of seeking us out and calling out to us to come to him. He can do this in a whole variety of ways.

27 January, Saturday, Third Week in Ordinary Time

Mark 4:35-41

There is a very striking image of Jesus in today's gospel reading. As a gale blew and the waves broke into the boat he is there in the stern of the boat asleep with his head on a cushion. There is a storm at sea and a storm within the disciples; they are filled with dread before the terror of the storm. Yet amid all this chaos in nature, and in his disciples, there is Jesus, a focal point of calm and stillness. He is at peace. His peaceful sleep when all seems lost speaks of his trust in God as one who is more powerful than the storm. The disciples focused on the storm and lost sight of God and therefore felt overwhelmed by the storm. Jesus focused on God rather than on the storm and therefore he was completely at peace as the storm raged. Jesus' demeanour teaches us to keep our focus on God even when we seem to be overwhelmed by forces before which we feel powerless. Our faith does not preserve us from the storms of life, no more than it preserved Jesus, but it can enable us to remain at peace in the midst of the storm. Jesus rebuked his disciples for their lack of faith in God, their lack of trust. Jesus was with them; that should have been enough for them, even as the storm howled. Jesus is with us too as Risen Lord, as we battle with our own storms in life. If we keep our focus on him at such times, we will come to share in his own peace and rest. It is a peace the world cannot give and the world cannot take away. It is a gift which empowers us to be peacemakers for others.

29 January, Monday, Fourth Week in Ordinary Time
Mark 5:1-20

The central character of the gospel story is one of the most disturbed people that we find in the gospels. He was someone out of control, completely alienated from himself and from others. He was more dead than alive, as is shown by his living among the tombs. He was the total outsider. Yet, Jesus engaged with him and, as a result of his encounter with Jesus, he was restored to himself and to the community from which he came. Having just calmed a storm at sea, Jesus calmed the storm in this man's psyche and spirit and sent him out as a messenger of good news to his community. We may never be as disturbed as this man evidently was, but we can all find ourselves disjointed from time to time, out of sorts with ourselves and with others, feeling only half alive within ourselves, tossed and thrown about. It is then that we need to come before the Lord as the man in the gospel did. His initial approach to the Lord was quite aggressive; it was full of anger, 'What have you to do with us, Jesus of Nazareth?' That can be our starting point too when we come before the Lord in prayer. Yet, he is never put off by our disturbance within. If we allow him, he will pour his peace into our hearts; he will calm us as he calmed the storm, and having done so he will send us out to share his peace and mercy with others, just as he sent out the man in the gospel reading.

30 January, Tuesday, Fourth Week in Ordinary Time
Mark 5:21-43

Today's gospel reading presents us with two interlocking stories. Two desperate people approach Jesus in their need, a man and a woman, a prominent person within the synagogue community, and someone excluded from that community because of her physical condition. Both stories make reference to touching. Jairus pleads with Jesus to come and lay his hands upon his seriously ill daughter, and Jesus goes on to take Jairus' daughter by the hand and lift her up. The woman reaches out and touches the hem of Jesus' cloak. In both stories, the act of touching brings life where there was death, healing where there was sickness. Both stories can speak to our own faith lives. The Lord wants to touch our lives in a healing and life-giving way, as he touched the life of Jairus's daughter. The Lord does not relate to us at a distance. As he entered the home of Jairus and took his daughter by the hand, so he enters our homes, our lives, and takes us by the hand. He has entered fully into our human condition and meets each one of us where we are. The Lord who comes to us also desires us to come to him, like the woman in the gospel reading. As he touches our lives with his presence, he looks to us to touch his presence with our faith, like the woman. Michelangelo's masterly painting of God creating Adam on the ceiling of the Sistine Chapel comes to mind. The Lord reaches out to touch our lives and, in doing so, moves us to reach out in faith and touch his presence to us.

31 January, Wednesday, Fourth Week in Ordinary Time
Mark 6:1-6

In today's gospel reading the people of Nazareth took offence to the fact that one of their own, someone whose family they knew well, someone whom they had known as a carpenter, was now displaying great wisdom in the words he spoke and great power in his deeds on behalf of others. 'What is this wisdom that has been granted to him, and these miracles that are worked through him?' They took offence, it seems, not to his actual wisdom and power, but to the fact that one of their own was displaying such wisdom and power. It was as if Jesus was too ordinary, too much like themselves, to be taken seriously. They were coming up against the scandal of the incarnation, the Word who was God became flesh as all of us are flesh. God chose to come to us in and through someone who was like us in all things, except sin. When Jesus went on to speak about God, he often pointed to the ordinary, to the familiar, to the normal – a farmer sowing seed, a man on a journey from Jerusalem to Jericho, a rebellious son in a family, a widow looking for justice from a judge. The life and teaching of Jesus shows us that God speaks to us in and through the ordinary events of life. What we need are the eyes to see and the ears to hear the extraordinary in the ordinary, the divine in the human.

1 February, Thursday, Feast of Saint Brigid

Luke 6:32-38

We know very little about the life of Brigid. She was probably born around the middle of the fifth century and died at the beginning of the sixth century. At a young age she seems to have devoted her life completely to God. She founded a monastery of Kildare which contributed to the spread of Christianity in Ireland. The stories that have come down about her in her various lives depict her as a woman of deep prayer and as someone whose life was characterised by great generosity and deep compassion, especially for the needy and the broken. In today's first reading from Paul's letter to the Romans, Paul mentions various gifts that can be expected to be found among the members of Christ's body. Two in particular seem to fit the profile of Brigid as it has come down to us in the literature about her, 'Let the almsgivers give freely ... and those who do the works of mercy do them cheerfully'. It seems that Brigid gave alms freely and did many works of mercy cheerfully. That lovely reading concludes with, 'If any of the saints are in need you must share with them, and you should make hospitality your special care'. Again Brigid shared with those in need and had a reputation for a very hospitable spirit. Her cult extended beyond the shores of this island. I was only reading recently that in England there were at least nineteen ancient Church dedications in her honour, the most famous being Saint Bride's in Fleet Street. It is clear that her great love of the Lord which was nourished by a life of prayer found expression in a very practical love of others, especially of those in any need. She can continue to inspire us to live the gospel to the full and to find joy in so doing.

1 February, Thursday, Fourth Week in Ordinary Time
Mark 6:7-13

When Jesus chose a group of twelve from among the larger group of disciples, he chose the number twelve very deliberately, as an echo of the twelve tribes of Israel. He seems to have seen the group of twelve as the nucleus of a renewed Israel. They were to have a special role in Jesus' mission of renewing God's people. In today's gospel reading, we have Mark's account of Jesus sending out the twelve for the first time to share in his mission. It is noteworthy that Jesus sends them out in pairs. Rather than twelve individuals going off in twelve different directions, there are six groups of two going off in six different directions. Some might think that it would have been more effective to send out the twelve individually; in that way twice the area could have been covered. However, Jesus clearly saw a greater value in sending out the twelve in twos. No one was to work alone; each would have someone else to work alongside. As disciples of the Lord today, we still need to work together, rather than as individuals or loners. When we work together we learn to receive from and give to each other and, thereby, the Lord is more fully present to others. He did say that where two or three are gathered he would be there in their midst. Even Paul, the great apostle to the Gentiles, was very aware of the debt he owed to what he called his co-workers. The Lord needs us to work together if his work is to be done in today's world. As members of the Lord's body, we are interdependent. In the life of faith, we never go it alone.

2 February, Friday, The Presentation of the Lord
Luke 2:22-40

Today we celebrate Jesus' presentation in the Temple in Jerusalem by his parents, in accordance with the Jewish Law. In the opening chapters of his gospel, Luke portrays Jesus' parents as faithfully observing the Jewish Law. In this way he wants to stress that the movement that became known as Christianity has its roots deeply in the Jewish faith. In the Jewish Scriptures, especially in the prophet Isaiah, Israel's role was to be a light to the Gentiles, to reveal the light of God to the world. According to our gospel reading, the elderly Simeon, a devout Jew, recognises Mary and Joseph's child as the one who is to embody this calling of Israel. He is to be a light to enlighten the pagans, and in being faithful to this role he will bring glory to Israel. Simeon had spent his life looking forward to 'Israel's comforting'. When Mary and Joseph entered the Temple with their newborn first child on that day, Simeon's longings and hopes were brought to fulfilment. It has been said that Simeon has become the patron saint of those who, having found meaning at last in their lives, are able to let go and surrender to the Lord. His prayer of surrender has become part of the Night Prayer of the Church. We pray that prayer as people who have been graced by God's light shining through Jesus. Like Simeon, we have come to recognise Jesus as the light to enlighten the pagans and the glory of Israel. We have candles blessed on this day; we light them and carry them as a sign of our joy of discovering Jesus as the light of the world. Indeed, every time we light a candle in church or at home, we are acknowledging Jesus as the light of the world and we are also recognising our own need for his gracious light as we struggle with the various forms of darkness in our lives.

3 February, Saturday, Fourth Week in Ordinary Time

Mark 6:30-34

In today's gospel reading, Jesus proclaims the value of rest from our labours. The apostles had been on a very busy period of mission and when they returned, Jesus insisted that they come away to a lonely place to rest awhile. However, this plan that Jesus had for himself and his disciples did not materialise. When they arrived at their destination, the hoped-for lonely place was full of people looking for Jesus and his disciples. Jesus responded to this interruption with compassion. He abandoned his plan for a quiet time with his disciples away from everybody and set himself to teach the people 'at some length'. It is often the case in our own lives that our plans do not work out. People have a way of scuppering our plans. We have something worked out in our head, but the unpredictability of life means it doesn't come to pass. Like Jesus, we can find ourselves helpless before a set of circumstances we had not anticipated. The question then becomes, 'How are to going to react to this demise of our plans and purposes?' We can react with annoyance or even anger. We can be tempted to get very discouraged. Jesus reacted with compassion to his plans not working out; he didn't turn away from the new and unexpected situation, but engaged with it compassionately. He heard God's call in this unexpected situation and responded generously. We too have to keep listening to the Lord's call even in those situations that are not of our making and that leave us feeling, initially at least, very put out. The unexpected interruptions can be where the Lord is present to us.

5 February, Monday, Fifth Week in Ordinary Time

Mark 6:53-56

The gospel reading today conveys a sense of the great popularity of Jesus among the ordinary people of Galilee. In particular, it was the sick and broken that he attracted, because God's healing power was at work through him. People begged him to let him touch even the fringe of his cloak, as the woman had done who was healed of her flow of blood. It was above all the broken and needy who were desperate to get to him and to connect with him. In our own lives too, it is often in our brokenness that we seek out the Lord with the greatest urgency. Something happens to us that brings home to us our vulnerability, our weakness, our inability to manage. It is often in those situations when we come face-to-face with our limitations that we seek out the Lord with an energy and an urgency we don't normally have. It is those moments when we experience life as a real struggle that bring home to us our need of the Lord and our dependence on him. It is often the darker and more painful experiences of life that open us up to the Lord. Saint Paul bears witness to that. When he was struggling with his 'thorn in the flesh', he said that he pleaded with the Lord three times to be rid of it, and he heard the Lord say to him, 'My power is made perfect in weakness'. The Lord can come powerfully to us in our weakness if, like the people in today's gospel reading, we hurry towards him.

6 February, Tuesday, Fifth Week in Ordinary Time
Mark 7:1-13
There are times in our lives as individuals and in the lives of our communities that we need to rediscover what is truly important. We can all lose sight of what really matters and give ourselves over to that which is of much lesser spiritual value. This is true in the area of our faith as well as in every other area of life. In the gospel reading, Jesus accuses the religious leaders of his day of giving more importance to various human religious traditions than to the word of God. 'You make God's word null and void for the sake of your tradition which you have handed down'. By 'God's word' Jesus meant what we would call today the Jewish Scriptures or the Old Testament. For us Christians, God's word also includes the gospels, the letters of Paul and the other documents that make up the New Testament. As

Christians, we too are prone to making God's word null and void for the sake of our tradition. We can give greater importance to traditions that have emerged in the history of the Church and have been handed down than to the word of God in the Scriptures. As people of faith, we can get very worked up about various Church traditions, giving them an authority that they do not deserve. This was the failing of the Pharisees and scribes in today's gospel reading. We all need to keep returning to the word of God, because it is the light generated by that word which allows us to see everything else, including our religious traditions, in proper perspective.

7 February, Wednesday, Fifth Week in Ordinary Time
Mark 7:14-23

In the gospel reading Jesus makes a distinction between what is on the outside of a person and what is within. The religious experts of the time were very concerned about certain external rituals that needed to be performed if a person was to be right with God. Jesus declares that what is much more important in God's eyes is what is within the heart of the person, because what is within a person determines a person's moral behaviour, how they speak and how they act. This is what matters to God, rather than various ritual washings of one kind or another or what people eat or don't eat. As in yesterday's gospel reading, Jesus is saying that the religious experts of the time are not getting their priorities right. Their priorities are not God's priorities. The most important part of a tree is its roots, which are invisible because they go down deep into the earth. Jesus is suggesting God wants us to look deeply into ourselves with a view to getting our depths right. Our inner life will determine the quality of our outer, observable life. Our underlying attitudes and values are what really matters. We need to keep working on our inner core, or, rather, allow the Lord to keep working on it, asking him to keep on renewing our heart so that it corresponds more to his heart.

8 February, Thursday, Fifth Week in Ordinary Time
Mark 7:24-30

Today's gospel reading gives us an insight into a mother's instinct to leave no stone unturned when the well-being of her child is at stake. Jesus was in Tyre, a predominantly pagan city on the Mediterranean coast. Why had he moved so far beyond his usual area of ministry? The reference to Jesus going into a house and not wanting anyone to know he was there suggests that he may have been seeking some time away on his own. Yet, not for the only time in the gospels, his desire for solitude was frustrated. A pagan woman burst into the house and threw herself at Jesus' feet, begging him to heal her daughter. The reputation of this Jewish prophet had reached the ears of this pagan woman. Having somehow come to hear that Jesus was in Tyre, she wasn't going to miss her opportunity. Jesus appeared to give her short shrift, 'the children should be fed first' (the people of Israel), certainly before the house dogs (the pagans). Yet, the woman's determination that Jesus should heal her daughter was in no way deflected. With both humility and humour she retorted that the house dogs and the children can eat quite happily together. Jesus was disarmed. He recognised her tenacious faith and declared there and then that her daughter was healed. There is a story in the Jewish Scriptures of Jacob wrestling with God. This woman was, in a sense, wrestling with Jesus. There can be an element of wrestling with God in our own faith. Our faith can be put to the test when the Lord does not appear to hear our prayer. At such times we need to be as tenacious in our faith as the Syrophoenician woman was.

9 February, Friday, Fifth Week in Ordinary Time
Mark 7:31-37

The gospels often describe people bringing someone to Jesus. In particular, people bring those who cannot make their way to Jesus themselves. We are given a picture of people looking out for each other, especially for those who have some form of impediment or disability. We have a good example of that in today's gospel reading. People brought to Jesus a deaf man who had an impediment in his speech and they begged Jesus to lay his hands on the man. They lead him to Jesus and then they intercede with Jesus on his behalf because he cannot speak for himself. The people who brought the man to Jesus portray one element of our own baptismal calling. We are all called to bring each other to Jesus and, like the people in the gospel reading, to intercede for each other with the Lord, to pray for each other, especially for those who, for whatever reason, cannot pray for themselves. The Lord draws us to himself in and through each other. He needs us if he is to do his life-giving work, just as he needed people to bring the deaf man who couldn't speak to him. Each of us is an important labourer in the Lord's field. The Lord is dependent on every one of us.

10 February, Saturday, Fifth Week in Ordinary Time
Mark 8:1-10

There are two questions asked in today's gospel reading. The question of the disciples is a somewhat despairing one, 'Where could anyone get bread to feed these people in a deserted place?' The question of Jesus is much more hopeful and already points to how the crowd will be fed, 'How many loaves have you?' When we are faced with a situation that seems beyond our resources to deal with, it is important to ask the right kind of question. Some questions only increase our sense of powerlessness. Other questions encourage us to take whatever step we can take, no matter how small. Jesus wanted his disciples to take whatever step they could take to address the hunger of the crowd. There were some resources there which they could place at the Lord's disposal. They could not feed the crowd on their own, but their contribution was essential to the Lord's feeding of the crowd. As people of faith, we believe that the Lord wants to work through us for the good of humanity. It may seem as if our resources are very limited before the task at hand. Yet, if we are generous with those resources and invite the Lord to work with them, he can accomplish far more through us than we could ever imagine.

12 February, Monday, Sixth Week in Ordinary Time
Mark 8:11-13

Mark makes greater reference to the emotions of Jesus than any of the other evangelists. In today's reading, Mark states that Jesus responded to the Pharisees' request for a sign from heaven 'with a sigh that came straight from the heart'. That sigh issued forth in a question, 'Why does this generation demand a sign?' We can almost sense the frustration and weariness of Jesus in that phrase, 'with a sigh that came straight from the heart'. The religious quest often takes the form of a search for heavenly signs, a longing for the extraordinary and unusual. The Jesus of the gospels, however, will always redirect us towards the ordinary. He speaks of the sower who goes out to sow his field, the woman who looks for her lost coin, the care that a Samaritan traveller gives to a stranger on the road from Jerusalem to Jericho, the man who unexpectedly finds treasure in his field, the merchant who finds the pearl he has been seeking and so on. It is in the ordinary that the mystery of God's kingdom is to be found, because heaven and earth are full of God's glory for those who have eyes to see. Since the death and resurrection of Jesus, the kingdom of God is among us.

13 February, Tuesday, Sixth Week in Ordinary Time
Mark 8:14-21

In today's gospel reading, Jesus speaks about the yeast of the Pharisees and the yeast of Herod. In that culture 'yeast' or 'leaven' was often used as a symbol of evil and with reference to how the evil of a few can infect a large group. However, the disciples interpret Jesus' reference to 'yeast' in a very literal way, with reference to bread. 'It is because we have no bread', they said. As a result, Jesus goes on to address them as having no understanding or perception, having eyes and not seeing, having ears and not hearing. Jesus often speaks in the language of image, metaphor and symbolism. Sometimes, to take what he says literally is to misunderstand him, like the disciples in today's gospel reading. Today's gospel reading suggests that the meaning of what Jesus says is not always obvious. If we presume too quickly that we know what Jesus says, we can dismiss it too quickly if it does not make immediate sense to us. As we listen to what Jesus says, we need to take time to ponder his words so as to hit upon the real meaning of what he says. We need to approach the word of God in a spirit of humility, recognising that we can easily be blind and deaf, like the disciples. We listen, in the awareness that we are learners before the Word and that we need the Spirit to enlighten us.

14 February, Ash Wednesday

Matthew 6:1-6, 16-18

In a few moments, we will all come forward to receive some ashes on our foreheads and, as we do so, we will hear the words, 'Repent and believe in the gospel'. It is the beginning of Lent. It is a seven-week period which ends with the Easter Triduum, Holy Thursday evening to Easter Sunday. It is a sombre season within the Church's year. The celebrant at Mass wears purple vestments instead of green or white. No flowers will appear to beautify our altar. At Mass on Sunday there will be no 'Glory to God in the highest' after the penitential rite. There is a general toning down. In musical terms, we are in a minor key. Lent is a season when the whole community of believers, the Church, is invited to go on a kind of retreat. It is not a retreat in the normal sense of going off to a retreat house for a period of time. Very few are in a position to do that. It is more of a retreat in the midst of life. It is a time to come back to the Lord with all our heart, in the opening words of today's first reading from the prophet Joel. As Joel reminds us in that reading, the Lord to whom we are invited to come back is one who is all tenderness and compassion, slow to anger, rich in graciousness. It is a time to be reconciled to God in the words of Paul in the second reading, so that we can become what Paul calls in that reading 'the goodness of God'. This coming back to the Lord with all our heart will involve in some shape or form the three traditional Jewish practices which Jesus endorses in the gospel reading, almsgiving, prayer and fasting. Our coming back to the Lord will mean a deepening of our prayer life. It will entail a form of fasting, of abstaining, from whatever it is that is pulling us away from the Lord. Our turning towards the Lord will show itself in some form of almsgiving, a more generous way of life towards others, a readiness to give out of what has been given to us. This is the journey on which we are being invited to set out together as we begin Lent. Our receiving of ashes proclaims our desire to enter into this journey with a willingness of heart and spirit.

15 February, Thursday after Ash Wednesday
Luke 9:22-25

There are two little words in today's gospel reading that often strike me every day. Jesus says, 'if anyone wants to be a follower of mine, let him renounce himself and take up his cross every day and follow me'. Jesus is saying that following him is something we need to do *every day*, and, *every day*, this will involve some form of renunciation and taking up the cross, some saying 'no' to what may often seem an easier path, all in the service of saying 'yes' to Jesus' call to follow him. It is as if Jesus is saying that we never take a holiday from trying to follow him more closely. There are no days off. It is something we need to do every day. Every day, the Lord calls us to follow him, to take the path he has shown us by his life and his teaching, and, indeed, by his death, and every day we try to respond to that call. It is because the following of the Lord is daily that Jesus teaches us to ask the Father to 'give us this day our daily bread'. Daily, we need the resources that only God can provide if we are to be faithful to the Lord every day. Of course, we all have our off days. We recognise at the end of some days that we were not at our best. Yet, we just begin again the next day. Each day the Lord says to us what Moses says to the people in the gospel reading, 'choose life'. Jesus assures us in the gospel reading that in seeking to follow him every day we are choosing life, we are saving our lives.

16 February, Friday after Ash Wednesday

Matthew 9:14-15

The gospels suggest that people often asked Jesus the question, 'Why?' In particular, the religious leaders asked him why he was doing this or that or not doing this or that. There was clearly something new and different about the ministry of Jesus which gave rise to this repeated question, 'Why?' In today's gospel reading, it is the disciples of John the Baptist who ask, 'Why?' They wonder why Jesus and his disciples do not follow the fasting practices of the disciples of John the Baptist and of the Pharisees. In the gospel reading for Ash Wednesday, Jesus affirmed the value of the key Jewish practices of fasting, prayer and almsgiving, provided they are not done to attract attention. In today's gospel reading, he indicates that the celebratory aspect of his ministry means that fasting cannot have the same significance as it does for the disciples of the Pharisees and John the Baptist. Jesus' ministry is more like a wedding feast than a funeral, with himself as the bridegroom and his disciples as the bride. Jesus goes on to say that this celebratory element of his ministry does not exclude fasting. However, it does give it a different tone and focus. That celebratory element of the Lord's ministry continues today in the Church. The Risen Lord wants his joy to be in our lives, a joy the world cannot give. Our fasting is with a view to entering more fully into the Lord's joy; it is in the service of deepening our loving relationship with the Lord so that the joy of his Spirit may be in our lives.

As Isaiah in the first reading reminds us, and as Jesus would confirm, our fasting is also in the service of a more loving relationship with others, especially those in greatest need.

17 February, Saturday after Ash Wednesday
Luke 5:27-32

The first people Jesus called to follow him were fishermen. He went on to call people from other walks of life to follow him. In today's gospel reading he calls a tax collector, Levi, someone in the pay of the Romans, to follow him. On another occasion he called a rich man to follow him. The gospels also inform us that he had many women followers. Jesus looked on all people as his potential followers. His call to 'follow me' was addressed to all who would respond to it. It was addressed to people who were considered sinners by those who did their utmost to live by God's law. Jesus got close to those he was calling to follow him, sharing table with them, regardless of how they were regarded by others. The gospel reading reminds us that the Lord is always drawing close to us, to all of us, even when we think of ourselves as sinners. He never ceases to draw near to us and to call on us to follow him. We may think that we have to put a distance between ourselves and the Lord, but the Lord never puts a distance between himself and us. He is always standing at the door of our lives and knocking, calling out to us to follow him, to walk in his way so as to share in his mission in the world.

19 February, Monday, First Week of Lent
Matthew 25:31-46

Both groups in today's gospel reading are surprised when they are told that they were encountering the Son of Man, the King of Kings, in their ordinary daily encounters with the people who crossed their path in life, in particular, the broken, the vulnerable and those in greatest need. Although both groups dealt very differently with those they encountered in life, both asked the same question, 'When did we see you...?' The gospel reading suggests that there is always more to our various meetings with people in life than we realise. There is a sacred dimension to all our encounters; in dealing with each other, we are dealing with the Lord. In serving each other, we are serving the Lord. In neglecting to serve each other, we are neglecting to serve the Lord. There is a sacramental quality to all of life, and to all our human encounters. The Lord is really and truly present to us in others, especially in those who are experiencing the cross that Jesus himself experienced. On the cross he was hungry, thirsty, a stranger, naked, sick, imprisoned. He identifies himself fully with those who share his cross. The gospel reading suggests that we can find ourselves before the Lord on the cross more often than we might think.

20 February, Tuesday, First Week of Lent

Matthew 6:7-15

The prayer that Jesus gave to his disciples to pray is the one prayer that Christians of all denominations are comfortable praying. Perhaps that is because this prayer is really about the basics. It focuses on what really matters. Jesus had a way of zooming in on the essentials and that is evident in this prayer, the only prayer he is recorded as asking us to pray. For Jesus the primary essential was, of course, God his Father, which is why the first three petitions all relate to God. They are really variations of one petition: 'your kingdom come'. When God's kingdom comes to earth, God's name will be held holy and God's will finally come to pass. At the beginning of this prayer, Jesus is teaching us to look beyond ourselves to God's programme, God's agenda. Within that setting, Jesus focuses on the remaining petitions on the essentials for human living and human relationships. We are to pray for our daily bread, all that we need each day for our journey through the present world. It is an imperfect world, we ourselves are imperfect and we have to deal with imperfect people and so we will always stand in need of God's forgiveness and we will always need the freedom to allow the forgiveness we receive from God to flow through us and embrace those who offend and hurt us. In this world, we will be assailed by evil in various forms, which will often put us to the test, as disciples and human beings. Jesus teaches us to ask God to keep us faithful when the test, the temptation, comes, so that we don't succumb to evil but, rather, as Paul says, overcome evil with good. In many ways, this prayer, the Lord's prayer, displays the fundamental shape of our lives as followers of Jesus.

21 February, Wednesday, First Week of Lent

Luke 11:29-32

People are often drawn to what Jesus in today's gospel refers to as 'signs', unusual manifestations of a religious nature. We have had our own examples of these in recent times. Yet, the very people who were asking Jesus for signs were failing to recognise the great sign that was there before them, Jesus himself. He speaks of himself as greater than Solomon, greater than Jonah, and yet, some of his contemporaries were taking him less seriously than the contemporaries of Solomon and Jonah had taken them. Sometimes in our search for the unusual and the extraordinary we can miss the wonder of what is there before us. The Lord is present to us as fully as he was present to the people of Galilee and Judea; he is present to us as someone greater than Solomon, Jonah and all the other great characters of the Jewish Scriptures. He is present to us in his Word, in the Eucharist, in each other, deep within ourselves. The Lord dwells among us full of grace and truth and we are invited to receive from his fullness. We don't need signs and wonders. Lent is a good time to become more aware of the many ways the Lord is present to us in all his greatness and wonder.

22 February, Thursday, Feast of the Chair of Saint Peter

Matthew 16:13-19

Today's feast celebrates the teaching authority of the Bishop of Rome, who is the Pope of the Universal Church. When Jesus declares to Peter in the gospel reading that whatever he binds on earth shall be considered bound in heaven and whatever he loses on earth shall be considered loosed in heaven, he is using terminology that was associated with teaching authority in the Jewish world of the time. Part of the role of the teachers of the Jewish law was to determine which aspects of the law were binding and which could be interpreted more loosely. Jesus is portrayed in the gospel reading as giving to Peter the role of determining which aspects of the teachings of Jesus were binding and which could be interpreted more loosely. Jesus himself in the course of his ministry was a teacher in this sense, declaring some parts of the Jewish Law binding and showing that other parts could be interpreted more loosely. Jesus wants Peter to continue his own teaching role into the future. As Catholics, we believe that this same teaching role resides with the Bishop of Rome today, whom we recognise as the successor of Peter. In that sense our church is a teaching church and that teaching finds expression in the Catechism of the Catholic Church. This teaching is given as a resource to help us to understand what we believe in and to guide us in the living out of that faith. Apart from the Catechism, each Pope also gives his own distinctive understanding of the faith in his personal teaching. Today we thank God for Pope Francis whose teachings in their various forms have been an inspiration not only to people of faith within the Catholic Church but to people of faith in other churches, in other religious traditions, and to those of no particular religious faith. We pray that we ourselves would be attentive to what this particular successor of Peter is saying to us today.

23 February, Friday, First Week of Lent

Matthew 5:20-26

Action – behaviour – was very important to Jesus. Yet, in his teaching, he often focused on what resides in the human heart, the wellspring of our actions. In today's gospel reading, he goes beyond the action of murder to the anger that so often lies behind that action. The Jewish Law declares, 'You must not kill'. Jesus goes further and declares that whoever is angry with his brother will answer for it before the court. A relatively small proportion of the human race commits murder. However, we are all familiar with the emotion of anger. All kinds of things can make us angry. Sometimes our anger is a sign that some injustice is being done to ourselves or to others. Our anger can be a signal that all is not well with our world, and, to that extent, it can serve a good purpose. At other times, our anger can be saying more about us. Because of the particular space in which we find ourselves, we get angry at what would pass bt most people. Whatever the cause of our anger, Jesus in the gospel reading is alerting us to the damaging potential of our anger. It can negatively impact how we speak to others. Jesus makes reference to those who call others names in anger. It can impact on how we behave towards others. Jesus suggests that it is an emotion that is worth attending to, because it can lead us to become estranged from others. In the second part of the gospel reading, Jesus encourages us to do all we can to heal such estrangement when it does happen. He even goes so far as to say that prayer and worship may have to take second place to whatever initiative we can take to bring about reconciliation with those who are estranged from us.

24 February, Saturday, First Week of Lent

Matthew 5:43-48

Occasionally we come across people who have taken Jesus' teaching in today's gospel reading to heart and have lived it out. They have suffered at the hands of their enemies, those who hate them and reject all they stand for. Yet, they appear to hold no bitterness towards those who have persecuted them. They have no desire to inflict on their enemy what their enemy has inflicted on them. They wish their enemy well and pray to God for their present and ultimate well-being. Whenever we come across such people, we feel a profound respect and admiration for them. We know that there is something remarkable about their attitude. We sense that it demonstrates what is best in human nature. We feel ennobled and empowered by such people. The teaching of Jesus in the gospel reading to love our enemy and pray for them can seem very unrealistic, but when we see the Lord's teaching take flesh in a human life we recognise its value, we sense its attractiveness. It has been said that if we can learn to love our enemy, then no one is beyond our love. Jesus identifies the love that he calls for as a divine love. If you love like this, Jesus says, you will be like your Father in heaven. Saint Paul says that God demonstrates his love for us in that while we were still sinners, Christ died for us. The cross reveals God's love even for his enemies. If something of this divine love can be in our lives, through the power of the Spirit, then we will indeed show ourselves to be sons and daughters of God.

26 February, Monday, Second Week of Lent
Luke 6:36-38
The first reading from the Book of Daniel is one of the great acts of sorrow to God for sin in the Bible. It is prayed on behalf of the whole people. It is a prayer that expresses both a great sorrow for sin and a great confidence in God's mercy, 'We have sinned against you. To the Lord our God mercy and pardon belong, because we have betrayed him'. Humility and trust are very clearly revealed in the prayer. We need both when we come before the Lord, the humility to acknowledge that we have not always lived as God calls us to live, and the total trust in God's mercy which is always stronger than sin. In the gospel reading, Jesus speaks of God as a compassionate Father. There

is a close connection between compassion and mercy. When we feel with others and for others, it is easier to forgive their failings towards us. When we suffer with them, when we enter into their situation, then forgiveness comes easier to us. God suffered with us, entered fully into our human situation, through the incarnation of his Son. As Christians, we have an even clearer understanding of God as compassionate and merciful than the writers of the Jewish Scriptures because we believe that God became like us in all things, except sin. In the gospel reading, Jesus asks us to be as compassionate and as merciful as God is, which will mean being slow to judge, slow to condemn others. We live in a culture where there is so often a rush to judgement. Jesus calls on us to take our lead not from the culture but from God who never rushes to judgement.

27 February, Tuesday, Second Week of Lent
Matthew 23:1-12

The words of Jesus in today's gospel reading suggest that preaching can be a dangerous business. It leaves the preacher open to the criticism that Jesus levelled against the religious leaders of his day, 'They do not practise what they preach'. Those who preach need to see themselves as preaching to themselves as much as to others. We are all pilgrims on a shared journey of faith. None of us have arrived; we are all on the way. Hopefully, we are all trying to help each other on this shared journey of faith, with each of us giving from what we have received and receiving from what others have been given. This egalitarian vision of church is reflected in the words of Jesus in the second part of today's gospel reading. He tells us that we are all brothers and sisters with one heavenly Father and with one Lord and one teacher, Jesus. Behind this lies Jesus' vision of his followers as a family. Elsewhere in the gospels Jesus speaks of his disciples as his brothers and sisters. Within this family, Jesus declares that there can be no room for attention seeking, much less honour seeking. Rather, within this family of faith, loving service of others is the golden norm. 'The greatest among you must be your servant'. As a church, we still have some way to go before this vision of Jesus for his followers comes to pass. Yet, the important value is to keep this vision of Jesus in our sights and to keep coming back to the path he sets before us whenever we stray from it.

28 February, Wednesday, Second Week of Lent
Matthew 20:17-28
In today's gospel reading Jesus asks James and John, 'Can you drink the cup that I am going to drink?' He was asking them if they were prepared to share his cup, to throw in their lot with him, to follow where he leads, even though it may mean the cross. In the garden of Gethsemane Jesus prayed, 'Father, if it is possible, let this cup pass from me'. Yet, he went on to drink that cup to the full on the cross. At the last supper, he drank of the cup, and then gave the cup to his disciples, who also drank from it. Yet, a little later, they deserted him and fled. In spite of James's and John's expressed desire to drink from the Lord's cup in today's gospel reading, they would not follow where he would lead when the time came. In a few minutes we will be invited to drink from the Lord's cup, the cup of the Eucharist. In doing so, we are expressing our willingness to going where the Lord leads, walking in his way, even when it means the way of the cross. In today's gospel reading, Jesus speaks of that way as the way of self-giving service of others, as against lording it over others. We pray that in taking the body and the cup of the Lord at this Eucharist, we would be faithful to what that action signifies, walking in the footsteps of the Son of Man who came not to be served but to serve.

1 March, Thursday, Second Week of Lent

Luke 16:19-31

Today's parable reflects the great gulf between the exceedingly wealthy and the completely destitute in the time and place where Jesus lived and worked. The scenario is not without its contemporary equivalents. Jesus in his teaching and in his practice challenged this huge social disparity. In the parable, the physical hunger and thirst of the poor man Lazarus was only satisfied beyond death, at the banquet of life where Abraham was host and Lazarus had a place of honour. Yet, Lazarus need not have waited that long and should not have had to wait that long. If the rich man had given even a little from his abundance, even the scraps that fell from his table, that would have been enough to satisfy Lazarus. Then something of God's kingdom would be coming to pass on earth as it is in heaven. God will see to it that justice is done in the end, even if beyond this earthly life, but God wants something of his justice to become a reality in the here and now. We all have a part to play in making this happen. We may not be fabulously rich like the man in the parable, but many of us have some surplus that could greatly benefit others. Yet, so often we lack the freedom to share it, because we have come to rely on it, to trust in it. If, in the words of today's response to the Psalm, we can place our trust in the Lord more, then we will be freer to live in ways that help to make God's kingdom more of a reality on earth.

2 March, Friday, Second Week of Lent

Matthew 21:33-43, 45-46

As Jesus approaches the hour of his passion and death, he tells a parable about a vineyard owner's son who is killed by the tenants to whom the vineyard was entrusted. Jesus must have seen in this story something of his own story that was unfolding, in particular, his death that was fast approaching. In his comment on the parable, Jesus quotes a passage of Scripture which contained an image about a stone, a kind of a mini parable. The stone that was rejected by the builders as worthless went on to become the most important stone, the keystone, of a building. Again, Jesus would have recognised himself in the stone that was rejected by the builders, just as he recognised himself in the son of the vineyard owner who was killed. However, there is also a suggestion of Jesus' resurrection from the dead in the image of the rejected stone that became a keystone. Jesus would be rejected in the most violent way imaginable. Yet, God raised him from the dead, thereby establishing him as the keystone of a new spiritual building, the Church. The image of the rejected stone becoming a keystone is a powerful image of how God can work powerfully in situations of weakness, to use the language of Paul. For Paul, God worked powerfully through the weakness of Christ crucified on behalf of all humanity. God can turn our own rejected stones into keystones. God can work powerfully through those experiences in our lives which we reject as useless, worthless, of no value. As Paul declares in his letter to the Romans, 'all things work together for good for those who love God'.

3 March, Saturday, Second Week of Lent
Luke 15:1-5, 11-32
This is a story that is very familiar to us. It lives long in our memory. It has inspired artists down through the ages. There are three characters in the story, the father and his two sons. One son was totally rebellious and the other son was dutiful. Yet, each son rejected the father, even if in very different ways. The rebellious son rejected his father by demanding his share of his inheritance before he was entitled to it and then wasting it on self-indulgent activity. The dutiful son rejected the father by refusing to join the celebration when his brother returned and by then addressing his father in tones that were full of self-pity and very judgemental of both his father and his younger brother. The father went out in love to both of his sons. He ran to his

rebellious son when he saw him coming into view on the horizon; he then left the celebratory meal to go out to his dutiful son and to plead with him to come and join the feast. The father speaks to us of God and of Jesus, of God seeking us out through his Son, Jesus. The two sons suggest different ways in which we can isolate ourselves from God, through our self-indulgence which causes pain to others, and through our self-pity which causes us to judge others harshly. In the story, the younger, rebellious son was able to receive the father's love, whereas we do not know if the older son was able to receive the father's love. The story ends with the father pleading in love with his older son and we are not told how the older son responded. One of the messages of this profound story with its many meanings is the importance of being able to receive God's love for myself and of being able to rejoice in God's love for others who are very different to myself.

5 March, Monday, Third Week of Lent
Luke 4:24-30

In his sermon on the mount, Jesus warns against the danger of anger, an emotion that can have deadly consequences if it is nurtured and stoked. Jesus went behind the commandment 'do not kill' to the emotion of anger that can lead to the action that the commandment prohibits. Today's gospel reading gives an example of the kind of deadly anger that Jesus warned against. It is said that the people of Nazareth who heard Jesus preach in their synagogue were enraged at him. Their anger was such that they took Jesus up to the brow of the hill on which their town was built with the intention of throwing him down the cliff to his death. On this occasion Jesus escaped from the deadly power of their anger. Group anger, as is portrayed in the gospel reading, can be even more deadly than individual anger. Why were people so angry at Jesus, so enraged? Jesus reminded his townspeople of what was in their own Scriptures, the Jewish Scriptures.

He was simply showing them that the God of Israel was the God of all humanity and that God often sent his prophets to care for people beyond Israel, indeed, to care for those who would have been considered Israel's enemies. This was the dimension of the God of Israel that Jesus wanted to highlight in his ministry. Because the one true God cares for all of humanity, all the members of the human race are our brothers and sisters, including those who are very different from us. History, past and present, suggests that this is a lesson we have to keep on relearning.

6 March, Tuesday, Third Week of Lent

Matthew 18:21-35

Today's first reading from the Book of Daniel is one of the great acts of sorrow for sin in the Jewish Scriptures. It is a communal act of sorrow. Although prayed by an individual, it is prayed on behalf of all the people. 'Now we are despised throughout the world today because of our sins'. That confession of sin is followed by a firm promise to take a new path, 'Now we put our whole heart into following you, into fearing you and seeking your face once more'. The prayer expresses confidence in God's mercy, 'Treat us gently, as you yourself are gentle and very merciful'. The people can make this prayer for mercy, in the confidence that the God of mercy will hear it. Although it is a Jewish prayer, it could be prayed by any Christian, as is the case with so many Jewish prayers. This prayer is reflected in the request of the servant in the gospel reading who threw himself at his master's feet, imploring him, 'Give me time and I will pay the whole sum'. He owed a very large sum of money to his master and needed time to pay it off. The master in the parable gave him more than he asked for. He simply cancelled the vast debt so that the time asked for was superfluous. There is an image here of God whose response to our prayer for mercy is always more generous than we could imagine. Having been graced so abundantly, the servant refused to grant a much smaller grace to a fellow servant who also asked for time to pay off a much smaller debt. As a result, the first servant lost the forgiveness he had been granted. Jesus is reminding us in this parable, that we are to give as we have received. The abundant mercy we have received from God obliges us to pass some of it on to others. That is why Jesus taught us to pray, 'Forgive us our trespasses, as we forgive those who trespass against us'.

7 March, Wednesday, Third Week of Lent
Matthew 5:17-19

The first reading shows us that the people of Israel understood their laws as a great gift from God given through Moses. For the people of Israel, their laws embodied a great wisdom and they traced out a path that was well worth taking because it would bring life to oneself and to others. According to Matthew, Jesus declared that he did not come to abolish these laws, but to bring them to completion, to fulfilment, through his teaching and his way of life. If the Jewish Law embodied a great wisdom, Jesus' teaching embodied an even greater wisdom because Jesus himself was the Wisdom of God. If the Jewish Law was the way to life, Jesus' teaching was life-giving to an even greater extent, because it is the way that leads to eternal life beyond this earthly life. If according to today's first reading from the Book of Deuteronomy, the people of Israel are blessed – 'what great nation is there that has laws and customs to match this whole law?' – we are even more blessed. As Jesus declares in today's gospel reading, those who keep Jesus' words and teach others to do the same will be considered great in the kingdom of heaven. We thank God for what we have received through his Son, and we pray that we would always treasure it and seek to pass it on to others.

8 March, Thursday, Third Week of Lent

Luke 11:14-23

It is always an inspiration to meet people who recognise the good in others, while not being blind to their failings. They have an eye for the presence of God in the lives of others. They can perceive the 'finger of God' at work there, in the image of today's gospel reading. As a result, the good that is there is affirmed and strengthened. In contrast, it can be very dispiriting to be in the company of someone who can only see the negative in the life of someone else. The exclusive focus on what is wrong makes them blind, and can make others blind, to the good that is also there. An extreme example of this kind of seeing is to be found in today's gospel reading. Jesus had healed someone with a speech impediment and some people concluded that this showed the working of Beelzebul (or Satan) in Jesus' life. If the finger of God could be seen anywhere, it was in the ministry of Jesus, and yet these people were blind to it. It is often the case that we see what we want to see rather than seeing what is really there, because to see what is really there would be to allow our basic assumptions to be challenged. At the end of the gospel reading Jesus calls on us to be with him in a wholehearted way, 'he who is not with me is against me'. Being with Jesus entails seeing with his eyes, recognising the finger of God even in places and people where it seems absent.

9 March, Friday, Third Week of Lent

Mark 12:28-34

In the time of Jesus it was understood that there were 613 regulations of the Jewish Law. In that context, the question of the scribe to Jesus in today's gospel reading is an important one, 'Which is the first of all the commandments?' He was asking Jesus what was the cornerstone on which all of the rest of the law rested. In a sense he was asking, 'What is the core of our Jewish faith?' He wanted Jesus to help him to get to the heart of the matter. We are all searching for that core.

We all want to know what really matters in our faith, in life. We are aware that we can get hung up on non-essentials and neglect what really matters. The answer Jesus gave to the scribe is valid not just for the Jewish faith but for our own Christian faith. It is God who is central, and the most important commandment is to love God. Jesus does not say to fear God or to obey God but to love God. God's nature is love and the appropriate way to relate to God is through love. Jesus declares that this is to be a love that embraces all of our being, all our heart, the seat of will and intellect, all our soul, the seat of desire, all our mind, the seat of understanding and all our strength, understood as spiritual strength. This is a unique love which is due to God alone and which will find expression in prayer and worship. In response to the scribe's question about the first of all the commandments, Jesus goes on to give what he considers to be the second most important commandment, to love our neighbour as if he or she were an extension of ourselves. An authentic love of God will embrace the neighbour, whoever he or she may be. Jesus implies that if we truly love God we will be caught up into God's love of all humanity.

10 March, Saturday, Third Week of Lent
Luke 18:9-14
The parable in today's gospel reading relates to prayer. One man prayed a prayer of thanksgiving and the other a prayer of petition. We all pray in petition and thanksgiving at different moments in our lives. Indeed, probably the prayer of petition comes easier to us. It is often when we are in need that we pray with greatest fervour and when we are in need our prayer is generally one of petition. We can neglect the prayer of thanksgiving. At one level, the Pharisee's prayer of thanksgiving was very appropriate. He thanked God that he had kept God's Law, which suggests that he understood that his keeping of God's Law was due to God. It was God who enabled him to live according to God's will. However, his prayer was fatally tainted

by his disdain for a fellow human being, the tax collector who was present in the Temple at the same time. He seems to have forgotten that love of God was inseparable from love of neighbour, even if the neighbour left a lot to be desired. There was no disdain for anyone in the tax collector's prayer of petition, except perhaps for himself. His prayer reminds us of the little speech of the prodigal son when he arrived home, 'Father, I have sinned against heaven and against you'. The gospels assure us that such a prayer for mercy when prayed with sincerity of heart will always be heard by God. As today's responsorial psalm expresses it, 'a humbled, contrite heart, O God, you will not spurn'.

12 March, Monday, Fourth Week of Lent

John 4:43-54

We are only two weeks away now from Holy Week. Between now and Holy Week the weekday gospel readings are taken from the gospel of John. In today's gospel reading, the court official showed faith in coming to Jesus and asking him to cure his seriously ill son. Yet, rather than responding to the official's request immediately, Jesus challenges his faith. Jesus suggests that the official's faith is dependent on his seeing signs and wonders, in particular, the sign and wonder of his son being healed by Jesus. Yet, the official's son turned out to be deeper than that kind of faith. Jesus did not go to the home of the official to cure his son. Instead, he simply said to him, 'Go home, your son will live'. In response to what Jesus said, the gospel reading tells us that 'the man believed what Jesus had said'. He believed on the basis of Jesus' word, before he had seen any signs or wonders, before he knew whether or not his son would be healed on his return home. His faith in Jesus' word was vindicated. Before he reached home, word came to him that his son had recovered. This royal official exemplifies the faith we all need to have, a faith that is based on the word of Jesus, on the promise of Jesus, a faith that is not dependant on signs and wonders. We won't always see signs and wonders, but we always have the word of Jesus preserved for us in the gospels. The Lord's word is enough for us. It is what we are asked to believe.

13 March, Tuesday, Fourth Week of Lent
John 5:1-3, 5-16

Many people benefit from Jesus' healing ministry across the four gospels. Most of them respond appropriately to the gift they have received. They give praise to God; they announce to others what God has done for them; some even become followers of Jesus. The man who was healed in today's gospel reading seems to respond somewhat inappropriately. Jesus took the initiative to heal him. The question Jesus asked him, 'Do you want to be well again?', may seem strange to our ears. Yet, in asking this question Jesus was giving him the opportunity to be involved in his own healing. Jesus healed the man on the Sabbath day which put him at odds with the religious leaders of the time. They wanted the man who had been healed to tell them who it was that healed him on the Sabbath. The man didn't know who had healed him until Jesus took another initiative towards him and revealed his identity to the man. The healed man then sought out the religious leaders to tell them it was Jesus who healed him. In a sense, he appears to betray Jesus to his enemies. As a result, the religious leaders began to persecute Jesus. The good that he did for this man did not serve Jesus well. Sometimes the good we do does not always serve us well either. When we give of ourselves to others, we don't always receive something good in return. Jesus would make this discovery more than once. Yet, he continued doing good, giving of himself, until his last breath. He teaches us to do the same. We serve, we give, not in order to get back something, but simply because it is the right thing to do, what God wants of us.

14 March, Wednesday, Fourth Week of Lent

John 5:17-30

At the end of today's gospel reading, Jesus declares, 'My aim is not to do my own will, but the will of him who sent me'. Jesus' life is shaped by the will of his Father, and that will is that all men and women would find life through believing in Jesus. As the evangelist says a little earlier in his gospel, 'God did not send the Son into the world to condemn the world, but in order that the world might be saved through him.' In the words of today's gospel reading, 'The Father, who is the source of life, has made the Son the source of life'. God wills life and that is why Jesus says elsewhere in John's Gospel, 'I have come that they may have life and have it to the full'. This is also the image of God we find in today's first reading. Just as a mother cherishes the child of her womb and gives life to her child, even more so does God cherish us and work to bring us to fullness of life. God guides us to springs of water. When we pray 'your will be done' in the Our Father we are praying that a culture of life would prevail over a culture of death. We are also committing ourselves to doing God's will by protecting life, by bringing life to others, by helping others to life fully-human lives, lives that are shaped by the Holy Spirit and that lead ultimately to eternal life.

15 March, Thursday, Fourth Week of Lent

John 5:31-47

Very few of us probably could say with Jesus in today's gospel reading, 'As for human approval, this means nothing to me'. Very few of us are indifferent to what other people think of us. If we meet with disapproval, we tend to think that there is something wrong with us. We sometimes measure our worth in relation to how others see us. Human approval can confirm our sense of self-worth; similarly human disapproval can undermine our sense of self-worth. Jesus was not like us in that respect. His sense of self-worth was rooted less in how others saw him and very much in how God saw him. In the gospel reading, Jesus goes on to challenge his critics, 'How can you believe, since you look to one another for approval and are not concerned about the approval that comes from the one God?' Many of Jesus' critics went along with undermining Jesus' ministry because this is what their peers were doing. They were more concerned with the approval of their peers than with the approval of God. Peer pressure is a permanent feature of life in any age. We can all find ourselves going along with the emerging consensus, because not to do so would be to risk the disapproval of others. Yet, Jesus suggests in the gospel reading that the more important question is not 'what do others think?' but rather 'what does God think?' or 'how does God see me?' In the gospel reading, Jesus suggests that one of the places where we can discover what God thinks, what God approves or and doesn't, is in the Scriptures, 'these same Scriptures testify to me', and for us that includes above all the Christian Scriptures. As believers, it is from there we try to take our lead, even if it leaves us at odds with our peers.

16 March, Friday, Fourth Week of Lent
John 7:1-2, 10, 25-30

In the gospel reading, Jesus speaks of himself as the one whom God has sent: 'There is one who sent me and I really came from him.' He goes on to claim that because he came from God, he knows God: 'I know him because I have come from him and it was he who sent me.' It is only Jesus who can make the claim to know God, because it is only Jesus who, according to this fourth gospel, was with God in the beginning, who came from God to earth and who remains close to the Father's heart while on earth. It is Jesus who is uniquely placed to make God known. 'No one has ever seen God. It is God the only Son, who is close to the Father's heart, who has made him known' (*Jn 1:18*). It is because Jesus is the only one who can make God fully known that he is at the centre of our faith. We all have a deep desire to see and know God. In this fourth gospel, Philip speaks for us all when he says to Jesus, 'Lord, show us the Father, and we will be satisfied' (*Jn 14:8*). On that occasion, Jesus had to remind Philip, 'Whoever has seen me has seen the Father'. Jesus shows us the face of God because he is God in human form. If Jesus shows us the face of God, it is above all the gospels that show us the face of Jesus. The gospels are our bread of life because there we meet Jesus who reveals the God who alone can satisfy our deepest hungers.

17 March, Saturday, Feast of Saint Patrick

Mark 16:15-20

Today on the feast of St Patrick, we celebrate the beginnings of the Christian story in Ireland. We remember Patrick as the one who lit a flame that has remained lighting for nearly 1,600 years. Today we give thanks that the flame of faith that Patrick first lit has been kept alive among us. Two of Patrick's own writings have been preserved for us. It is above all from his 'Confessions' that we get the fascinating story of his life. He was probably a citizen of Roman Britain. His father was a town councillor, part of the local Roman administration. Patrick came from a Christian family. He tells us that his father was a priest and that his grandfather was a deacon. Yet, in his youth Patrick's faith was lukewarm. Then at the tender age of sixteen, his rather comfortable world came crashing down around him. Writing in his confessions, he says: 'I was taken into captivity in Ireland with many thousands of people ... this is where I now am, among strangers'. Patrick became an emigrant, against his wishes. Many of our young people today find themselves in a similar situation. We probably all know one or two people who have recently emigrated without it being their first choice. Patrick's forced emigration was of a very rough kind. He was wrenched from the family that loved him, taken from his home, friends and culture by captives, and thrown into a foreign land as a slave. An experience like that could destroy a young man. Yet, Patrick tells us that in this harsh exile, he had a powerful experience of God's presence. He writes about, The great benefits that the Lord saw fit to confer on me in my captivity'. In the wilderness of exile, when everything was taken from him, his faith started to fan into a living flame. When we experience some devastating loss, the suffering can be bitter indeed; we find ourselves at the foot of the cross. Yet, like Patrick, we can also find, perhaps to our surprise, that the Risen Lord is there to lift us up.

Patrick goes on to tell us that six years after first coming to Ireland as a slave, at the age of twenty-two, he escaped from his captivity and made his way home. What a homecoming that must have been for his parents, who thought they would never see him again. Patrick states that, 'They earnestly begged me that I should never leave them'. Yet, some years later, Patrick tells us, he had a vision of a man coming from Ireland with a large number of letters. As he began to read one of them, he heard a crowd shout with one voice: 'We ask you, boy, come and walk once more among us'. That vision touched him deeply, and there and then decided to answer the call. He writes,'I came to the Irish heathen to preach the good news'. Patrick was prepared to endure voluntary exile to bring the gospel to the very people among whom he had experienced captivity. He brought the precious gift of the Christian faith to those who had taken away his freedom many years earlier. The gospel reading refers to the Lord working powerfully through his disciples. He certainly worked powerfully through Patrick. He continues to work powerfully today through our own efforts to proclaim the gospel by what we say and how we live. All the Lord asks of us is that we may remain faithful and generous. We could easily make our own the prayer of Patrick, 'I ask God for perseverance, to grant that I remain a faithful witness to him for his own sake until my passing from this life.'

19 March, Feast of Saint Joseph

Matthew 1:16, 18-21, 24

We know relatively little about Joseph. In the gospel of Matthew, when Jesus preached for the first time in his home town of Nazareth, those who knew him asked, 'Is not this the carpenter's son?' Jesus was known to them as the son of the carpenter, the son of Joseph. Joseph had a skill which not everybody in Nazareth had; he could make useful things from wood. He used his skill to provide for his family, including his son Jesus. Jesus would go on to provide for many people in the course of his public ministry. He gave everything he had, including his very life, for God's people, for all of us. Yet, before Jesus could provide for others, he needed to be provided for, and Joseph played a key role in providing for him. With Mary, Joseph made it possible for Jesus to get to the point where he could leave home a fully formed adult and begin in earnest the work that God gave him to do. Jesus was able to do his work in Galilee and Judea because Joseph did his work in Nazareth. Joseph's work might seem insignificant compared to the work Jesus went on to do and still does as Risen Lord. Yet, Joseph's work was vitally important because without Joseph's work, Jesus would not have gone on to do the work of God. Joseph teaches us the importance of doing what we have to do as well as possible, even if what we are doing seems of little significance in the greater scheme of things. We are all interdependent. If we do what we have to do as well as we can, we make it easier for everyone else to do what they are called to do. Everything we do has greater significance that we realise. We all have vital roles to play within God's greater purpose. We are all called to do God's work, at every stage of our lives, each of us in our own particular way.

20 March, Tuesday, Fifth Week of Lent
John 8:21-30

As we draw close to Holy Week, Jesus speaks of his forthcoming death in today's gospel reading, 'I am going away... Where I am going, you cannot come'. Jesus speaks of his death as a journey. He is soon to leave this world and go to his heavenly Father. His being lifted up on the cross is a crucial moment in this journey. Those who crucified Jesus believed they were doing away with him. In reality, they were sending him on a journey back to his Father from whom he came. His going to the Father made it possible for him to send the Holy Spirit to all who believe in him. His departure, his leaving this world and going to his Father, was a life-giving journey not just for himself but for all his disciples. Artists down the centuries have often depicted the cross of Jesus, the wood of the cross, as a source of life. They sometimes depict water flowing from the foot of the cross or the tendrils of a vine growing out from the wood of the cross. This is very much in keeping with the understanding of the death of Jesus in the gospels, and in John's gospel in particular. The crucifixion of Jesus was the revelation, the explosion, of God's love for the world, a love that is supremely life giving for all who open themselves to it. From the cross flows the Spirit of God's love for all humanity.

21 March, Wednesday, Fifth Week of Lent
John 8:31-42

'Freedom' is very much a buzzword of our time. Freedom, as we know, can mean different things to different people. What one person's exercise of what they consider to be their 'freedom' can result in slavery or oppression or death for someone else. In today's gospel reading, Jesus speaks of freedom. He declares, 'the truth will make you free'. A little further on in the gospel, Jesus will declare, 'I am the truth'. Jesus declares himself to be the source of true freedom. As he says in our reading today, 'If the Son makes you free, you will be free indeed'. It is Jesus who can free us from the enslavement of sin; through the gift of the Spirit, he can empower us to live as God wants us to live, to love as God loves, to be perfect as God is perfect. This is what Paul calls 'the glorious freedom of the children of God', the freedom to live in accordance with God's purpose for our lives. This is authentic freedom, and Jesus – and the Spirit he pours into our hearts – is the source of such freedom. Saint Paul expresses this truth very simply, 'Where the Spirit of the Lord is, there is freedom' (*2 Cor 3:17*).

22 March, Thursday, Fifth Week of Lent

John 8:51-59

In the gospel reading Jesus makes an extraordinary claim that leads the Jewish leaders to want to stone him, 'Before Abraham was, I am'. This claim of Jesus in the fourth gospel is in keeping with the opening line of that gospel, 'In the beginning was the Word and the Word was with God'. Jesus existed with God in the beginning, before the creation of the world. He was before Abraham was, indeed, before anything had come into being. Yet, the Word who was with God in the beginning became flesh. He became like us in all things, except sin. While on earth, he remained with God. Having returned to God through his death and resurrection, he remains with us. He is now both with God and with us. He is uniquely placed to bring us the life of God, a life without end. That is why he can make the promise he makes in today's gospel reading, 'Whoever keeps my word will never know the taste of death'. It is an extraordinary promise. Surely, we will all know the taste of death. Yes, we will all know physical death, as Jesus did, but Jesus is speaking about spiritual or ultimate death. He is promising us that those who keep his word will never know this kind of death. They will begin to share in God's life here and now, a life that endures beyond physical death. If we entrust ourselves to the Lord, if we allow his word to shape our lives then, according to the gospel reading today, we will begin to live with a life which will not be interrupted by physical death. This life, which begins now, is a life of communion with the Lord, and that communion will not be broken by death but, rather, it will be deepened beyond it.

23 March, Friday, Fifth Week of Lent

John 10:31-42

In today's gospel reading, Jesus is accused of blasphemy: 'You are only a man and you claim to be God'. From a Jewish perspective, for any man to claim to be God was blasphemy. The accusation of blasphemy seems to have been levelled against Jesus on more than one occasion. At the very beginning of his public ministry, Mark's Gospel informs us that Jesus was accused of blasphemy because he declared to the paralytic, 'Your sins are forgiven'. The response of the experts in the Jewish Law was to say, 'It is blasphemy! Who can forgive sins but God alone?' Jesus was judged to be speaking in ways that were associated exclusively with God. In response to the accusation of blasphemy in today's gospel reading, Jesus speaks of himself as the one whom the Father consecrated and sent into the world and as the one who is doing the work of God his Father. That expresses what we believe about Jesus. He is the one whom God has sent into the world to do the work of God. He has a unique relationship with God; he is Son of God. He is not only a man who claims to be God; he is a man in whom God is to be found in a unique way. In the centuries after the gospels were written the Church would say that Jesus was fully human and fully divine. In the coming week we will be contemplating the humanity of Jesus in all its pain and brokenness, his passion and death. Today's gospel reading reminds us that in looking upon the broken humanity of Jesus we are also looking upon the face of God, the God who so loved the world that he gave his only Son.

24 March, Saturday, Fifth Week of Lent

John 11:45-56

At the end of today's gospel reading, a decision is made by the Jewish authorities to put Jesus to death. He was considered a threat to the status quo, from which the authorities benefited. In every age and culture, those who are perceived to be disturbing the way things have always been are silenced in one way or another. Jesus was disturbing the status quo just by being true to his deepest calling from God. He came to bring God's life to the world. He had just raised Lazarus from the dead and brought joy to a grieving family. It was this liberating, life-giving work that was perceived as threatening. It was because Jesus came as the life-giver that he was put to death. In giving life to people like Lazarus, Jesus lost his own life. Yet, the further paradox was that in losing his life, in having his life taken from him, Jesus continued his life-giving work. Jesus was the life-giver on the cross, as much as when he walked the paths of Galilee and the streets of Jerusalem. In today's gospel reading, the evangelist declares that Jesus' death had a gathering effect. He died 'to gather together in unity the scattered children of God'. Jesus' death was an even fuller revelation of God's life-giving love for the world, than his life had been. God's love pouring from the broken body of Jesus drew people to Jesus and gathered them together around him. This is one of the ways his death was life-giving for others. That is why we call the Friday on which Jesus was crucified Good Friday and why we venerate the wood of the cross on that day, rather than simply grieving over it.

26 March, Monday in Holy Week

John 12:1-11

The gospel reading for next Thursday, Holy Thursday, is the account of Jesus washing the feet of his disciples with a basin of water and wiping them with a towel. It was an act of loving service that pointed forward to the greater act of loving service he would perform for them and for all humanity on the following day when he would lay down his life as the good shepherd. In today's gospel reading, Mary performs an act of loving service for Jesus that looks ahead to his act of loving service on Holy Thursday. Rather than washing the feet of Jesus with water, she anoints his feet with very costly ointment, and rather than wiping his feet with a towel she wipes then with her hair. During the following six days, Jesus would be treated with total disrespect; he would be made to suffer the most ignominious death imaginable by crucifixion. However, at this meal, Jesus is shown a tender love and respect by Mary, the sister of Lazarus. Jesus interprets her gesture as preparing him, strengthening him, for what lies ahead. Mary was anointing him in advance of his death and burial. As Jesus entered his darkest hour, a ray of light shone through Mary. This woman inspires us to become a ray of light in whatever darkness others may be experiencing. Whenever we do something, no matter how small, to support those who are walking through their own valley of darkness, it is the Lord that we are serving.

27 March, Tuesday in Holy Week
John 13:21-33, 36-38

There is a very dramatic verse in today's gospel reading: 'As soon as Judas had taken the piece of bread he went out. Night had fallen.' Jesus had offered Judas bread that had been dipped in the dish as a sign of affection and friendship. Judas took the bread but not the love that it expressed. After taking the bread, he walked out into the darkness of the night, having turned away from the light of the world. This scene happens in John's Gospel immediately after the scene of Jesus washing the feet of his disciples. He washed the feet of all his disciples, including the feet of Judas. He showed the same love to Judas that he showed to the other disciples. Judas, however, did not receive Jesus' love. He chose to turn his back on it. We see the mystery of human freedom at work here. The Lord needs our free response to the offer of his love and friendship. If it is not forthcoming, he cannot force it. Yet, as Risen Lord he continues to seek out the lost. His seeking us in our weakness and sin is never in doubt. The only question is whether we will allow ourselves to be found. This Holy Week is a good time to allow ourselves to be found by the Lord who has laid down his life for us. As we contemplate the final journey of Jesus, as we celebrate it liturgically, we allow ourselves to be touched by the love which that journey expresses. It is the love of the good shepherd for all the scattered children of God.

28 March, Wednesday in Holy Week

Matthew 26:14-25

The early Church was very aware that Jesus was betrayed to his enemies by one of his closest associates. Even though this was a very uncomfortable reality for the first generation of believers, there was no attempt to gloss over the disturbing truth that, in the words of today's gospel reading, Jesus was betrayed by someone who dipped his hand into the dish with Jesus, someone who broke bread with Jesus. The gospel reading declares that when Jesus announced that one of those sharing table with him would betray him, everyone present was 'greatly distressed'. To be betrayed by someone you trust is very distressing both for the one betrayed and for all those associated with that person. Some of us may have had the experience of our trust being betrayed. We confide in someone and they use that information against us. This week tells us that, in the case of Jesus, the human betrayal that led to Jesus' crucifixion did not have the last word; God had the last word by raising his Son from the dead. God brought good out of the evil of betrayal and the many other evils that Jesus endured in the last week of his life. God can also bring good out of the painful experiences that come our way because of others. These days of Holy Week invite us to trust that God can work in life-giving ways even in those dark experiences that might make us cry out in the words of today's psalm, 'I have reached the end of my strength'.

Easter Triduum: 29–31 March

2 April, Easter Monday

Matthew 28:8-15

We have been hearing a lot about 'fake news' in recent times. There is an example of such fake news in today's gospel reading. When the soldiers who had guarded the tomb of Jesus went to the chief priests and told them what they witnessed, the chief priests, with the elders, told the soldiers to spread a fake news story, according to which Jesus' disciples came during the night and stole the body of Jesus while the soldiers slept. This story, false as it is, nonetheless presupposes that the tomb of Jesus was empty on the morning of the first day of the Jewish week, our Sunday. In yesterday's gospel reading, when Mary Magdalene saw the tomb was empty, she came to the conclusion that someone had stolen the body, 'They have taken the Lord out of the tomb and we do not know where they have put him'. This was simply a misunderstanding, which was clarified when the Risen Lord appeared to Mary. There is a big difference between misunderstanding and the propagation of a deliberate falsehood. There is nothing false about Easter, it is the truth that grounds all other Christian truths. As Paul declares in his first letter to the Corinthians, 'If Christ has not been raised, then our proclamation has been in vain and your faith has been in vain'. An essential part of the Church's mission is to proclaim the truth of Easter and all that it implies. In raising his Son from the dead, God demonstrates his faithfulness to his Son and his faithfulness to all humanity, in spite of its sinful rejection of his Son. Easter announces, again in the words of Saint Paul, that 'God is for us'. This is a truth which the world needs to hear.

3 April, Easter Tuesday

John 20:11-18

In today's gospel reading, the evangelist traces Mary Magdalene's journey towards Easter faith. Initially she is weeping at the empty tomb of Jesus. She then saw Jesus standing there but didn't recognise him, assuming he was the gardener. Then in response to Jesus calling her name, she recognised the figure standing before her as Jesus. She was not yet at Easter faith. She called Jesus 'Master', which was the title she had given him before his death, and she clung to him. She had to learn to let Jesus go. He would no longer be with his disciples as he was before his death. He would be with them in a new way in and through the Holy Spirit. Only when she had let go of her former relationship with Jesus could she finally be sent out as a messenger of Easter faith, 'I have seen the Lord'. At the beginning of the gospel reading, Mary was a disciple weeping for the dead Jesus. At the end of the reading, she was a joyful messenger of the Easter good news. We are all on a similar journey towards a fully mature Easter faith. Part of that journey will involve for us, as it did for Mary, a letting go of Jesus. Mary had to learn that she could not possess Jesus. There was more to Jesus as Risen Lord than she imagined. We too have to let go of Jesus as we might want him to be. We cannot possess the Risen Lord, no more than Mary could. We can only allow ourselves to be possessed by him who said of himself, 'I am the Truth'. I have recently been reading *Last Testament: In His Own Words* by Benedict XVI and Peter Seewald. Towards the end of this extended interview he says, 'We cannot say, "I have the truth", but the truth has us, it touches us. And we try to let ourselves be guided by this touch.'

4 April, Easter Wednesday

Luke 24:13-35

One way of hearing today's gospel reading is as having something to say to us about prayer. We always come to pray as we are, rather than as we think we should be. The two disciples on the road to Emmaus were clearly discouraged and downcast. We can all find ourselves in that place from time to time, in the shadow of the cross. If that is where we are, that is the self we bring to prayer. When the Risen Lord first spoke to his unsuspecting disciples, it was to invite them to share what was in their hearts, to tell him their story, a story that was full of sadness and devoid of hope. The Lord invites us in prayer to tell our story, to share with him whatever might be in our hearts. It is only when the Lord had listened to their story that he told them his story, the story of his journey from suffering to glory as told in the Scriptures. Having opened their hearts to this stranger, it was now their turn to listen. There comes a time in our prayer when, having opened our hearts to the Lord, we too need to listen to his word to us. A passage from scripture can help us to be attentive to what the Lord might want to say to us. This prayerful moment of sharing with the Lord and listening to him 'on the way' led to another prayerful moment at table. There Jesus prayed a prayer of blessing over the bread, broke it and gave it to his disciples. Jesus' prayerful words and actions led to a prayer of recognition on the part of the disciples. They recognised the Lord at the breaking of bread. Our prayer of sharing and listening will often lead us to the prayer of the Eucharist. There we enter into the Lord's own prayer of blessing and thanksgiving to the Father as we prayerfully recognise the Lord who comes us in the breaking of bread. After these prayerful encounters, the two disciples left the table and shared with others their Easter faith. At the end of every Eucharist, we are sent out to do the same.

5 April, Easter Thursday

Luke 24:35-48

Today's gospel reading is Luke's account of the first appearance of the Risen Lord to the disciples as a group. His first words to the disciples after rising from the dead were, 'Peace be with you'. It is a greeting that has made its way into our celebration of the Eucharist. The Risen Lord was offering his disciples the gift of his peace. He was making peace with those who had slept on the Mount of Olives when he had asked them to pray. He was making peace with Peter who had denied him publicly three times. He was taking the initiative to be reconciled with those who had failed him. Like the father in the parable of the prodigal son, he was welcoming back into communion with himself those who had strayed. He went on to express his communion with his disciples by eating in their company. The resurrection proclaimed the faithfulness of Jesus to his flawed disciples. It was a moment of grace which the disciples struggled to receive. According to the gospel reading, they were agitated and full of doubt. They were dumbfounded. In a striking phrase, it is said of them that 'their joy was so great they still could not believe it'. The Risen Lord continues to stand among us offering us his peace. Our many past failings do not make his presence any less powerful or his offer of peace any less generous. He comes among us to call us into a renewed communion with himself. As Risen Lord he shows us the face of God as mercy. When we allow ourselves to receive the peace of God he is offering, then he will send us out, as he send out his first disciples, as his peacemakers, as messengers of God's love and mercy.

6 April, Easter Friday

John 21:1-14

We have packets of charcoal in the Sacristy. On solemn liturgical occasions, the charcoal is placed in the Thurible and, after it is lit, incense is sprinkled on the lighted charcoal. In today's gospel reading, mention is made of a charcoal fire. The Risen Jesus appeared to his disciples by the Sea of Galilee as a host. When the disciples came ashore, they saw that there was some bread there and a charcoal fire with fish cooking on it. Jesus said to them, 'Come and have breakfast'. The charcoal fire was a symbol of the Lord's hospitality to his disciples who, at the hour of his passion, had scattered, each to his own home, leaving him alone. The only other reference to a charcoal fire in this gospel, the Gospel of John, is in connection with the story of the denial of Peter. After the first denial of Peter, the evangelist says that the police who had earlier arrested Jesus were standing around a charcoal fire warming themselves, and Peter was standing with them, warming himself. He was in the company of Jesus' enemies That charcoal fire was a symbol of the failure of the disciples, their lack of courage, and of Peter's failure, in particular. The second charcoal fire symbolises the Lord's faithfulness to his failed disciples. He wanted their company, even though they fled from his company in his hour of need. The Lord continues to call us into communion with himself, 'Come and have breakfast', even though we may break off communion with him. The smell of the incense on the burning charcoal at our liturgies might serve to remind us of the Lord's faithful love.

7 April, Easter Saturday
Mark 16:9-15

Today's gospel has a focus on the unwillingness of the disciples to initially believe the Easter story. Mary of Magdala went to them to announce that the Risen Lord had appeared to her, and they did not believe her. Two of the disciples went to the other disciples to announce that the Risen Lord had appeared to them and their story was not believed either. Jesus himself finally appeared to those who had refused to believe the story of Mary of Magdala or the story of the two disciples and rebuked them for their reluctance to believe those who had seen the Risen Lord. The gospel reading suggests that the disciples were very slow to believe the news that Jesus had risen from the dead, until the Risen Lord himself appeared to them. Nothing less than a personal appearance of the Risen Lord to them would bring them to Easter faith. It is evident that Jesus' closest associates did not expect him to rise from the dead and had great difficulty in really believing it. However, the first reading shows that once the Risen Lord appeared to them and they knew in their hearts that the Lord had risen from the dead, nothing would stop them from proclaiming this wonderful news. When the Jewish authorities warned them to make no further statements about Jesus, the disciples stood their ground, 'We cannot promise to stop proclaiming what we have seen and heard'. Once doubt and incredulity gave way to Easter faith, after the Lord appeared to them, their faith was unshakable. It is because of their eventual, unshakable, faith and their courage in proclaiming it that we are here today to celebrate our Easter faith. The Risen Lord has touched all our lives through the preaching of those eye witnesses of the Risen Lord, and for this we give thanks.

9 April, Monday, Annunciation of the Lord

Luke 1:26-38

The gospel reading portrays Mary as saying 'yes' to God's call on her to become the mother of God's Son. Yet, the gospel suggests that her response to God's call did not come easily to her. Initially she was 'deeply disturbed' by the greeting of the angel. She was full of questions in response to the further words of the angel. 'How can this come about?', she asked. She eventually arrived at the point where she could say, 'Let what you have said be done to me'. However, she only came to that point after a lot of struggle. We are reminded of Jesus in the garden of Gethsemane. His prayer eventually brought him to the point where he could say, 'Not my will but yours be done'. Again, that was only after a great struggle, in the course of which he had prayed, 'Remove this cup from me'. The experience of Mary and of Jesus remind us that responding to God's call, remaining faithful to God's will for our lives, will always involve a struggle of some kind. The nature of that struggle will be different for each of us. We engage in that struggle knowing that we are not alone in it. The power of the Most High will overshadow us; the Holy Spirit will come upon us, as it came upon Mary. In our struggle to be faithful, we are also encouraged by the words of Gabriel to Mary, 'Nothing is impossible to God'. In the words of Paul's first letter to the church in Thessalonica, 'The one who calls you is faithful, and he will do this'. Mary is also a resource in our struggle to remain faithful, which is why we ask her to intercede for us, 'Pray for us sinners, now and at the hour of our death'.

10 April, Tuesday, Second Week of Easter
John 3:7-15

In today's gospel reading, Jesus speaks of the wind as having a mysterious quality. Although we can hear the sound of the wind, it is not always easy to judge the direction the wind is blowing from and the direction towards which it is blowing. In the language that the gospels were written, and the language Jesus spoke, the same word could refer to both the physical wind and the Spirit of God. Jesus argues that if there is a mysterious quality about the wind, there is an even more mysterious quality about the Spirit of God. The origin and destination of the Spirit, the Holy Spirit, is wrapped in the mystery of God. We cannot fully grasp the Holy Spirit and we certainly cannot control the Holy Spirit. The Holy Spirit is the Spirit of God's love, a love whose breadth and length and height and depth cannot be fully comprehended. Yet, God pours this Spirit of his love into our lives. Our calling is to surrender to this Spirit in our lives, to allow ourselves to be born of this Spirit, to be born from above, in the words of Jesus to Nicodemus. This being born of the Spirit will take more than nine months, the period of human birth. The opening of our lives more fully to the Spirit of God is the journey of a lifetime, a journey we are asked to be faithful to until the end of our earthly lives.

11 April, Wednesday, Second Week of Easter
John 3:16-21

The words of Jesus to Nicodemus in today's gospel reading are one of the strongest and most positive statements in the New Testament about God. It speaks of God's love for the world, of God's generous way of expressing his love by giving the world his Son and of God's desire that all people would experience eternal life through receiving God's Son in faith. It is a hugely positive image of God and of how God relates to the world. It is a verse worth pondering and reflecting upon at length. Yet, the gospel reading we have just heard acknowledges another reality. It recognises that people can refuse God's love, God's gift of his Son, God's offer of life. In the words of the gospel reading, 'Though the light has come into the world, people have shown that they prefer darkness to the light, because their deeds were evil.' God can only do so much. We have to open ourselves to God's love, receive God's Son, enter into the light and allow it to shine upon us. God wants our response, but God cannot force it. Yet, God is prepared to wait, as Jesus was prepared to wait for Nicodemus. He only gradually came to believe in Jesus as God's Son given to the world out of love. His first tentative step was to come to Jesus by night. His last appearance in the gospel is alongside Joseph of Arimathea, as they both arrange for Jesus to have a dignified burial.

12 April, Thursday, Second Week of Easter
John 3:31-36

One of the questions that Jesus is often asked in John's Gospel is, 'Where do you come from?' When people ask that question they generally mean, 'Where about in Judea or in Galilee do you come from?' However, the attentive readers of John's Gospel will recognise that there is more to that question than those who ask it seem to realise. The real answer to the question addressed to Jesus, 'Where do you come from?', is that Jesus comes from heaven or from God. This is what we find stated very clearly in today's gospel reading, which declares that Jesus comes from above or from heaven. The gospel reading goes on to declare that because Jesus comes from heaven, he is able to bear witness to what he has seen and heard in heaven, what he has seen and heard from God his Father. He is uniquely placed to bear witness to who God is because, according to John's Gospel, he has been with God from all eternity and has come from God. Indeed this gospel would go further and state that Jesus is God in human form. That is why we take Jesus so seriously and is why we pay such close attention to what he does and says, to his life, death and resurrection. That is why we treasure the books of the gospels so much, because if Jesus bears witness to God, the gospels bear witness to Jesus. Jesus brings God to us and brings us to God. The risen Jesus, therefore, has to be at the centre of our faith lives and at the centre of the life of the Church.

13 April, Friday, Second Week of Easter
John 6:1-15

In today's gospel reading, Andrew, noticing that a small boy has barley loaves and two fish, asks the question, 'What is that between so many?' His assessment was that the resources available were much too small to meet the need. We can all find ourselves asking a similar kind of question to Andrew, 'What is that between so many?' We see some need or other and we recognise that our own personal resources or those of the group are not sufficient to meet the need. Andrew, Philip and the other disciples went on to discover that the Lord worked powerfully in and through the few resources that the small boy made available. The hunger of the crowd was satisfied and there was food left over. The gospel reading reminds us that the Lord can work powerfully through humble and meagre resources if they are made available to him. We are all aware of our limitations, our weaknesses, and yet, we are not always so aware of the many ways that the Lord can work through us, in spite of that, if we trust him to do so. The small amount of food that the boy had was not enough to feed the crowd in itself, and yet, Jesus could not have fed the crowd without it. The Lord needs what we have, even if it seems slight to us, and he can accomplish far more than we could imagine with the little we have if we make ourselves available to him.

14 April, Saturday, Second Week of Easter
John 6:16-21

At the end of yesterday's gospel reading, we heard that Jesus, having fed the multitude in the wilderness, withdrew to the mountain by himself. The evangelist, John, suggests that Jesus needed to be alone with God the Father who had sent him into the world. While Jesus was alone, the disciples set out to cross the sea of Galilee without Jesus. In his absence they found themselves struggling with a strong wind and a rough sea. Even after evening had given way to night they had rowed only three or four miles. They seemed lost without Jesus. It was then that they discovered that Jesus' withdrawal to pray did not remove him from them. They saw him coming towards them, speaking words of reassurance, 'It is I. Do not be afraid'. Almost immediately, they arrived at the destination that they had just been struggling to reach. The gospel reading is suggesting that the Lord who lives forever to intercede for us is always coming towards us. If we are to reach our destination, we cannot do it on our own. We need the Lord's help. A little later in this same gospel, Jesus will say to his disciples, 'Those who abide in me and I in them bear much fruit, because apart from me you can do nothing'. The gospel reading is on our own journey, our journey of faith, in which we depend on the Lord to reach the goal of our life's journey. We depend on him especially when the wind is against us and the waters of life get stormy. Today's gospel reading assures us that the Lord comes to us in those difficult and threatening moments. If we are open to his coming and receptive to his presence we will move on through the storms that come our way and reach the shore.

16 April, Monday, Third Week of Easter

John 6:22-29

It is probably true to say that we are all searching for something. In today's gospel reading, the crowd who had been fed by Jesus in the wilderness go to great lengths to seek him out. When they find him, Jesus reveals to them what it is that motivates their seeking. They are looking for more of the bread that Jesus had given them the day before. He tells them, 'You are looking for me because you had all the bread you wanted to eat.' Jesus challenges them to look for something more enduring. He calls on them to work not just for food that cannot last, the food which satisfies their physical hunger, but to work for food that endures to eternal life, the food that can satisfy their deeper, spiritual hunger. Jesus was concerned about people's physical needs, their physical hungers. That is why he took action to feed the crowd in the wilderness when he saw that they were hungry. However, he was just as concerned, if not more concerned, with people's spiritual hungers. He presents himself to the crowd as someone who can satisfy not just their physical hunger but their spiritual hunger. He wants the crowd and all of us to pay attention to that deeper, spiritual hunger, by believing in him as the one sent by the Father so that we may have life and have it to the full. This deeper hunger is more easily neglected than our physical hunger. It is also true that just as we can eat poor quality food in an effort to satisfy our physical hunger, we can try to satisfy our spiritual hunger on poor quality fare. In today's gospel reading, Jesus presents himself as the only one who can truly satisfy the deeper, spiritual hunger in our lives.

17 April, Tuesday, Third Week of Easter

John 6:30-35

The children who make their first Holy Communion are familiar with the term 'bread of life' that Jesus uses with reference to himself in today's gospel reading. They understand that what they receive is bread, but it is not ordinary bread; it is the bread of life. When Jesus says, 'I am the bread of life', it is the first of seven 'I am' expressions that Jesus uses with reference to himself in the fourth gospel. He will go on to say, 'I am the light of the world', 'I am the gate', 'I am the good shepherd', 'I am the resurrection and the life', 'I am the vine' and 'I am the way, the truth and the life'. The fact that the fourth evangelist has Jesus speak of himself in this way seven times is not by accident. The number seven in the biblical world is always a symbol of completion or fullness. Each time Jesus uses any of these seven expressions with reference to himself in this gospel, he is identifying himself as God's life-giving presence in human form. More specifically, in declaring himself to be the Bread of Life, he is saying that he alone can satisfy the deepest hungers of the human heart. That is why Jesus' invitation to us in this gospel of John is the simple invitation, 'Come', 'Come and see' and 'Come and eat'. We spend our earthly lives trying to respond to that life-giving invitation.

18 April, Wednesday, Third Week of Easter

John 6:35-40

In today's gospel reading, Philip preaches the gospel in Samaria and the people there unite in welcoming the message Philip preached. In Luke's first volume, Jesus had attempted to preach the gospel to a Samaritan village but they rejected Jesus because he was heading for Jerusalem. Now the Risen Lord, through Philip, preaches the gospel to the Samaritans and this time they welcome the gospel. The Lord continues to offer the gospel even to those who have rejected it. Even though we may turn from the Lord at times, he never turns from us.

This is in keeping with what Jesus says in today's gospel reading, 'Whoever comes to me I shall never turn away'. Easter celebrates the faithfulness of God to his Son Jesus, and the faithfulness of Jesus to all of us. The Lord's faithfulness encourages us to keep turning back to him, to keep coming to him, even after we have turned away from him. Even when we fail to respond to his coming, he remains for us the bread of life and he continues to promise that if we come to him we will never hunger and if we believe in him we will never thirst.

19 April, Thursday, Third Week of Easter
John 6:44-51

If we look across the two readings today we find an interesting sequence. We begin with an Ethiopian, who was clearly drawn to Judaism in some way. He is coming from Jerusalem and is reading from the text of the prophet Isaiah, without really understanding what he is reading. He is a seeker after truth, after God. On his search he meets with a companion who helps him to find an answer to some of his questions, who throws light on the word of God that has so intrigued him. Having been touched by God's word, he is ready for baptism. Philip, who helped to open up God's word for him, goes on to baptise him. The proclamation of the word leads to baptism and then in the gospel reading Jesus speaks in language that is clearly Eucharistic, 'The bread that I shall give is my flesh for the life of the world'. As the search for God leads to the hearing of the word and as the hearing of the word leads to baptism, so baptism leads us to the Eucharist. The sequence for us has been a little different, because it began with baptism. We then received the Eucharist at a relatively early age. We can easily miss out on that earlier stage that we find in our readings, the stage of engaging with the Scriptures, questioning them and searching for answers to our questions. That stage is more appropriate to adulthood. When we engage in it, it helps us to appreciate more fully both the sacrament of baptism and of the Eucharist.

20 April, Friday, Third Week of Easter

John 6:52-59

The question the Jews ask in today's gospel reading – 'How can this man give us his flesh to eat?'– is an understandable one. The language Jesus had used about eating his flesh was shocking. After the question, Jesus went on to speak not only of eating his flesh but of drinking his blood, which would have sounded even more shocking. Yet, it is language which expresses the depth of communion which Jesus wants to create between himself and his disciples. In fact, Jesus wants our relationship with him to be as close as his relationship with God the Father. As he says in our gospel reading, 'As I draw life from the Father, so whoever eats me will draw life from me'. Just as Jesus was always in communion with his Father so he wants us to be always in communion with him. The Eucharist is a very special expression of our communion with him and of his with us, but our communion with him is to extend beyond the Eucharist. In the language of John's Gospel, we are to remain in him, as he remains in us. We remain in him by remaining in his word, by keeping his word and allowing his word to shape our lives. Our communion with the Lord in the Eucharist calls us to this ongoing form of communion.

21 April, Saturday, Third Week of Easter

John 6:60-69

In the course of John's Gospel, Jesus is often portrayed as asking very probing questions. We find one such question in today's gospel reading. Jesus asks the twelve, 'What about you, do you want to go away too?' In the previous verses many of Jesus' followers are depicted as leaving Jesus because of his words about the need to eat his flesh and drink his blood. Their leaving Jesus is the occasion for Jesus to place the twelve before a moment of decision, 'Do you want to go away too?' Jesus was probing, looking for them to make a personal decision as to whether they would stay with him or leave him like so many others. The Risen Lord looks for a similar personal decision from us, asking us, 'Do you want to go away too?' In the culture in which we live not everyone has chosen to respond in faith to the Lord's presence and call. As a result, we each have to make a more personal and more deliberate decision for the Lord than was needed in the past, the kind of decision the Lord looks for in today's gospel reading. As we strive to make that decision we can do no better than to make our own the response of Peter to Jesus' question, 'Lord, who shall we go to? You have the message of eternal life, and we believe; we know that you are the Holy One of God.'

23 April, Monday, Fourth Week of Easter
John 10:11-18

In today's gospel reading Jesus uses an image drawn from the rural life of Galilee. There is a sheepfold or sheep pen. The sheep enter the sheepfold through the gate at night for protection. In the morning the shepherd enters the sheepfold through the gate and calls the sheep to follow him back out through the gate to pasture. Jesus identifies himself with two elements of that image, firstly with the gate, and then with the shepherd. The sheep go through the gate at night for protection and go through the gate in the morning for pasture. In this way the gate is both life-protecting and life-sustaining. This is the sense in which Jesus applies 'the gate' to himself. 'I am the gate'. If we pass through him, if we interact with him, he both protects us and sustains our life. He protects in that he delivers us from evil, in the words of the Lord's Prayer, and from the evil one who stands behind all evil. He sustains our life in that he works to give us life to the full, a sharing in God's own life. God's life is a life of love. Jesus sustains our life by working to make us as loving as God is loving. To the extent that we love as God loves we already share in God's life, here and now in this earthly life. Jesus is the gate who both protects and sustains our life. That is why he calls on us to keep entering through him, to keep interacting with him, to keep growing in our relationship with him.

24 April, Tuesday, Fourth Week of Easter

John 10:22-30

Many of us are concerned about break-ins; we are anxious lest some-one might steal from us. We take various security precautions to prevent that from happening. In the gospel reading today, Jesus makes reference to stealing. He declares that no one will ever steal his followers from him. It is as if Jesus is saying that he has such a strong grip on his followers that no one will ever take them from him against his will. When you reflect on that saying of Jesus, it is indeed very reassuring. Jesus will do all in his power to keep us united with him and to prevent us from being taken away from him or falling away from him. Yet, there is something that we must do as well. In the gospel reading, Jesus also declares, 'The sheep that belong to me listen to my voice'. We need to pay attention, in some way, to the Lord. We try to hear what he may be saying to us; we seek to follow where he is leading us. If we do that, the gospel reading suggests that we can be assured that the Lord will do the rest. The Lord's contribution to the relationship between us and him is much more significant than ours. Our ultimate salvation is much more the Lord's doing than ours. Therein lies our confidence and hope.

25 April, Wednesday, Feast of Saint Mark

Mark 16:15-20

Mark has the great distinction of being the first to write a gospel, the story of the life, death and resurrection of Jesus. Before Mark came to write, much of the tradition about Jesus circulated within the early Church in oral form; there were also some written traditions about Jesus. However, Mark was the first person to put this material together into a narrative of the life of Jesus. The other evangelists took their lead from Mark. There is a very early tradition in the Church, which first surfaced in the early part of the second century, according to which Mark was a companion of Peter. Mark never knew Jesus personally; he was not an eyewitness. However, he knew those who met Jesus and, in particular, he knew Peter. That is why the first reading for the feast of Mark is always from the first letter of Peter. At the end of that reading, Peter makes reference to 'my son Mark'. We are probably to understand 'my son' as 'my spiritual son'. The Mark that Peter refers to may well be the author of the first gospel. That same early tradition places Mark in the Church of Rome, the city where Peter was crucified and where the Church experienced the first real persecution lead by the Roman state. Mark may have written his gospel for the Church in Rome in the aftermath of that cataclysmic event. The gospel was perhaps intended as a word of encouragement to the Church, assuring them that just as they had travelled and were still travelling the way of the cross, Jesus had travelled that way before them. As Risen Lord, he was present among them, just as he had been present with the disciples in the boat as the storm raged at sea. In the words of today's gospel reading, the Lord was 'working with them (the disciples) and confirming the word by the signs that accompanied it'. That fundamental message of Mark's Gospel remains a word of encouragement to the Church, the community of the Lord's disciples, today as we battle with our own storms.

26 April, Thursday, Fourth Week of Easter
John 13:16-20

Jesus spoke the words we have just heard in today's gospel reading immediately after he washed the feet of his disciples. He washed the feet of everyone present, without distinction, and that included the feet of Judas. He refers to Judas in the gospel reading through an appropriate verse from the Jewish Scriptures, 'Someone who shares my table rebels against me'. A more literal translation of that verse would be, 'The one who ate my bread has lifted his heel against me'. In that culture, to show someone the heel of your foot was a sign of rejection and enmity. Jesus washed the feet of Judas and Judas showed Jesus the heel of his foot. The contrast between how Jesus related to Judas and how Judas related to Jesus could not be more sharply drawn. The gospel reading reminds us that the way Jesus relates us is not determined by how we relate to him. The Lord gave himself completely to all his disciples, including Judas, when he laid down his garments to wash their feet, and even more so when he laid down his life on the following day. He continues to give himself to us all, even when there is something of Judas in us. He loves us in the way he does so as to elicit our love in return. Even when that love is not forthcoming, he continues to give himself for us and to us. Saint Paul said that nothing can separate us from the love of Christ. Perhaps all that can separate us from that unconditional love is our own persistent refusal to receive it.

27 April, Friday, Fourth Week of Easter
John 14:1-6
Today's gospel reading is set in the context of Jesus' words to his disciples on the night before he died. He had been speaking about his going away. Understandably, his disciples are distressed by this prospect. Jesus seeks to reassure them that his going away, his going to the Father, is a journey that he is travelling for them, for all of us. In going to the Father, he is opening up a way for all of us to make the same journey. As he says in the gospel reading, he is going to prepare a place for us and then to come and take us to that place, to the many roomed house of his Father. Jesus is the Way; he is the way to the Father for all his disciples. As John the Baptist prepared a way for Jesus, so Jesus has prepared a way, opened up a way, for all of us. That is why his leaving this world and going to the Father is good news; his departure is the gateway to new life, not just for him

but for us all. Furthermore, in going to the Father, he will send the Holy Spirit, and through the Spirit he will remain with us and within us, until that day when we go where he has gone, and join him in the house of the Father.

28 April, Saturday, Fourth Week of Easter
John 14:7-14

Jesus makes a statement in today's gospel reading that seems extraordinary, 'Whoever believes in me will perform the same works as I do myself, he will perform even greater works, because I am going to the Father.' We might wonder how believers could perform even greater works than Jesus himself performed. Jesus suggests an answer to that question in saying 'because I am going to the Father'. In going to the Father, Jesus pours out the Holy Spirit on his disciples, on disciples of every generation. In and through the Holy Spirit at work in the lives of his followers, Jesus continues to do the works he did before his death and, indeed, is able to do even greater works. This is not a reference to greater miracles but to a much greater scope for mission. During his earthly ministry Jesus' mission was limited to Galilee, Samaria, Judea and adjoining areas. However in returning to the Father and sending his Spirit upon his disciples, the Risen Lord is able to continue his mission through his disciples in a much wider geographical area. The pouring out of the Spirit after the death and resurrection of Jesus will empower his disciples' mission in the world. The Lord wants to continue his mission through us. As the Father sent him, so he sends us and he gives us his Holy Spirit to empower us to continue his mission. This is our calling, our privilege and, also, our responsibility.

30 April, Monday, Fifth Week of Easter
John 14:21-26

The verb *to love* occurs frequently in today's gospel reading. It speaks of our love for Jesus, Jesus' love for us and God the Father's love for us. God the Father expresses his love for us by giving us the Son. Jesus expresses his love for us by laying down his life for us, and by making known to us all he has learnt from the Father. We express our love for Jesus by keeping his word, by living according to his teaching, which, in John's gospel, is summed up as 'love one another as I have loved you'. The gospel reading also makes reference to the Advocate, the Holy Spirit. As the Father expresses his love for us by giving us the Son; the Father and Son together express their love for us by giving us the Holy Spirit. The role of the Holy Spirit, according to our reading, is to be our teacher, to keep bringing to our minds the teaching, the word, of Jesus. The Holy Spirit helps us to keep Jesus' word, especially his command to 'love one another as I have loved you'. In that short gospel reading, there is a whole vision of the Christian life, of God's relationship with us as Father, Son and Spirit and of our relationship with each other.

1 May, Tuesday, Fifth Week of Easter
John 14:27-31
In today's gospel reading, Jesus is portrayed as speaking on the night of the last supper, the night before he was crucified. His disciples are understandably troubled and fearful. Jesus has been telling them that he is going away. His death will take him from them. Yet, Jesus wants to reassure them that his leaving them, through death, is actually to their advantage. Yes, it is a great tragedy, but God is going to bring something wonderful out of this human tragedy. In and through his death, Jesus will give them the gift of peace, a peace the world cannot give, a peace that is deeper than any peace that those who are in power in the world can bring. The peace Jesus brings is peace with God, a reconciled relationship with God, and this will come to pass precisely through his leaving them, through his death. Jesus says that even though the prince of this world is on his way, namely, Satan who has taken hold of Judas and others, what is about to unfold will reveal

Jesus' love for his heavenly Father, and his Father's love for Jesus and the world. These are powerful, life-giving words that Jesus speaks to his disciples in their distress and anxiety. It is said of Paul and Barnabas in the first reading that they put fresh heart into the disciples. What Jesus does for his disciples at the Last Supper, Paul and Barnabas do for later disciples. It is what we are all asked to do, as disciples of Jesus. By what we say and do, we are called to put fresh heart into one another, to encourage one another. We are to be messengers of the Lord's refreshing, encouraging presence. If that is to happen, we ourselves need to listen to and absorb the Lord's life-giving words, those same words we have just heard in our gospel reading.

2 May, Wednesday, Fifth Week of Easter

John 15:1-8

As part of children's instruction for the Sacrament of Confirmation, they are told about the fruits of the Holy Spirit. It is Saint Paul in his letter to the Galatians who gives us the fruits, or what he terms the 'fruit', of the Holy Spirit: 'Love, joy, peace, patience, kindness, generosity, faithfulness, gentleness and self-control'. Paul was articulating there the fundamental attitudes of heart that the Holy Spirit works to form within us. He is saying that if we open ourselves to the gift of the Spirit we have received, our life will show forth this rich fruit. In the gospel reading today, Jesus also speaks about fruit in connection with the image of the vine. At the end of the gospel reading he declares that it is to the glory of God his Father that we should bear much fruit. A little beyond this reading Jesus identifies this fruit with love, the kind of love that Jesus gave expression to in his own life, what Paul also identifies as the fruit of the Spirit. Jesus declares in our reading that if we are to bear this fruit we must remain in him as branches in the vine. Paul identifies the Spirit as the source of this fruit; Jesus identifies himself as its source. It is our union with the Lord through the Spirit that empowers us to live in a way that reflects how the Lord lived. We cannot live this way on the basis of our own resources alone. We need to be in union with the Lord and his Spirit

3 May, Thursday, Feast of Saints Philip and James
John 14:6-14

We celebrate the feast of two of the twelve, Philip and James the son of Alphaeus. We know a little bit more about Philip than we do about James from the gospels. The first chapter of John's Gospel tells us that Philip was from Bethsaida, on the northern shore of the Sea of Galilee, the same town that Peter and Andrew were from. According to that first chapter of John it was Philip who went to Nathanael to declare, 'We have found him about whom Moses ... and also the prophets wrote, Jesus son of Joseph from Nazareth'. He was met with very little enthusiasm from Nathanael, 'Can anything good come out of Nazareth?' Yet, Philip wasn't put off by this rather brusque response; he simply replied to Nathanael, 'Come and see'. Nathanael eventually came, saw and stayed. Philip encourages us not to be too easily thrown when our enthusiasm for our faith is not shared by others. In today's gospel, Philip makes a request of Jesus, 'Let us see the Father and then we shall be satisfied'. He had yet to learn that, as Jesus said in reply, 'To have seen me is to have seen the Father'. Philip was full of faith when he went to Nathanael and his witness was very effective. Yet, it is clear that he was only at the beginning of his own faith journey; he had only begun to see. He had a great deal more to learn from Jesus. Philip reminds us that we don't have to know it all to be effective witnesses for the Lord. We are called to share the Lord with each other while we are still on the way.

4 May, Friday, Fifth Week of Easter
John 15:12-17

Friendship is one of the great blessings of life. Friendships don't just happen; two people have to choose each other as friends, on the basis of a mutual attraction of some kind, a set of common interests, a shared way of looking at things. Friends tend to share deeply with each other. In today's gospel reading, Jesus calls his disciples friends, 'I shall not call you servants any more ... I call you friends'. He goes on to say to them, 'You did not choose me, no, I chose you'. The Lord has taken the initiative to befriend them; he has chosen them as friends. The Lord has chosen to befriend all of us. He has demonstrated his friendship by sharing deeply with us; he has revealed to us what is most personal to him, his own relationship with God his Father. He has also demonstrated his friendship by emptying himself on our behalf, by laying down his life for us. He has done his part, but if the friendship is to happen, we need to do our part. We need to choose him as he has chosen us; we need to befriend him as he has befriended us. We need to remain in his love, his friendship. According to the gospel reading, that will entail loving one another as he has loved us, befriending one another as he has befriended us.

5 May, Saturday, Fifth Week of Easter
John 15:18-21

John's Gospel speaks about God's love for the world. God so loved the world that he sent his only Son. In today's gospel reading Jesus speaks about the world's hatred for him and for his followers. In Luke's Gospel Jesus calls on his disciples to love their enemies and to do good to those who hate them. The gospels suggest that Jesus was realistic about the hostility that would come his own way and the way of his followers. Yet, he wanted his followers to relate to the world not on the basis of how the world relates to them but on the basis of how God and Jesus relate to the world. In the gospel reading Jesus says, 'A servant is not greater than his master'. That can be read in two ways. One way is, 'If the master experienced hostility so will the servants'. The other way is, 'If the master washed the feet of the servants, including the feet of Judas, the one who betrayed him, the servants must do likewise; they must reveal the love of God to others regardless of how they relate to them.' That saying of Jesus, 'A servant is not greater than his master', gives us much to ponder. It is only with the help of the Holy Spirit that we can be like the master in every respect.

7 May, Monday, Sixth Week of Easter
John 15:26-16:4

On the day before he was crucified, the night of the Last Supper, Jesus speaks in very stark terms to his disciples. He names some of the trials that lay ahead of them. The time will come when those who try to kill them will think that they are doing a holy duty for God. That warning has a strangely contemporaneous ring in these times when religious fundamentalists can take people's lives in the name of God. At this moment in certain parts of the world Christians are being persecuted by those who believe they are doing God's work. Jesus says to his disciples that he is telling them what is to come so that when it does come their faith may not be shaken. The more painful and darker experiences of life have the potential to leave our faith shaken. Jesus was aware of that. We may be aware of it from our own experience. Even if we do not suffer the kind of persecution Jesus speaks about, some kind of suffering will come the way of all of us and it can shake our faith. In that same reading, as well as issuing a warning, Jesus also makes a promise to his disciples, and to all of us. He promises to send the Spirit of Truth, the Holy Spirit, and he tells us that this Spirit will enable us to witness to him, even in the dark experiences of life. The Spirit will keep us faithful in the face of whatever may threaten to undermine our faith. We need the Spirit that Jesus speaks about; we need to keep on praying, 'Come Holy Spirit'.

8 May, Tuesday, Sixth Week of Easter

John 16:5-11

In today's gospel reading, Jesus explains to his disciples that his leaving them will ultimately be to their advantage. Although they will experience a great loss at no longer being able to see Jesus' bodily presence, this loss will make possible a greater good. In going back to the Father, Jesus will send the Holy Spirit and through the Spirit he will be present in a new way to his disciples and to disciples of every generation. The experience of loss will be life-giving because Jesus' going away will result in a new coming. Jesus' departure is a necessary loss if God's purposes are to be realised. It is often the way in life that we find ourselves having to deal with certain necessary losses, losses that are unavoidable and that are somehow part of God's purpose for our lives. At the time, such losses can be very painful, but over time we can begin to see some new life emerging out of the loss. The going away that the loss entails can often give way to a new coming, a new birth, new life. The gospel reading invites us to trust that the Lord can and will bring good out of the necessary losses we have to suffer in the course of our lives.

9 May, Wednesday, Sixth Week of Easter

John 16:12-15

There is only so much that people can learn at a certain stage of their lives. The great truths of life take a long time to absorb. This is certainly the case with the truths of our faith. We enter into those truths gradually over time, with experience of life. Jesus seems to acknowledge that in today's gospel reading. He tells his disciples that he has many things to say to them but that they are not yet ready to hear them, 'they would be too much for you now'. Jesus declares that the Paraclete, the Spirit of Truth, who will be sent to them after Jesus' death and resurrection, will begin to reveal these things to them and will lead them towards the complete truth. The Holy Spirit is given to us all to lead us to the complete truth, the truth about Jesus, God, our world, ourselves. This is a lifelong journey. Indeed, there is a sense in which we never attain the complete truth in this life. We are always on the way. We can never really afford to say, 'I have the complete truth'. Rather, we must always leave ourselves open to being led by the Spirit ever more closely towards the complete truth, towards the one who said of himself, 'I am the truth'.

10 May, Thursday, Sixth Week of Easter
John 16:16-20

When Paul went to Philippi and preached the gospel he was offered hospitality by one of the women who responded to Paul's preaching, Lydia, a dealer in purple cloth. According to today's first reading, when Paul entered Corinth he received hospitality from a Jewish Christian married couple, Aquila and Priscilla. Paul would have understood that it was the Lord who was supporting him in and through these people who offered him hospitality when he was most in need of it. Paul experienced the presence of the Risen Lord at the heart of his life and work. In the gospel reading, Jesus tells his disciples that in a short time they will no longer see him, and then that they will see him again a short time later. Jesus will be taken from them in death, but he will return to them when he is raised from the dead and, having returned, he will remain with them as they engage in the work of witnessing to him. He will be with them above all in and through the members of the faith community. This was Paul's experience; Paul experienced the Lord's presence, especially in and through those who supported him and stood by him. This can be our experience too. The Risen Lord stands at the heart of our day to day life. He journeys with us as he journeyed with the two disciples on the road to Emmaus. He comes to us in and through the members of his body. He comes to bring us hope when we are downhearted, to give us strength in our weakness, to bring us joy in our sorrow. This is the good news of Easter which we are celebrating at this time.

11 May, Friday, Sixth Week of Easter

John 16:20-23

In the gospel reading, Jesus is very honest about the impact which his death on the following day will have on his disciples, 'I tell you most solemnly, you will be weeping and wailing ... you will be sorrowful'. The death of someone close to us always generates strong feelings of sadness and loss within us. Jesus speaks to his disciples in the awareness that they will experience all these feelings when he is taken from them in death. Yet he also assures them that these feelings won't last forever. Their sorrow will turn into joy, a joy that no one will take from them, because Jesus will see them again when he rises from the dead. He reassures them that because his death will be an opening to new life, their sorrow and pain will be a prelude to joy, just as the pain of a pregnant woman is the prelude to the joy of new life. Jesus is assuring us all that sorrow and pain and death will not have the last word in our lives either. Because he has triumphed over death and has passed from death to new life all our sorrows, pains and losses will be ultimately transformed by him. Because he is present to us here and now in the power of his risen life this transformation can begin to be experienced here and now. Because he journeys with us as Risen Lord, he can say to us, 'your sorrow will turn to joy', not just in the life beyond death but on our present life journey. This was something the two disciples on the road to Emmaus discovered, and that we can all discover for ourselves.

12 May, Saturday, Sixth Week of Easter

John 16:23-28

Today's gospel reading is again set in the context of the last supper. Jesus tells his disciples that a day is coming when he will no longer need to pray to the Father on their behalf, 'I do not say that I shall pray to the Father for you'. This is because on that day the disciples themselves will enjoy an intimacy and communion with God that up until then has belonged to Jesus alone. The 'day' that Jesus refers to there is the day of Easter, the day of Pentecost, the day of the Church. Through the outpouring of the Spirit we are brought into a relationship with God, which is a sharing in Jesus' own relationship with God. As Saint Paul says, the Spirit that has been poured into our heart cries out 'Abba, Father' as Jesus does; through the Spirit we receive adoption as sons and daughters of God, sharing in Jesus' own relationship with God. Through the Spirit we can pray directly to the Father as Jesus does. Such is the depth of our communion with God through the Spirit that Jesus does not have to stand between ourselves and God to make representation on our behalf. One of the principal messages of John's Gospel is that Jesus has come to draw us into that same communion with God the Father that he has enjoyed from all eternity. That is why what Jesus says of himself can often apply to all of us. At the end of the gospel reading Jesus says, 'I came from the Father and have come into the world and now I leave the world to go to the Father'. This is the essential truth about Jesus' life, but it is also the essential truth about our lives as well. We have come from God the Father and we are on a lifelong journey to the Father.

14 May, Monday, Feast of Saint Matthias

John 15:9-17

On this feast of Saint Matthias, the two readings are linked by the verb 'to choose'. In the first reading, the early disciples gather to complete the number of the twelve apostles after the betrayal and death of Judas. Having nominated two candidates, Barsabbas and Matthias, they turn in prayer to the Lord and ask him, 'Show us which of these two you have chosen to take over this ministry and apostolate, which Judas abandoned'. They used their judgement to narrow the field down to two, but they needed the Lord's guidance to make the final choice. They wanted their choice to be in harmony with the Lord's choice. Their question was not just 'who should we choose?' but 'who is the

Lord choosing?' In the gospel reading, Jesus says to his disciples, 'You did not choose me, but I chose you and I commissioned you to go out and to bear fruit'. Again the Lord's choice of his disciples takes priority over their choice of him. What Jesus says to his disciples there, he says to all of us, 'I chose you'. The Lord's choice of us is prior to all else. Yes, we have to choose the Lord for ourselves, but our choice of the Lord is always in response to his choice of us. To express it in another way, the Lord is always seeking us out, and our seeking of him is a response to his seeking us. The Lord loves us first and our love of him is in response to his love of us. The Lord's initiative towards us is there before our initiative towards him. In our dealings with each other, we may choose someone as a friend, but we cannot be sure that they will choose us. However, in our dealings with the Lord, we know that the Lord has already chosen us as a friend, 'I call you friends', he says to his disciples. He cannot be sure that we will choose him as he has chosen us, but he earnestly desires us to do so.

15 May, Tuesday, Seventh Week of Easter
John 17:1-11
Today's gospel reading is the beginning of Jesus' great prayer that we find in John's Gospel. We will be reading from that prayer for the next couple of days. Jesus begins his prayer by praying for himself, 'Father ... glorify your Son'. As he prays to be glorified, Jesus is aware that the path to glory is through the cross. There is a lifting up on the cross that is prior to the lifting up in glory. Jesus is ready to return to the Father from whom he came because, as he says in that prayer, 'I have finished the work that you gave me to do'. We all have some work to do while we are on this earth; we have all been given some sharing in the Lord's own life-giving work. Each day, we try to be faithful to the Lord's work, to the mission that the Lord has given each of us, the mission to make him known by the way we live. In

the carrying out of that mission we are not left to our own devices. The Lord works with us and is praying for us. In the gospel reading, having prayed for himself, the Lord prayed for his disciples, who are to be his witnesses in the world. He continues to pray for his disciples today. Saint Paul in his letter to the Romans speaks of Christ who is at the right hand of God, who, indeed, intercedes for us. The Lord lives forever to intercede for all us, so that we may be faithful to the work he gives us. When we find it a struggle to pray for ourselves, we can be sure that the Lord is praying for us and, also, that his Spirit is praying within us.

16 May, Wednesday, Seventh Week of Easter

John 17:11-19

In today's gospel reading we hear a further section of Jesus' prayer for his disciples on the evening of the last supper. There is a great deal of realism in Jesus' prayer. He asks the Father to protect his disciples from the evil one. We are reminded of one of the petitions of the prayer that Jesus gave to his disciples, the Lord's Prayer, 'Lead us not into temptation but deliver us from evil' or 'from the evil one'. The prayer that Jesus asks us to pray for ourselves in the gospels of Matthew and Luke is the same prayer that Jesus prays for us in the Gospel of John. Jesus prays in the awareness that our relationship with him is prone to assaults of various kinds. Our faith will be put to the test. Yet, the gospel reading reminds us that we have the assurance of Jesus' prayer for us and of his supportive presence as the Good Shepherd who protects his flock from harm. The Holy Spirit at work in our lives is stronger than any temptation. Jesus prays that his disciples would be protected from evil so that they can share in his mission in the world. As God sent Jesus into the world, so Jesus sends us into the world. The mission of Jesus was to reveal God's love for the world and that is our mission too. As God consecrated Jesus for that mission, set him apart and empowered him for it, so Jesus prays that God would consecrate us for our mission. Jesus identifies himself with his disciples, with us, in a very striking way in our gospel reading.

17 May, Thursday, Seventh Week of Easter
John 17:20-26

The prayer of Jesus for all future disciples in today's gospel reading has been the inspiration of the ecumenical movement, especially since the Second Vatican Council. Jesus prays, 'May they all be one'. It is clear that the unity Jesus prays for is not just the fruit of human effort. Having prayed, 'May they all be one', Jesus immediately prays, 'may they be one in us'. Our unity flows from our relationship with Jesus and his Father. Our union with the Lord is the source of our union with each other. The closer we grow towards the Lord, the closer we will grow towards each other. It is by growing in our relationship with the Lord and with the God whom he reveals that that we will grow in our relationship with each other. The unity that Jesus prays for is a unity in the Lord – 'May they be one in us'. For Jesus this unity among his followers is vitally important because without it those who do not believe will not come to faith. The goal of the unity that Jesus prays for is a missionary one, 'So that the world may believe it was you who sent me'. As we grow in our communion with the Lord and with each other, we will become more effective missionaries. Jesus said earlier in John's Gospel, 'When I am lifted up from the earth, I will draw all people to myself'. He was speaking of the drawing power of love, the divine love revealed from the cross. When this love finds expression in the lives of his followers, in a community of love, it has the same drawing power. The Lord's love present among us draws people to faith.

18 May, Friday, Seventh Week of Easter

John 21:15-19

According to the fourth gospel, at the last supper Jesus said to his disciples, 'As the Father has loved me, so I have loved you. Remain in my love'. However, at the time of his passion and death, the disciples did not remain in Jesus' love; they deserted him, and Peter, in particular, denied him three times. It is understandable, then, that the only question the Risen Lord asks Peter is, 'Do you love me?' There is no need for Jesus to state again, 'As the Father has loved me, so I have loved you'. That is self-evident. What needs to be established is whether Peter is ready to love Jesus in return. The Lord loves all of us, as the Father loves him; our calling is to respond to that love in kind; to love the Lord as he loves us. It is only when Peter publicly professed his love for the Lord that he was given pastoral responsibility for other disciples, for the Lord's flock. His relationship with the Lord had to be healed first before he could serve those who are dear to the Lord. We all have pastoral responsibility for each other, in one way or another. We are called to accompany each other on our pilgrimage through life, to feed one another with the Lord's presence on that journey. We can only do that if our own relationship with the Lord is in order. The Lord is to be our first love, and it is that love which finds expression in our care for one another.

19 May, Saturday, Seventh Week of Easter

John 21:20-25

This is the final weekday of the Easter season. The season of Easter concludes with tomorrow's feast of Pentecost. We are back to Ordinary Time on Monday. As we conclude the Easter Season the two readings of today's Mass are also conclusions. The first reading is the conclusion of the Acts of the Apostles from which we have been reading since Easter Sunday. It speaks of the arrival of Paul in Rome as a prisoner of the Roman authorities. Yet, even while under house

arrest, Luke describes him as continuing to do what he had been do-
ing since his meeting with the Risen Lord on the road to Damascus,
'Proclaiming the kingdom of God and teaching the truth about the
Lord Jesus Christ'. The gospel reading is the conclusion of John's
Gospel, from which we have also been reading since Easter Sunday.
Two other key figures in the early Church feature in that conclusion,
Peter and the beloved disciple. Peter has just been given his work by
the Risen Lord of shepherding the Lord's flock. It just remains for the
work of the beloved disciple to be clarified. His work was causing
the gospel to be written that we have come to know as the Gospel of
John. This gospel is his legacy to the Church. These three very different figures were key people in the Lord's work in the world. They
each made a very distinctive contribution to that work. We all have a
part to play in that work of the Lord, in accordance with our gifts and
our abilities. To each of us, Jesus says what he said to Peter in today's
gospel reading, 'You are to follow me'.

21 May, Monday, Seventh Week in Ordinary Time
Mark 9:14-29

In today's gospel reading, Jesus seems very frustrated with his disciples, 'You faithless generation. How much longer must I be with
you? How much longer must I put up with you?' Something of Jesus'
humanity comes through here. He was annoyed with his disciples
because they were arguing with the scribes instead of working to heal
a seriously disturbed boy. Jesus goes on to make up for the failings of
his disciples by restoring the boy to health, raising him from a kind
of death. At the end of the gospel reading, Jesus traces the failure of
the disciples to their lack of prayer, 'That is the kind that can only be
driven out by prayer'. Jesus was clearly frustrated at his disciples'
argumentative spirit and lack of prayer. Both were inhibiting the work
he had sent them to do, and empowered them to do. We all have a
share in the Lord's work. We are all sent and empowered by the Lord

to do his life-giving work in our world. That work of the Lord will be inhibited by an argumentative spirit and a lack of prayer in our lives. Indeed, it is the lack of prayer that can contribute to our argumentativeness. We cannot blame the disciples in the gospel reading, because there go all of us. Perhaps it is the disturbed boy's father who has most to teach us. In this crisis, which affected him more than anyone else, he managed to find a space for prayer, 'Lord, I do have faith. Help the little faith I have'. It is a prayer we can all make our own, especially when we feel powerless before some distressing experience.

22 May, Tuesday, Seventh Week in Ordinary Time
Mark 9:30-37
There are some issues worth arguing about and then there are other arguments that serve very little purpose. In today's gospel reading, Jesus identifies the argument the disciples are having with each other as serving no useful purpose. They were arguing about which of them was the greatest. Sensing that Jesus is going to inaugurate the kingdom of God, they were discussing their place in it. Who would have the more prominent place? It was an argument about status and position. It seems very out of place just after Jesus had spoken of himself as the Son of Man who would be delivered into the hands of men and be put to death. We are all prone to the wrong kind of arguments. When we put our own personal interests to the fore, as the disciples were doing, it can lead to unhelpful arguments. Jesus responded to this argument among his disciples in a very deliberate way. He sat down, taking up the position of the teacher, and in an acted parable he took a little child and placed his arms round him, and went on to identify himself completely with the child. Jesus is saying to his disciples and to us that in the kingdom he is proclaiming the central value is recognising and serving Jesus in the most vulnerable and most dependant members of society. The kind of self-promoting behaviour of the disciples that leads to unhelpful

argument is always going to be at the opposite end of the spectrum to that core kingdom value.

23 May, Wednesday, Seventh Week in Ordinary Time
Mark 9:38-40

In Mark's Gospel we often find a clash between Jesus and his disciples. Today's gospel reading is one example of that. The disciples had a somewhat black and white view of people. Only those who were 'one of us', as they put it, could be trusted to do the Lord's work. Jesus had a much more nuanced view of people than his disciples. He could see that even those whom he had not formally called to become one of his disciples could be doing God's life-giving work. Indeed, he makes the very generous statement, 'Anyone who is not against us is for us'. That might be a good principle to take to heart in the times in which we live. There are a lot of people who are not explicitly *for* the Church, in the sense of practising their faith in the way we have come to understand that, and, yet, they are not against the Church or the gospel either. The attitude of Jesus in today's gospel reading encourages us to build bridges with all those who in some way share the Church's mission to bring life where there is death, wholeness where there is brokenness, relief where there is suffering. We can be partners in mission with those who are 'not one of us' in the strict sense. In these times we need the generous vision that Jesus displays in today's gospel reading rather than the much narrower one displayed by his disciples.

24 May, Thursday, Seventh Week in Ordinary Time
Mark 9:41-50

In the gospel reading the word translated as 'hell' is '*Gehenna*', a valley just below the city of Jerusalem which stood on a hill. It served as the city dump and so was characterised by worms and fire. This is the imagery that is behind the translation 'hell'. In language that is deliberately provocative and exaggerated, Jesus is saying that it is better to end up in Jerusalem's rubbish dumb than to give in to forces within ourselves that lead us astray and turn us away from God. The hand, the foot and the eye are metaphors for those faults and failings that are very close to us, as close as those limbs of our body. We all have faults and failings that come between us and God, that take us in a direction other than the one God desires for us. Jesus is declaring very clearly that they need to be dealt with. The wider context of the gospels suggests that we can only deal with our faults and failings with the Lord's help. We come before him in our weakness and open ourselves up to the strength that only he can give. As Jesus will go on to say in the next chapter of Mark's Gospel, 'For God all things are possible'. Growing in virtue is a daily struggle but it is not one that we engage in on our own. We need the support of the Lord and we will find his support above all in and through the community of believers. We have a responsibility for each other in the faith, which is why Jesus is so critical in the gospel reading of those believers who undermine the faith of others, those who are an obstacle or stumbling block to other believers, those who give scandal.

25 May, Friday, Seventh week in Ordinary Time
Mark 10:1-12
Today's first reading from the book of Sirach has some lovely things to say about true friendship, 'A faithful friend is a sure shelter, whoever finds one has found a rare treasure. A faithful friend is something beyond price… a faithful friend is the elixir of life.' The author also says in that reading that those who fear the Lord will find a faithful friend. In other words, when we relate well to the Lord we will find faithful friends. When our relationship with the Lord is right it helps us to find and to form good human relationships that are marked by faithfulness and self-giving. In the gospel reading, Jesus speaks of a special kind of friendship, the relationship between a husband and

wife in marriage. His vision of marriage has something in common with the vision of friendship in the first reading. Jesus presents the ideal of two people, man and woman, remaining faithful to each other for life to the point where they become no longer two but one. Whether we are married or single, we can all taste the joy of a faithful friendship, through which we come to experience the Lord's faithful love in others and reveal that faithful love of the Lord to others.

26 May, Saturday, Seventh Week in Ordinary Time
Mark 10:13-16

This is the only passage in all of the gospels where Jesus is described as being indignant. The gospel reading says that Jesus was indignant with his disciples. He had been investing himself in instructing them but they do not seem to be absorbing Jesus' mindset. In the previous chapter of Mark's Gospel Jesus had declared to his disciples that whoever welcomes a child in his name welcomes him. Yet now the disciples try to turn children away when people brought them to Jesus for him to lay his hands on them. Jesus is understandably indignant at his disciples' unwelcoming attitude towards children. He corrects his disciples, 'Let the children come to me; do not stop them'. Jesus wanted people to bring children to him. They have as much of a right to the gift of God's kingdom as anyone, 'It is to such as these that the kingdom of God belongs'. If children have a right to all God is offering us through Jesus, we have a duty to lead children to Jesus. Every effort we make to open up children to the person of Jesus and to help them respond to his presence in faith is pleasing to Jesus. It is what he wants. Children are receptive to faith in the Lord in ways that adults often are not. If the Lord wants to be generous towards children and they are naturally receptive to what the Lord is offering, then it falls upon us to bring children to Jesus. Indeed, Jesus goes further in the gospel reading. He declares that adults have a lot to learn from the openness and readiness of children to receive his gift of the kingdom of God, 'Anyone who does not welcome the kingdom of God like a little child will never enter it'.

28 May, Monday, Eighth Week in Ordinary Time
Mark 10:17-27

In the gospel reading a man of great wealth runs up to Jesus with a burning question, 'What must I do to inherit eternal life?' Here was someone who clearly wanted to take the path of life, God's path that leads to eternal life. He subsequently declares to Jesus that he has kept God's commandments since his earliest days. He has been serious about his faith life, since his early youth. He was a good man who wanted to be better. He seems to have made an impact on Jesus. The gospel reading declares that 'Jesus looked steadily at him and loved him'. Jesus looks steadily at all of us and loves us as we struggle to take the path of life that God is calling us to take. It was out of his love for this man that Jesus now invites him to take another step on his faith journey, a more generous and demanding step. Jesus calls him to walk away from his great wealth and to follow him as a disciple on the road to Jerusalem. Jesus knew that this was the path that would be truly life-giving for this man. Yet, it proved a step too far for him. In response to Jesus' call, we are told that 'he went away sad'. It is one of the saddest verses in the gospels. It is because the Lord loves us that he is always calling us to take that extra step in our relationship with him. Like the man in the gospel, we too can hesitate to take that extra, more generous, more demanding, step on our journey of faith. We may feel it is more than we are able for. Yet, if we take the step the Lord is calling us to take, God will be our help and our strength. In the power of God's help and strength we will be able to do what we cannot do on our own. As Jesus declares at the end of the gospel reading, 'Everything is possible for God'.

29 May, Tuesday, Eighth Week in Ordinary Time
Mark 10:28-31

At the beginning of today's gospel reading, Peter declares to Jesus, 'We have left everything and followed you'. He spoke the truth. He and his companions had left their family and their fishing business to follow Jesus. Jesus goes on to acknowledge that Peter and the others did indeed leave their household, family and possessions for his sake. He assures them that leaving their family will open them up to an experience of a new kind of family, brothers, sisters, mothers and children in the here and now. Jesus is talking here of the family of disciples, what we have come to call the Church. Most of us have not been asked by the Lord to leave our families and livelihood in order to follow him. Yet, our following the Lord will often require some form of letting go on our part. By the standards of this age, there may appear to be a loss involved in our remaining faithful to the way of the Lord. Yet, Jesus assures us in the gospel reading that in losing our lives for his sake we will gain something new. Our faithful following of the Lord, even at a cost to ourselves, will open us up to an experience of a new spiritual family, the family of the Church. In giving our lives to the Lord we will receive abundantly from him in and through the community of his followers, the Church. This is a community that extends beyond this life into eternal life.

30 May, Wednesday, Eighth Week in Ordinary Time
Mark 10:32-45

People make requests of Jesus in the gospels. If the request is for healing of some kind, he always responds. However, if the request is tainted with self-interest he doesn't respond. In the gospel reading today two of the disciples make a request of Jesus to which he does not respond. There was certainly an element of self-interest in the requests of James and John; they wanted the best seats in Jesus' kingdom. Our own requests of the Lord have to be purified of self-interest if he is to respond to them. If we ask something of the Lord for ourselves it needs always to be with a view to others. Our asking has to be in the service of the Lord's work in the world. Towards the end of the gospel reading Jesus defines the greatest in God's kingdom in terms of service of others, 'Anyone who wants to become great among you must be your servant'. Jesus points to himself as the model servant, declaring that he came not to be served, which is what James and John wanted, but to serve. His service of others involved a painful self-emptying, as all service in his name will often involve. That is why in response to the self-serving question of James and John, Jesus asks them a question which points in the direction of self-emptying service, 'Can you drink the cup I must drink, or be baptised with the baptism with which I must be baptised?' There is an implicit reference to both Eucharist and baptism in Jesus' question. Every time we drink the cup of the Lord at the Eucharist we are saying 'yes' to our baptismal calling to share in the Lord's work of giving of ourselves in the service of others.

31 May, Thursday, The Visitation of the Blessed Virgin Mary
Luke 1:39-56

I have often been struck by that line in today's gospel reading, 'As soon as Elizabeth heard Mary's greeting, the child leapt in her womb'. The child in Mary's womb evoked a response from the child in Elizabeth's womb, a response of joy. The meeting of Mary and Elizabeth was, at another level, a meeting between the Son of the Most High and the prophet of the Most High, between Jesus and John the Baptist. The meeting of these two women had a deeper dimension that would not have been obvious to an external observer. However, the text suggests that both Mary and Elizabeth were very aware of this deeper dimension. Elizabeth addresses Mary as the mother of my Lord; Mary proclaims the great things that the Almighty has done for her. Any meeting between two people, especially between two disciples of the Lord, has a deeper dimension beyond what is clearly visible. We each bring something of the Lord to those we meet and the Lord comes to us in and through those who meet with us. We are not always aware of that deeper dimension of our day-to-day encounters. We grow in our awareness of that dimension to the extent that we grow in what might be called a contemplative approach to all of life. Mary exemplifies such an approach. Twice in the opening chapters of his gospel, Luke says of her that she pondered and treasured these things, these seemingly ordinary things.

1 June, Friday, Eighth Week in Ordinary Time
Mark 11:11-26

In our gospel reading the evangelist, Mark, places the story of Jesus and the Temple in the middle of another story about Jesus and the fig tree. It is likely that Mark saw a connection between the fig tree and the Temple. When Jesus came to the fig tree looking for fruit, he found none on it. Likewise, Jesus did not find the kind of fruit in the Temple that he was expecting. According to the prophet Isaiah, whom Jesus quotes in the gospel reading, the Temple was intended by God to be a 'house of prayer for all the peoples'. It wasn't only for the Jewish people but for all peoples. Indeed, there was a special court within the Temple complex which was set aside for pagans. However, it seems that this court of the Gentiles, as it was called, had been taken over for all kinds of commercial activities such as the selling of animals for sacrifice and the exchange of money from the normal Roman coinage into one that was acceptable within the Temple area. All this was necessary work but it should not have been happening in the court of the Gentiles, thereby preventing pagans from gathering in the place assigned to them. When Jesus saw what was happening he became angry and began clearing the court of the Gentiles. The Temple was not being administered in the way God intended; it was like the barren fig tree. The gospel reading reminds us that the Lord calls every institution to account, including every religious institution. The institution of the Church is always in need of reform so that it reflects God's purpose for it. We can never allow ourselves to become complacent. What is true of the Church as a whole is true of each one of us who make up the church. We have to continually open ourselves to the reforming and purifying work of the Lord. Such work is always a work of love because it comes from a heart which seeks our present and ultimate well-being.

2 June, Saturday, Eighth Week in Ordinary Time
Mark 11:27-33

Yesterday's gospel reading was Mark's account of Jesus' cleansing of the Temple in Jerusalem. It was a daring and provocative action which could not but antagonise those who were responsible for overseeing what went on in the Temple, the chief priests, the scribes and the elders. In today's gospel reading, this group confronts Jesus and asks him what authority he had for acting the way he did. Generally, when a question is put to Jesus in the gospels he answers it. On this occasion, however, he refused to answer the question of the chief priests, scribes and elders. Jesus recognised that their question was not a genuine search for truth. They had already closed their hearts to Jesus, just as they had earlier closed their hearts to John the Baptist. We, the readers of Mark's Gospel, know the answer to the question that was put to Jesus. Jesus derived his authority from his relationship to God. He was the earthly representative of God, the beloved Son of God, the one in and through whom God was acting and speaking. Jesus is the authority of God made visible. The word 'authority' can have negative connotations today. Jesus' authority is ultimately a life-giving power that works to bring God's good purpose for humanity and all of creation to pass. That is why we can submit to Jesus' authority over us with joy, trust and thanksgiving.

4 June, Monday, Ninth Week in Ordinary Time

Mark 12:1-12

There is a lot of violence in the parable we have just heard. A vineyard owner sends several servants to collect the produce at the appropriate time. The tenants beat up many of the servants and kill some of them. The owner then sent what was most precious to him, his beloved son, and he too was killed by the tenants. What motivated the final killing was greed. In killing the son the tenants saw a way of taking over the owner's inheritance. There is so much violence and death in the parable that we might be tempted to wonder if there is any redeeming feature there at all. When we look at the violence and death in our world at the moment we can be tempted to ask the same question. Yet, there is always some redeeming feature even in the darkest of situations. There are always to be found people at work trying to bring some light into the darkness, creating opportunities and spaces for others to grow and flourish. In Jesus' parable the positive feature that comes through is the determination of the owner of the vineyard to ensure that his vineyard is properly managed and that the fruit of its harvest is carefully disposed of. As Jesus says in his comment on the parable, even a rejected stone can be turned to a good purpose. God is always at work in a life-giving way, even in the most unpromising of situations. Our calling is to allow ourselves to become channels of that life-giving work of God, especially in those contexts where it is most needed.

5 June, Tuesday, Ninth Week in Ordinary Time

Mark 12:13-17

Jesus was asked many questions in the course of his public ministry and when the question came from a heart that was genuinely searching he took it very seriously. The question that is put to Jesus in today's gospel reading – 'Is it permissible to pay taxes to Caesar or not?' – is not a sincere question. It is an effort to trap Jesus. If he were to say, 'Yes, pay your taxes to Caesar', he would lose the esteem of many of the Jewish people who resented the Roman presence; if he were to say, 'No, do not pay your taxes to Caesar', he would be liable to arrest and trial by the Romans. Yet, Jesus did not stay silent before this question, insincere as it was. In a succinct and somewhat enigmatic answer he declared that people should give back to Caesar what belongs to Caesar and give back to God what belongs to God. Jesus seems to be saying that a certain loyalty is due to the political authorities but an even greater loyalty is due to God. A little later in that same chapter of Mark's Gospel, Jesus will spell out what is due to God. God is to be loved with all our heart, soul and mind. God is to be our first and greatest love. That certainly can never be said of any human authority, be it political or otherwise. Our primary loyalty is to the God whom Jesus reveals to us by his life, death and resurrection; all other loyalties are shaped by that primary loyalty.

6 June, Wednesday, Ninth Week in Ordinary Time
Mark 12:18-27

In our own time different people take different positions on the question of whether or not there is life after death. Those who believe in God, especially the God of Jesus Christ, will believe in life after death. Professed atheists will not, as a rule, believe in life after death. In the time of Jesus some of those who believed in the God of Israel believed in life after death; others who also believed in the God of Israel did not believe in life after death, and one such group was the Sadducees who question Jesus in today's gospel reading. They put a scenario to Jesus which is intended to show the foolishness of belief in life after death. In his reply, Jesus declares that the premise of the Sadducees' objection to life after death is faulty; they presume that life after death will be similar to life before death. Jesus, however, declares that it will be fundamentally different. Heaven is not just another version of earth. The way people relate in heaven is not just a reflection of how they relate on earth. Jesus in the gospel reading says what heaven is not without really saying what it is. It is easier to say what it is not than what it is, but the images for heaven that Jesus uses elsewhere in the gospels, such as the banquet, suggests an experience of communion, both with the Lord and with each other. To the extent that we can build communion on earth, this present life will be an anticipation of what awaits us in heaven.

7 June, Thursday, Ninth Week in Ordinary Time
Mark 12:28-34

We live in a world with all kinds of competing demands on us. There can be a great deal coming at us more or less at the same time. This is all the more so since the advent of the various forms of digital communications. We need to prioritise when we are faced with such an array of stimuli. The need to prioritise is there in today's gospel reading. One of the scribes asks Jesus which of the (more than 600) commandments in the Jewish Law takes priority over all others. Jesus is clear in his response. The first commandment is the commandment to love God with all our being, heart, soul, mind and strength. We don't often think of love as a commandment. We are more likely to think of it as a feeling or an emotion. Yet, for Jesus and the Jewish tradition, love could be commanded because it was about behaviour; it was a way of life. Loving God with all our being involved certain forms of behaviour related to prayer and worship. However, Jesus gives his questioner more than he asked for, not just the most important commandment, but the second most important commandment. He thereby declared that these two commandments are inseparable. The second commandment also commanded love, the love of neighbour. This love could also be commanded because it was more than a feeling; it was a way of behaving towards the other which placed the well-being of the other before one's own. Jesus implies that if we truly love God with all our being we will be caught up into God's love for all humanity.

8 June, Friday, Feast of the Sacred Heart of Jesus

John 19:31-37

Many of us will have grown up with the image of the Sacred Heart in the house. One of the strongest memories I have as a child is the picture of the Sacred Heart in the kitchen of my grandmother's house, with a little red light in the form of a cross lighting in front of it. It always seemed to be on. It was indication of how significant that image of the Sacred Heart was for people. Here was an image of Christ that spoke to people. It is an image that is very much rooted in the gospels. It is only John's Gospel that gives us the scene in today's gospel reading, the piercing of the side of Jesus and the resulting outpouring of blood and water. In John's Gospel, 'water' is always a symbol of life. Earlier in this gospel, Jesus offered living water to the Samaritan woman, and he promised her that whoever drinks the water he gives will never be thirsty again. The water Jesus offers can quench the deepest thirst of the human heart because it is the water of eternal life, the water of God's life, of God's love. God's love is life-giving, as the fourth evangelist declares, 'God so loved the world that he gave his only Son so that whoever believes in him may have eternal life'. That life-giving love of God became flesh in Jesus. The water of life that pours from the side of Jesus, from the heart of Jesus, on the cross is the symbol of God's love present in Jesus, a love which, according to Paul in our second reading, 'is beyond all knowledge'. The love which pours from Jesus on the cross draws us powerfully to the Lord – as Jesus said earlier in John's Gospel, 'When I am lifted up from the earth, I will draw all people to myself'. Today's feast calls on us to allow ourselves to be drawn to the heart of Jesus from which pours God's life-giving, renewing and healing love.

9 June, Saturday, Feast of Saint Colum Cille

Matthew 8:18-27

Colum Cille was born in Gartan, Co Donegal in AD 521 and was of royal lineage. He founded monasteries in Derry, Durrow, and possibly Kells. In AD 565 he left Ireland with twelve companions and founded a monastery on the island of Iona off the South West of Scotland, which was given to him for a the purpose of establishing a monastery by the ruler of the Irish Dalríada. Colum Cille remained the rest of his life in Scotland, mainly Iona, returning to Ireland only for occasional visits. He lived in Iona for over thirty years and died on 9 June AD 597. Colum Cille and his companions preached the gospel in the western part of Scotland. They made the word of God fully known wherever they went. In the course of their ministry they went through many a stormy sea, like the disciples in today's gospel reading. Yet, just as Jesus was with the disciples in the storm and brought them through it, he was with Colum Cille and his companions through all their difficult moments, and they discovered, like those disciples, that the Lord was stronger than the storm. Colum Cille regarded himself as a man of peace, and his spirit lives on in the Iona community which is based on the island. The Iona Community is a Christian ecumenical community of men and women from different walks of life and different traditions in the Church. They are committed to working together for peace and social justice, the rebuilding of community and the renewal of worship. In the Eucharist we celebrate God's reconciling love revealed fully in the death and resurrection of Jesus. We are then sent from the Eucharist to be instruments of that reconciling love in our own sphere of influence today.

11 June, Monday, Feast of Saint Barnabas

Matthew 10:7-13

Barnabas does not feature in the gospels but he is a significant presence in the Acts of the Apostles, Luke's story of the early years of the Church. He was originally a leading member of the Church in Jerusalem. According to today's first reading he was instrumental in encouraging a new development that took place in the city of Antioch, where the gospel was preached to pagans for the first time. He clearly saw the hand of the Lord in this new phenomenon. According to our reading, Barnabas encouraged Saul or Paul to leave the church in Tarsus, Paul's home city, and to come to the church in Antioch because he recognised that Antioch would be an ideal location for this great apostle to the pagans. Barnabas himself seems to have become a leading member of the church of Antioch. He worked alongside Paul there and together they were sent out on mission by the church of Antioch, travelling to Cyprus and beyond. Barnabas is portrayed in the Acts of the Apostles as an enabler, an encourager. What he enabled and encouraged others to do turned out to be just as significant as what he did himself. In the gospel reading, Jesus says to his followers, 'You received without charge, give without charge'. One of the ways we give is by creating a space for others to give and to grow. This is where Barnabas comes into his own. He recognised and encouraged the workings of the Spirit in the lives of others. He didn't try to do everything himself; he stepped back and allowed the Lord to work through others. That takes a certain generosity of spirit, a willingness to rejoice in the gifts of others and allow them to find expression. We can all learn from Barnabas that delicate art of creating space for others to flourish.

12 June, Tuesday, Tenth Week in Ordinary Time

Matthew 5:13-16

Salt has something of a negative press at the moment. Some of our foods have too much salt in them, more salt than is healthy. Yet, in the time of Jesus, salt had a very positive profile. It was used to preserve and flavour food. When Jesus said to his disciples, 'You are the salt of the earth', he was reminding them of their identity and of their calling as his disciples. Jesus does not spell out what he means by the image of salt when he applies it to his disciples. He may be implying that just as salt enhances the flavour of food, they are to enhance the lives of others by the values that they proclaim and live by. As disciples, we are called to be present to our world in a way that helps to preserve what is best there and that adds a dimension, a flavour, that would not otherwise be there. We are called to make a difference for the better. That saying about salt comes immediately after the beatitudes. Jesus seems to be saying that in so far as we are people of the beatitudes, in so far as we live by the values proclaimed in the beatitudes, we will make a difference for the better in our world; we will enhance the lives of those who come within our sphere of influence.

13 June, Wednesday, Tenth Week in Ordinary Time
Matthew 5:17-19

In the gospel reading, Jesus the Jew shows himself to be respectful of his own Jewish tradition, 'Don't imagine that I have come to abolish the Law and the Prophets'. However, he also declares that he has come to complete the Law and the Prophets, to bring their true intention to fulfilment. Jesus valued the good in his religious tradition, but was also open to the ways that God was working to enrich that tradition. We too are called to value the good in our own religious tradition. There can be an overly critical stance towards tradition, including religious tradition, today. People can dismiss the tradition of their faith without having really explored it. There are resources and riches in our religious tradition that can continue to nurture and enhance our lives today. Yet, while valuing the riches of our religious tradition, we also need to critique the shadowy side of that tradition. There are elements of the tradition that do not serve us well today. We need to be open and receptive to the ways that the Lord is constantly renewing and enriching our faith tradition. God is like the potter who takes what is there and reshapes it so that it serves his purposes more fully. God is always ahead of us in that sense; our task is to keep up with what God is trying to do.

14 June, Thursday, Tenth Week in Ordinary Time
Matthew 5:20-26

In today's gospel reading, Jesus declares that if any of his Jewish contemporaries were bringing their offering to the altar in the Jewish temple and they remember that someone has something against them they should first be reconciled with their brother or sister and only then present their offering. The Lord will always send us out to work to be reconciled with those who have something against us. We may not succeed in our efforts, but the Lord calls on us to be prepared always to make the first move. 'Go and be reconciled', Jesus declares. We are not just to wait for others to take the initiative; we have to make the move, even if in doing so we fail. In behaving like this, we are reflecting how God has related to us through his Son. God took the initiative to reconcile us to himself, through the life, death and resurrection of his Son. In his letter to the Romans, Paul declares, 'God proves his love for us in that while we were still sinners Christ died for us'. The Lord calls on us to be as ready as he was to take the same initiative when a relationship needs reconciling. Jesus even declares in today's gospel reading that the readiness and willingness to take such an initiative is a prior condition of worship.

15 June, Friday, Tenth Week in Ordinary Time
Matthew 5:27-32

The gospel reading today presents Jesus as going further than the Jewish Law in his teaching. He forbids not just the act of adultery but the lustful look that leads to it, not just the action but the intention. At the time, Jesus' teaching would have been perceived by many Jews as unnecessary challenging. That is the way that much of Jesus' teaching would be perceived today, too. The gospel will always be counter-cultural, counter the dominant culture, to some extent. If we are trying to be faithful to the gospel we will sometimes find ourselves at odds with the prevailing culture. Not only is the culture working against us as Christians, but we know our own weakness, our vulnerability and frailty, can work against us as well. Paul alludes to that in the first reading today when we declares that, 'We are only the earthenware jars that hold this treasure'. We have the treasure of the gospel and we are trying to live it, sometimes against an opposing tide. At the same time, we are like earthenware jars that were used in the time of Jesus and Paul to hold oil and a wick to make a light. They were very expendable; if they fell they broke, but they were cheap to buy. However, Paul goes on to say that the overwhelming power of the gospel does not come from us but from God. God is powerfully at work helping us to live the treasure of the gospel, and his power is greater than our weakness and greater than the pressures that oppose the gospel. That realisation encourages us to keep on fighting the good fight, as Paul says elsewhere.

16 June, Saturday, Tenth Week in Ordinary Time
Matthew 5:33-37

At the root of the prohibition of oaths in today's gospel reading is Jesus' desire that, among his followers, unqualified truthfulness is required. This is one further dimension of life within God's kingdom. The teaching of Jesus here is reflected in the letter of James, 'Do not swear either by heaven or by earth or by any other oath but let your "Yes" be yes and your "No" be no' (*James 5:12*). Most of us would acknowledge that we do not always follow the injunction of Jesus in today's gospel reading, 'All you need say is "Yes" is you mean yes and "No" if you mean no'. We don't always find it easy to be truthful, to be true to what is in our heart. Our lips do not always express what is in our heart. Throughout this section of the Sermon on the Mount there is a focus on getting what is in our heart right and allow what is in our heart to shape all that we say and do. The first and most demanding task is the former, getting what is in our heart right. We need to allow the values and attitudes of the gospel to take root in our hearts. We then need the courage to be true to those values in our daily lives. This will require 'yes' and meaning it to certain calls and choices and saying 'no' and meaning it to other calls and choices.

18 June, Monday, Eleventh Week in Ordinary Time
Matthew 5:38-42

We are all aware that there is great evil in the world. We only have to listen to or look at the news in the evening to be reminded of the terrible evil that can be inflicted on people. A person goes into a peaceful setting where people are engaged in ordinary social activities and shoots at random and takes human life. Someone's life is changed forever by the evil and irresponsible actions of others. Jesus was very aware of this darker side of human nature; he came to see that he would suffer the ultimate loss of his own life because of it. In today's gospel reason he makes reference to the wicked person who seeks to do people harm; he mentions the greedy person who would take someone to court to get their tunic. His real concern is how his followers would react to such experiences when it affects them. Jesus' call to his disciples in today's gospel reading is summed up in the call that Paul makes in his letter to the Church in Rome, 'Do not be overcome by evil, but overcome evil with good'. Jesus declares that we are not to meet wickedness with wickedness, evil with evil, but rather with generosity of heart and spirit. So, if a Roman soldier unfairly orders a disciple to carry his rucksack for one mile, the disciple is to carry it for two miles. This attitude that Jesus is promoting goes against all human reasoning; it is not the way the world operates. Yet, it is the way of Jesus and he calls on us to make it our way too. We cannot possibly live this way by our own strength alone. We need the Lord's strength, the strength of the Holy Spirit, which the Lord gives to those who ask for it.

19 June, Tuesday, Eleventh Week in Ordinary Time
Matthew 5:43-48

It is clear from the gospels that nature spoke powerfully to Jesus about God and God's way of relating to us and our way of relating to him. When Jesus noticed that the sun was shining and the rain was falling on all people equally, regardless of their moral standing, it spoke to him of God's love which was given equally to all. Just as the sun and the rain do not discriminate between the good and the sinner, so God's love does not discriminate between the morally good and immoral. God loves all equally; what differs is people's willingness to open themselves to this love and allow it to transform their way of being and living. In the gospel reading, Jesus calls on his disciples to be God-like in the way they relate to others. We are to love indiscriminately. How we relate to others is to be shaped by how God relates to us rather than by how others relate to us. This is how Jesus understands perfection. He himself embodied fully this way of relating that he calls for in the gospel reading. He loved others as God loved him, regardless of how others related to him. He prayed for his friends and his enemies alike. In his letter to the Ephesians, Paul prays that Christ would live in our hearts through faith. This is the essence of our baptismal calling, to allow the Lord to live in us and to love through us. When that happens we become perfect as God is perfect.

20 June, Wednesday, Eleventh Week in Ordinary Time
Matthew 6:1-6, 16-18

There often appears to be a tension between the various sayings of Jesus in the gospels. At the beginning of the Sermon of the Mount, Jesus calls on his disciples to, 'Let your light shine before others, so that seeing your good works they may give praise to your Father in heaven'. In today's gospel reading, also from the Sermon on the Mount, he calls on his disciples to, 'Be careful not to parade your good deeds before others to attract their notice'. Do you let your light shine or not? The answer to that question has to be yes. We have been enlightened by Christ and we must let that light shine by doing works inspired by the gospel, the kind of works Jesus himself did. However, today's gospel reading raises the question of motivation. We do not let our light shine to be noticed; we don't do good works to draw attention to ourselves. In all that we do, we work to bring glory to God and not to ourselves. One of the great temptations that people of faith come up against is the temptation to do the right thing for the wrong reason. As Paul says in his first letter to the Corinthians, 'Whatever you do, do everything for the glory of God'.

21 June, Thursday, Eleventh Week in Ordinary Time
Matthew 6:7-15

In today's gospel reading Jesus makes a contrast between how the pagans pray and how his followers are to pray. He characterises pagan prayer as a form of babbling, as if the use of many words is more likely to catch the attention of their gods. This approach to prayer presumes that the gods have no interest in human affairs and they have to be pressured into giving us their attention. The more words and the louder they are spoken the better. Jesus reveals a very different God, a God who is already intimately involved with our affairs before we turn to him in prayer. As Jesus says in the gospel reading, 'Your Father knows your need before you ask him'. Prayer is not so much a matter of trying to get the attention of God who has no interest in us, but rather, it is about opening ourselves more fully to what God is already doing within us and among us. Many words are not needed; it is the attitude of the heart that matters. The prayer that Jesus gives his disciples in the gospel reading expresses that proper attitude of the heart which opens us up more fully to God's life-giving work in the world. We begin by focusing on what God wants, what God is doing. We pray that God's kingdom would come, not ours. We then acknowledge our dependence on God for our most basic needs, namely, nourishment, both material and spiritual, forgiveness when we fail, and strength when we are put to the test. In what has become known as the Lord's Prayer, Jesus not only gives us one prayer, but a whole way of praying.

22 June, Friday, Eleventh Week in Ordinary Time
Matthew 6:19-23

We all recognise the truth of Jesus' saying in today's gospel reading, 'Where your treasure is, there will your heart be also'. We give our heart to whatever or whoever we treasure or value. We spend our lives trying to discern what it is that is truly valuable, valuable enough to give our heart to, to give our life to. In the course of our lives we meet people whom we come to value and treasure, people who mean a great deal to us, to whom we give our hearts, in one way or another. It is people who tend to be our greatest earthly treasures. People will always mean more to us than the material possessions we might accumulate. In today's gospel reading, Jesus suggests that he is our ultimate treasure, the one who is worthy of all our heart and mind and soul. When he becomes our greatest treasure, then, in the words of the gospel reading, we store up treasures for ourselves in heaven. He is the treasure beyond all human treasures because he is Emmanuel, God-with-us. He is the pearl of great price. In his letter to the Philippians, Paul declares, 'I regard everything as loss because of the surpassing value of knowing Christ Jesus my Lord'. Jesus was Paul's greatest treasure; it was to him that Paul gave his heart. Because he gave his heart to Jesus, he had a heart for others, for all those for whom Jesus died and rose to new life. When we give our heart to Jesus, it is not withdrawn from others. Rather, he comes to dwell in our heart and our heart expands to embrace all whom he embraces.

23 June, Saturday, Eleventh Week in Ordinary Time
Matthew 6:24-34

We all have worries and anxieties and preoccupations. It is part and parcel of living. In the gospel reading, Jesus suggests that there needs to be a sense of proportion about our anxieties. We need to be more preoccupied about what is more important and less preoccupied about what is less important. What is most important is what Jesus refers to in the gospel reading as the kingdom of God and his righteousness. We are to set our hearts on those realities first. In comparison to those realities the material needs of life for food and clothing are much less important. What Jesus says here corresponds to the prayer that he gave his disciples to pray, where we are taught to pray first for the coming of God's kingdom and that God's will would be done on earth as in heaven, and only then to pray for our own material needs, our daily bread. What Jesus refers to in the gospel reading as God's righteousness is simply another way of referring to the doing of God's will. If everyone did God's will on earth, as it is done in heaven, then the kingdom of God would be fully present on earth. It is clear what Jesus' own priorities are and he wants us to make his priorities our own. Our primary preoccupation is to be the seeking and doing of God's will. This priority of Jesus is there again in the Beatitudes, 'Blessed are those who hunger and thirst for righteousness'. If we were to ask, 'What does doing God's will mean?', Jesus would point to himself, and he would say to us, 'Learn from me'. He is the one human being in whom God's will was done on earth as it is in heaven.

25 June, Monday, Twelfth Week in Ordinary Time
Matthew 7:1-5

We live in a society which tends to rush to judgement very quickly. When some damning report is issued there is an immediate search for people to blame. It can be very easy for those who have never been in a particular situation to blame others for their actions in that situation.

Condemning others can come all too easily to us. The gospel reading today suggests that Jesus was very aware of that. He warns against rushing to premature judgement, 'Do not judge and you will not be judged'. Perhaps Jesus was more aware than we are of the danger that in judging others we can easily get it very wrong. He understood that our limited vision can make it very difficult for us to judge fairly. Our limited vision comes from the many failings in ourselves. That seems to be the point of the humorous image in the second part of the gospel reading. We cannot attempt to take a splinter out of the eye of someone else while all the time we have a plank in our own eye. We need to attend to the plank in our own eye first. We need to put our energies into renewing ourselves rather than condemning others. Only then can we begin to see as the Lord sees.

26 June, Tuesday, Twelfth Week in Ordinary Time

Matthew 7:6, 12-14

The command in today's gospel reading to 'treat others as you would like them to treat you' is not unique to the gospels. It is often termed the 'golden rule' and there are versions of this command among Greeks, Romans and Jews. There is nothing specifically Christian about it. It has been said that the command calls for an exercise of moral imagination as a preliminary to action. We are to ask ourselves, 'What do I really want from another person?' Then I try to ensure that all my actions in their regard reflect those qualities. The fact that we find this 'golden rule' in the gospels indicates that the teaching of Jesus incorporates the best of the moral wisdom of the ancient world. Jesus could affirm that wisdom as well as challenge it. In our own times it is equally true that many of the values of the gospel are appreciated and lived by people who would not describe themselves as disciples of Jesus, as Christians. In these threatening times for our world, we need to find the common ground that allows people of different faith perspectives, and of no faith, to work together in the service of humanity and of our planet. As well as challenging culture with the values of the gospel, we also need to build bridges towards it. In a similar vein, Paul in his letter to the Philippians exhorts, 'Whatever is true, whatever is honorable, whatever is just, whatever is pure, whatever is pleasing, whatever is commendable, if there is any excellence and if there is anything worthy of praise, think about these things.'

27 June, Wednesday, Twelfth Week in Ordinary Time
Matthew 7:15-20

Many of the images Jesus uses in the gospels have a striking quality to them. Such is the case with the image in today's gospel reading of a wolf disguised as a sheep. The wolf was the enemy of the sheep. In John's Gospel, Jesus speaks of the hired hand who, in contrast to the shepherd, leaves the sheep and runs away when he sees the wolf coming and, as a result, the wolf snatches the sheep and scatters them. The contrast between appearance and reality could hardly be expressed more forcibly than with that image of a wolf in sheep's clothing, an image that has made its way into modern parlance. Jesus then shifts imagery from the animal world to the plant world, declaring that the quality of the fruit reveals the quality of the tree that produced it. In other words, going back to the animal imagery, even if the wolf appears in sheep's clothing, eventually the wolf will out. The pretence cannot be kept up indefinitely. The quality of our heart will be revealed in the quality of our lives. Paul speaks of the fruit of the Spirit as love, joy, peace, patience, kindness, generosity, faithfulness, gentleness and self-control. If this kind of fruit is visible in a human life, then it is evident that the person's core is sound. Their heart is in some way in tune with the Lord's own heart.

28 June, Thursday, Twelfth Week in Ordinary Time
Matthew 7:21-29

When people were building houses in Palestine at the time of Jesus, during the dry season when the weather was fine and warm, it was tempting to build them in a way that did not take into account the wilder weather to come during the winter, when heavy rain and strong winds could affect that part of the Near East. It was easier to build on sand than on rock but it was also shortsighted. What serves in good times does not always serve in bad times. Building on rock ensures that the house will stand regardless of the weather. The gospel reading suggests that we have to build our lives in such a way that we will stand firm when life gets difficult, when the storms come our way and threaten to engulf us. We are to build for the worst of times. Jesus declares in the gospel reading that if we not only listen to his words but act on them, we will be doing just that. If we embrace his life and message and allow our own lives to be shaped by it, then we will be building our lives in such a way that we will stand firm when trials come. We need a firm foundation, we need resources to fall back on, when our vulnerability is exposed by life's storms. Jesus tells us that he is our primary resource. He will be our firm foundation if we keep on trying to take the path he sets before us by his life and teaching.

29 June, Friday, Feast of Saints Peter and Paul
Matthew 16:13-19

According to the gospel reading, what singled Peter out from the other disciples was his God-given insight into the identity of Jesus. It was because of his unique insight that Jesus gives Peter a unique role among his followers. He is to be the rock, the firm foundation, on which Jesus will build his church. Peter's role is further spelt out by Jesus giving him the keys of the kingdom of heaven. The image of the keys suggests authority. The nature of that authority is expressed in terms of binding and loosing. This refers to a teaching authority.

Peter is being entrusted with the task of authoritatively interpreting the teaching of Jesus for other members of the Church. Yet, this same Peter immediately tries to deflect Jesus from taking the way of the cross, and when Jesus did take that way, Peter would deny any association with him. Jesus gives a significant role to someone who remains very flawed. If the gospel reading associates teaching with Peter, the second reading associates preaching with Paul. In that reading, Paul refers to the Lord who, 'Gave me power, so that through me the whole message might be preached for all the pagans to hear'. Paul was the great preacher of the gospel to the pagans throughout the Roman Empire. He preached it for the last time, in the city of Rome, where, like Peter, he was martyred for his faith in Christ. Our second reading today may well have been written from his Roman imprisonment, 'I have fought the good fight to the end; I have run the race to the finish; I have kept the faith'. The image of the fight and the race suggest that 'keeping the faith' was a struggle for Paul; it did not come easily to him, just as keeping the faith did not come easily to Peter either. Keeping the faith does not always come easily to any of us. Paul was very aware that keeping the faith was not due primarily to his own efforts; it was the Lord who enabled him to keep the faith. As he says in today's second reading, 'The Lord stood by me and gave me power'. It is the Lord who empowers all of us to keep the faith; his faithfulness to us enables us to be faithful to him. The faithful witness of Peter and Paul speak to us ultimately of the Lord's faithfulness to us all.

30 June, Saturday, Twelfth Week in Ordinary Time

Matthew 8:5-17

We recognise the words of the Roman centurion in today's gospel reading as a version of what we say together just before we receive Holy Communion. It is striking that the words of a pagan have become part of the text of the Mass. Here was a pagan who showed tremendous respect for Jesus, so much so that he did not want Jesus, a law abiding Jew, to enter his pagan household. He was aware of the sensitivities around such a visit for Jews. Not only did he show great respect for Jesus, but he also displayed tremendous trust in the power of Jesus' word, 'Say but the word and my servant will be cured'. Here was a pagan who was prepared to give himself over to the word of Jesus. What this pagan says to Jesus is not far removed from what Mary is reported as saying to the angel Gabriel, 'Let it be to me according to your word'. This Roman soldier has a great deal to teach us, not only about respect and reverence for the Lord, especially in the Eucharist, but also about the value of giving ourselves over to the word of the Lord. It is no surprise that Jesus turned to his disciples and said, 'Nowhere in Israel have I found faith like this'. Sometimes our teachers in the faith can come from the most unlikely quarters.

2 July, Monday, Thirteenth Week in Ordinary Time
Matthew 8:18-22

The scribe who approaches Jesus at the beginning of today's gospel reading speaks in a way that suggests that he has a generosity of spirit and the best of intentions, 'Master, I will follow you wherever you go'. In response, Jesus tempers his enthusiasm with the reality of what lies ahead for him if he becomes a disciple, 'The Son of Man has nowhere to lay his head'. He will be following someone who is always on the move, without a real home to call his own. Sometimes our generosity of spirit and our enthusiasm can come up against the harsher realities of life and in response we can become less generous and less enthusiastic. Jesus' closest disciples seemed full of enthusiasm when they left their nets by the Sea of Galilee to follow him, but when the cross came into view for Jesus and for them, they fell away. It is not always easy to retain our idealism, our enthusiasm, our generosity of spirit over the long haul, especially when the cross comes our way in one shape or form. It is then that we realise that our own enthusiasm and generosity of spirit is not enough. We need the Lord to be our strength when we lose heart, our inspiration when we are tempted to settle for less, and our refuge when we come face-to-face with the storms of life. We can only be faithful to our following of the Lord if we allow the Lord at the same time to be our resource, our food for the journey. That is what he wants to be. He does not ask us to go it alone but to rely on him every step of the way.

3 July, Tuesday, Saint Thomas, apostle
John 20:24-29

The disciple Thomas has come to be known as 'Doubting Thomas'. Yet, there was more to Thomas than his doubt. The Risen Lord's face-to-face meeting with Thomas dispelled all Thomas's doubts and led him to one of the most profound professions of faith in all the gospels, 'My Lord and my God'. Because we only live in hope of such a face-to-face meeting with the Lord, there will always be some element of doubt in our own faith. As Paul says in his first letter to the Corinthians, 'Now we see as in a mirror, dimly'. The questions and doubts we feel are an inevitable part of seeing dimly. Such questions and doubts are not an enemy of faith. They can lead, rather, to a deepening of our faith. If we face our doubts and our questions honestly, as Thomas did, and bring them to each other and to the Lord, we too can reach a point where we can make Thomas's confession our own, 'My Lord and my God'. In one of his encyclicals, *Faith and Reason,* the lately-canonised Pope John Paul II stated, 'The Church remains profoundly convinced that faith and reason mutually support each other ... they offer each other a purifying critique and a stimulus to pursue the search for a deeper understanding.' We can all learn to seek the Lord with humility, sincerity and honesty, like Thomas. The Lord considers anyone who is a seeker and who wishes to believe as a believer already. If we remain true to our spiritual search, the Lord has his own way to meet each one of us and to invite us, as he invited Thomas, 'Doubt no longer but believe'.

4 July, Wednesday, Thirteenth Week in Ordinary Time
Matthew 8:28-34

In today's gospel reading Jesus brings two demoniacs to a greater fullness of life. It is striking that after doing this, the people of the region implored him to leave the neighbourhood. It might have been expected that they would have wanted someone who could bring freedom to the enslaved, to stay among them for some time. Surely, there were others in this region who could benefit from the presence of God's power at work in Jesus. Perhaps the people were nervous of such power for good, fearing that it might make demands on them. We too can be tempted to ask Jesus to leave our neighbourhood, to leave our lives. We sometimes want to keep him at a distance. We sense that his nearness might be very demanding. He might call us to go out towards those who live on the edge of the community, as he himself went out towards the two demoniacs who lived among the tombs. Yet, if we welcome the Lord into our lives, rather than keeping him at a distance, we will discover that he gives us the strength to respond to the challenging call of his presence and, in responding to that call, we too will find a greater fullness of life.

5 July, Thursday, Thirteenth Week in Ordinary Time
Matthew 9:1-8

There are times in life when we need the faith of others to carry us because our own faith is weak or even non-existent. This is how most of us began our Christian lives. It was the faith of our parents that carried us to the baptismal font. We had no faith of our own. The faith of others carried us to the Lord. We find something similar happening in today's gospel reading. A paralysed man is carried to Jesus by the faith of others. The gospel reading says that when the people brought the paralytic to Jesus, he saw their faith. There is no reference to the faith of the paralytic. It was the faith of those who carried the paralytic that Jesus responded to. The opening words of Jesus to the paralytic suggest that, far from being full of faith, he was in need of God's for-giveness, 'Courage, my child, your sins are forgiven'. Having been car-ried by the faith of others at the beginning of our Christian lives, there will come a time when we will be called upon to carry others by our faith. We were initially brought to the Lord by the faith others. As we grow older, the Lord will often call us to bring others to the Lord by our faith. Faith sends out its own waves that touch the lives of others. Rath-er, the Lord works through our faith to bring others to him. Our faith is never without an impact for good on others. As we grow in our faith, we expand the opening for the Lord to bring others to him through us.

6 July, Friday, Thirteenth Week in Ordinary Time
Matthew 9:9-13

There was a book written some years ago called *The God of Surprises* by a Jesuit priest, Gerald Hughes. God can surprise us human beings. After all, as the prophet Isaiah said, 'God's ways are not our ways'. Jesus, as the revelation of God, was also full of surprises. The gospels record people being amazed at what he said and did. He didn't behave as the religious leaders of the time normally behaved. Something of his surprising ways is evident in today's gospel reading. Jesus calls Matthew, a tax collector, to follow him and he went on to share table with Matthew and other tax collectors. Matthew and people like him would have been regarded by religious people of the time as sinners who did not keep God's law. Such people were to be avoided for fear of contamination. Jesus did not follow this path. He was not afraid of being contaminated by others. On the contrary, he knew that his own goodness had the power to transform others for the better. When Jesus went on to say in the gospel reading, 'What I want is mercy not sacrifice', he was declaring that he wants his own merciful way of behaving to find expression in the lives of his followers. We too are called to transform others by our own goodness. We are all to be agents of the Lord's transforming love and mercy.

7 July, Saturday, Thirteenth Week in Ordinary Time
Matthew 9:14-17

The question that the disciples of John the Baptist put to Jesus in today's gospel reading suggest that they recognised a clear difference in style between the ministry of John and the ministry of Jesus. John the Baptist's ministry, and that of his disciples, was characterised by fasting and other ascetic practices. The ministry of Jesus and his disciples was marked more by celebration. Indeed, Jesus goes on to compare his ministry to a wedding feast. No one would ever think of fasting at a wedding feast. Wedding feasts in the villages of Galilee were one of the few occasions when people could eat well. There is a joyful, celebratory style to Jesus' ministry because he is revealing the mercy of God for all. Jesus was proclaiming through his ministry the God, who is rich in mercy; he was revealing a God who wanted to embrace all in his merciful love, especially those who felt outside the orbit of God's mercy. That is why Jesus so often shared table with tax collectors and sinners. His ministry was truly good news. This indeed was new wine to gladden the heart. Such a celebratory event called for new practices and patterns, new wineskins. In the gospel reading, Jesus is reminding us that at the heart of our faith is good news, the good news of God's faithful and merciful love for us all. We are all invited to what the last book of the Bible, the Book of Revelation, calls 'The wedding feast of the Lamb'.

9 July, Monday, Fourteenth Week in Ordinary Time
Matthew 9:18-26

In the Jewish Scriptures, one of the ways God speaks to people is through their dreams. In today's first reading we find one of the most memorable dreams in the Jewish Scriptures, Jacob's dream of a ladder reaching between heaven and earth with the angels of God ascending and descending upon it. When Jacob woke from his dream he said, 'The Lord is in this place and I never knew it ... this is the gate of heaven'. Jacob had a profound sense of God's presence. In the gospel reading today, two very different people also had a profound sense of God's presence, a synagogue official and a woman whose physical condition would have excluded her from the synagogue. They each experienced God's life-giving presence in a way that was not available to Jacob; they experienced God in the person of Jesus. Jesus is Emmanuel, God-with-us, and he is God-with-us until the end of time. Like the official and the woman, we too live in the presence of Jesus, God-with-us. Yet, like Jacob, we often have reason to say, 'The Lord is in this place and I never knew it'. We are not always aware of the Lord's presence. Yet, because the Word became flesh and dwelt among us, there is a sense in which we always stand before what Jacob calls 'the gate of heaven'. Heaven comes to earth in the person of the Lord, God-with-us. Like the woman in the gospel reading, we are invited to reach out in faith and touch the Lord who is always present to us.

10 July, Tuesday, Fourteenth Week in Ordinary Time
Matthew 9:32-38

There is a sharp contrast in today's gospel reading between the way the ordinary people responded to Jesus' healing ministry and the way the Pharisees responded. The people said, 'Nothing like this has ever been seen in Israel'. The Pharisees said, 'It is through the prince of devils that he casts out devils'. The people saw God at work in what Jesus was doing; the Pharisees saw Satan at work in Jesus' healing work. It is hard to imagine a more contrasting set of responses. It brings home to us that when people look at the same phenomenon, they can see it very differently. The people, in contrast to the Pharisees, were attuned to the presence and action of God in Jesus. The gospel reading invites us to ask ourselves, 'To what extent am I alert to the presence of God all around me, especially in the good that other people may be doing?' We can be prone to seeing what is lacking in some situation and to miss the good that is also there. We can be better at naming what is wrong than what is right. We can be more attuned to noticing evil than good. While never being blind to evil, sin and failure, the gospel reading encourages us to be open to the ways that the Lord is at work in our lives and in the lives of others. The Lord himself was sensitive to the good in others, even when they failed to see it for themselves, and others failed to see it. We need something of the Lord's generous way of seeing, especially in these times when the negative can be highlighted to the detriment of everything else.

11 July, Wednesday, St Benedict, Abbot, Patron of Europe
Matthew 19:27-29

Today's gospel reading for the feast of Saint Benedict begins with a question from Peter, 'What about us? We have left everything and followed you'. Peter and the other members of the twelve had given up a great deal to become followers of Jesus. They may have been wondering if it was really worth it all. We too have responded to the Lord's call, although not in the same very radical way that those intimate associates of Jesus or men like Benedict answered the Lord's call, leaving livelihood and family for a very uncertain future. Perhaps on our off days we might be tempted to ask a similar question to that of Peter; 'Is it worth the effort, this following of Jesus, this struggle to live by the values of the gospel day in and day out?' The answer of Jesus to Peter and to us all is that, 'Yes, it is worth the effort'. Jesus promises us in that gospel reading that when we respond to his call, when we give of ourselves for his sake, we will receive far more than we will give. In particular, he says that we will gain a new experience of family, far beyond the confines of our blood family, the family of believers. We will find ourselves co-travellers with others who are trying to take the same path as ourselves; we will experience the richness of the Church, the community of the Lord's followers. That community who journey with us embraces not only those still on their pilgrim way, but all who have passed beyond this life, including the saints, like Saint Benedict, what the letter to the Hebrew calls that 'great cloud of witnesses'.

12 July, Thursday, Fourteenth Week in Ordinary Time
Matthew 10:7-15

Today's first reading from the prophet Hosea is surely one of the most beautiful readings in all of the Jewish Scriptures. God speaks of his relationship with his people as loving parents would speak of their relationship with their child, indeed as a mother would: 'I myself taught Ephraim to walk, I took them in my arms … I was like someone who lifts an infant close against his cheek; stooping down to him I gave him food.' Yet, in spite of such tender love, Israel turned away from God and went after other gods. Jesus is the fullest revelation possible in a human life of this tender love of God. He too experienced the turning away of people from this love, their refusal to respond to it in any meaningful way. When Jesus sends out his disciples in today's gospel reading he warns them to expect the same. They are to proclaim the good news that the kingdom of God is at hand, the reign of God's life-giving love, but they will encounter those who will not welcome them and will not listen to what they have to say. This negative response is not to deter them from their mission of proclaiming God's loving presence by what they say and do. It certainly did not deter Jesus. When he suffered the ultimate rejection on the cross, he proclaimed the same good news as Risen Lord to those who had turned away from him and rejected him. We are to reveal the loving presence of God, regardless of how we are received by others.

13 July, Friday, Fourteenth Week in Ordinary Time
Matthew 10:16-23

The gospel reading today is very realistic about the kind of reception that the disciples of Jesus are likely to get from the world in which they are called to bear witness. The reception will be predominantly hostile, and some of that hostility will even come from within their own families. Yet, Jesus reassures them that they will not have to face into this hostile world on their own. The Holy Spirit will be given to them as a resource and will inspire their witness. It could be argued that the society in which we are living is not as hostile to the faith as the society into which Jesus sent the first disciples. Yet, we know that the values of the gospel are not always well regarded by the culture in which we live; many see those gospel values as a threat, especially a threat to a certain understanding of human freedom. We are just as much in need of the Holy Spirit today, as the first disciples were, if we are to bear witness to the Lord and all he stands for. We still need the Holy Spirit to inspire our witness to the Lord. The Church is as dependant on the Holy Spirit today as it ever was. The good news is that the Holy Spirit is just as available to us today as he was in the earliest days of the Church, because the Lord needs our witness today as much as he did then. Earlier in Matthew's gospel, Jesus had urged his disciples, 'Ask (keep on asking) and it will be given you'.

14 July, Saturday, Fourteenth Week in Ordinary Time
Matthew 10:24-34
The gospel reading today is part of what is often termed Matthew's missionary discourse. Jesus is speaking to his disciples as he sends them out on mission. In our reading Jesus twice calls upon them, 'Do not be afraid'. They are not to be afraid of those who will oppose their message, even to the point of killing their body. They are to be free of fear because Jesus has brought them, and disciples of every gener-ation, into an intimate relationship with God. We share in Jesus' own relationship with God. God the Father knows us as well as he knows his own Son, down to the number of the hairs on our head. If God cares for creation, even the humble sparrow, how much more does God care for those who have been made in God's image and likeness

and in whom God recognises his own Son. This sense of being valued and watched over by God frees us from fear. The first letter of John declares that perfect love drives out fear. Paul in his letter to the Romans reminds us, 'You did not receive a spirit of slavery to fall back into fear, but you have received a spirit of adoption'. We have been adopted as sons and daughters of God in the Spirit through Jesus. We enjoy a familiar relationship and intimacy with God our Father in heaven. The assurance which this privileged relationship gives us empowers us to declare ourselves for Jesus in the presence of all.

16 July, Monday, Fifteenth Week in Ordinary Time
Matthew 10:34-11:1

It is often the case that people who take a stand for what is right and good can find themselves at odds with their own group. There have been many examples of whistle-blowers who are ostracised because they brought to light some inappropriate behaviour that others would have preferred to keep hidden. It is against such a background that Jesus' sayings at the beginning of today's gospel reading could be understood. He declares that he has come not to bring peace, but a sword and to set members of families against each other. Jesus recognised that those who followed in his way would often find themselves at odds with their own family members who had not embraced the way of Jesus. Earlier in Matthew's gospel, Jesus declared blessed those who are persecuted for what is right. Now he acknowledges that such persecution could come even from within one's own family. That is why Jesus goes on to declare in this gospel reading that those who chose to follow him will have to keep preferring him even to their family members, when that is called for. To be excluded from one's family, or one's peer group, for the sake of Jesus and his values, entails a huge loss. Yet, Jesus declares that those who lose their life for his sake will find it. The gospel calls on us to risk everything, even our most significant relationships, for the sake of Jesus and all he stands for. It is a call that remains as challenging today as it did when Jesus first uttered it.

17 July, Tuesday, Fifteenth Week in Ordinary Time
Matthew 11:20-24

The words of Jesus against the Galilean towns of Chorazin, Bethsaida and Capernaum seem harsh to our ears. Behind the harsh woes lie the anguish of a love that is frustrated. His rejection by many in these towns foreshadows a great rejection that lies ahead by the people of Jerusalem. Jesus has given much to these Galilean towns. Miracles have been done in their midst. Yet, the response has been at best indifferent and at worst hostile. Are all the efforts Jesus made to make present the kingdom of God among them wasted? Jesus had spared nothing on their behalf and, yet, the return has been minimal. Such an experience could have left Jesus disheartened. Yet, in the passage immediately following, Jesus gives thanks to God for all those who have responded to his message and work. Jesus understood that in spite of some setbacks and disappointments, God was at work in and through him. Much of the seed he scattered appeared to bear no fruit, yet some of the seed would bear a rich harvest. As people of faith we can get very discouraged by the indifference or even hostility to the gospel message. Yet, we can be sure that the Lord continues to work in our midst, even when the signs are unpromising. Like Jesus in the gospel reading, we can get distressed and troubled by the gospel's lack of progress but, like him, we need never get discouraged. There always remains much to give God thanks for, because God's work is not ultimately thwarted by human resistance.

18 July, Wednesday, Fifteenth Week in Ordinary Time
Matthew 11:25-27

Occasionally the gospels give us a glimpse into the prayer life of Jesus. From time to time, they allow us to observe the content of

Jesus' prayers. Today's gospel reading is one example of that. We are familiar with Jesus' prayer of petition in the Garden of Gethsemane, 'Father, take this cup from me'. The prayer of Jesus in today's gospel reading is a prayer of praise, beginning, 'I bless you, Father, Lord of heaven and earth'. Jesus praises God for the mysterious ways that God works, ways that seem paradoxical to human observation. Jesus blesses God for hiding the message of Jesus from the learned and the clever and revealing them to mere children. It is not the religious experts, the teachers of the Jewish Law, who are coming to know God as Jesus is revealing him. Rather, it is those who would have been considered religiously and theologically illiterate who are coming to know God in and through Jesus' ministry. Those who claim to know are learning nothing about God from Jesus; those who are aware that they know little or nothing are receiving the revelation of God that Jesus brings. The gospel reading reminds us that it is those who are aware of their own need, their own poverty before God, who will be open to whatever God wants to communicate to us through his Son.

19 July, Thursday, Fifteenth Week in Ordinary Time
Matthew 11:28-30
In the gospel reading, Jesus addresses himself to those who were burdened. We can all find ourselves burdened for many reasons. We may feel overworked; some relationship in our lives may have become a burden over time; we may struggle with ill health occasionally. Jesus addresses his words to those who felt burdened by the demands of the Jewish Law. These were demands they struggled to meet, and in failing to meet them they felt themselves to be religious outcasts. To such people, Jesus does not offer a new law. Rather, he offers them himself; he calls them and all of us into a personal relationship with himself. 'Come to me,' he says, 'learn from me'. We are to come to him and learn from him; he is a teacher whose teaching is visible in his person, in who he is and how he lives. To learn from some-

one, we need to be around them over time. In saying 'come', Jesus is really saying, 'Come and remain'. We are called into an ongoing relationship with the Lord. It is in and through that relationship that we learn to live as he calls us to live, as he wants us to live. We live out of our relationship with him, or more fundamentally, out of his relationship with us, because it is he who initiates that relationship, it is he who keeps on saying 'come' to us. He promises us that if we come to him and remain with him, we will discover that his yoke is easy and his burden is light. Yes, his way of life is demanding, but his relationship with us and ours with him makes it much less demanding than it would otherwise be. As Saint Paul says in one of his letters, 'His power at work within us is able to accomplish immeasurably far more than all we can ask or imagine.' It is by remaining in Jesus, as branches in the vine, that our lives will bear much fruit.

20 July, Friday, Fifteenth Week in Ordinary Time
Matthew 12:1-8

In today's gospel reading Jesus says to his disciples, 'Here I tell you is something greater than the Temple'. In those days it would have been difficult to conceive of anything greater than the Temple. Herod's Temple in Jerusalem was considered to be one of the wonders of the world. It was revered as the focal point of God's presence. Yet Jesus claims to be greater than the Temple because he is the new focal point of God's presence. God was present no longer in a building but through a person, through Jesus, whose other name is Emmanuel, God with us. It is because he is Emmanuel that Jesus speaks of himself in our gospel reading as Lord of the Sabbath. He is not just Lord of the Sabbath, but Lord of all, Lord of the Church, Lord of our lives. Because he is Lord of our lives, we are called to submit to his word so that his priorities become our priorities. In today's gospel reading Jesus shows his priorities, declares that feeding the hungry takes priority over a certain narrow understanding of the Sabbath Law. His hungry disciples are entitled to pick ears of corn to satisfy their hunger, even on the Sabbath. Jesus' word, and his whole life, helps us to sort out what is really important from what is not so important.

21 July, Saturday, Fifteenth Week in Ordinary Time
Matthew 12:14-21

There is a sharp contrast between the opening line of today's gospel reading which refers to a group of Pharisees who began to plot against Jesus, discussing how to destroy him, and the description of Jesus provided by the quotation from the prophet Isaiah which refers to Jesus as someone who will not brawl or shout, and who will not break the crushed reed nor put out the smouldering wick. It is really a contrast between a kind of power that damages the innocent and a very different kind of power that protects and nurtures what is vulnerable. This second kind of power is the power of the Spirit; it is the power which filled the life of Jesus and which is to fill all our lives. In the course of our lives we all encounter crushed reeds and smouldering wicks. Indeed we ourselves at times can be the crushed reed and the smouldering wick. When we are at our weakest and most vulnerable, we need a power that can nurture, sustain and encourage us. Such is the power of the Risen Lord in all our lives, the power of the Spirit, and our calling is to be the channels of that life-giving power of the Lord to each other.

23 July, Monday, Feast of Saint Bridget of Sweden
John 15:1-8

Bridget was born in the year 1303. She was the daughter of a wealthy governor in Sweden. She married a well-to-do man and they had eight children. She went on to serve as the principal lady in waiting to the queen of Sweden. She had a reputation as a woman of great prayer. After her husband died, she became a member of the third order of Saint Francis. She then founded a monastery for sixty nuns and twenty-five monks who lived in separate enclosures but shared the same church. She journeyed to Rome in 1349 to obtain papal approval for the order, known as the Brigettines. She never returned to Sweden from Rome. She spent the rest of her life in Italy or on various pilgrimages, including one to the Holy Land. She impressed with her simplicity of life and her devotion to pilgrims, to the poor and the sick. She experienced visions of various kinds; some of them were of the passion of Christ. She died in Rome in 1373. She was canonised not for her visions but for her virtue. The gospel reading for her feast is Jesus' wonderful image of the vine and branches. By means of this image, Jesus shows how much he wants to be in communion with us and wants us to be in communion with him. It is that communion with him, through prayer, through the Eucharist, which enables our lives to bear fruit in plenty, the rich fruit of the Holy Spirit which so characterised the life of Bridget. The gospel reading strongly suggests that if we are to be channels of God's goodness to others, we need to keep in communion with God's Son.

24 July, Tuesday, Sixteenth week in Ordinary Time
Matthew 20:20-28

Blood ties are very important to us. We greatly appreciate the members of our family, our brothers and sisters, our mothers and fathers, our other relatives. In the gospel reading, Jesus points to a group of people who are even more important to him than the members of his earthly family. Pointing to his disciples, to all of us, he says, 'Here are my mother and my brothers and my sisters'. He defines his disciples as those who do the will of his Father in heaven, as Jesus himself has revealed it to us by his teaching and by his life, death and resurrection. Earlier in Matthew's gospel, Jesus in the beatitudes declared, 'Blessed are those who hunger and thirst for righteousness', in other words, 'Blessed are those who hunger and thirst to do God's will'. We may not succeed in doing God's will all the time, but if we hunger and thirst to do it, if our deepest desire is to do what God wants, then we are truly the Lord's disciples, and, in virtue of that, his brothers and sisters, and, even, his mother. Jesus calls us to be members of his new family, the family of his disciples. This is a family that is held together not by ties of blood but by the Holy Spirit. In hungering and thirsting to do God's will, we open ourselves to the coming of the Holy Spirit, and that Spirit makes us brothers and sisters of Jesus and of each other, and sons and daughters of God.

25 July, Wednesday, Saint James, apostle
Matthew 20:20-28
In today's gospel reading for the feast of Saint James, we find one of several clashes between Jesus and his disciples in the gospels, as they make their way to Jerusalem, the city where Jesus will be crucified. Jesus and his disciples are clearly on different wavelengths. The difference between them finds expression in the very different questions they ask of each other. The question the two disciples, James and John, ask Jesus through their mother focuses on glory, honour and status. The question that Jesus asks James and John focuses on the experience of rejection and suffering that he is about to face into, 'Can you drink the cup that I must drink, or be baptised with the baptism with which I must be baptised?' Jesus was referring to the cup of suffering and the baptism of fire. The question of James and John showed their interest in self-promotion. The question of Jesus showed that his priority was self-giving. At the heart of being his disciple is self-giving love, becoming the servant of others, and this will often mean taking the way of the cross, as Jesus knew from his own experience. James and John, and all of us, are being called to follow the one who did not come to be served but to serve, whose purpose in life was not to promote himself but to empty himself for others. It is only in following this way that we will receive that share in Jesus' glory that was the focus of James and John's request. In the end,

James drank the cup of suffering that Jesus had to drink. According to the Acts of the Apostles, King Herod Agrippa had James killed with a sword. He was the first member of the twelve to die for his faith in the Lord. According to an ancient tradition his bones were brought from Jerusalem to Compostela in North West Spain, as a result of which Compostela has been a place of pilgrimage for the past thousand years or more.

26 July, Thursday, Sixteenth Week in Ordinary Time
Matthew 13:10-17

Jesus asserts in today's gospel reading that not all looking leads to seeing and not all listening leads to hearing. Many of his contemporaries looked and listened without seeing or hearing. Jesus sees the reason for this in a passage from Isaiah. It is because their heart 'has grown coarse' that some people look without seeing and listen without hearing. An openness of heart, a willingness to convert, is needed if people are to really see what Jesus is doing and hear what he is saying. According to Isaiah, it is God's desire that all people see and hear in this way so that they may be 'healed by me'. In refusing to see and hear with repentant hearts, the people are denying themselves what Jesus most wants to give them, healing. At the end of the gospel reading, Jesus turns to his disciples and pronounces a beatitude over them because, unlike many of his contemporaries, they have seen and heard, 'Blessed are your eyes because they see, your ears because they hear'. We would all like to see ourselves included in that beatitude. Yet, there are times when we listen to what the Lord is saying to us without really hearing it and look upon what the Lord is holding out to us without really seeing it. We too can suffer from a kind of coarseness of heart that prevents us from receiving all that the Lord is offering us. We need to recognise that we still have a journey to go before our looking is always at the same seeing and our listening at the same time hearing.

27 July, Friday, Sixteenth Week in Ordinary Time
Matthew 13:18-23

The parable of the sower is one of the better-known parables in the gospels. In today's gospel reading, we are given not the parable itself but Jesus' interpretation of the parable. The different kinds of soil are interpreted as different kinds of human response to Jesus' presence and his word. We are being reminded that although the word of Jesus is powerful it needs to meet with some response from us if it is to be effective. We have to open ourselves to the word if it is to bear fruit. The parable identifies certain blocks to our opening ourselves to the Lord's word. One is the lack of understanding; we need some under-standing of who Jesus is and what he has done and said if we are to respond to him. Another block is our tendency to keep the Lord at arm's length, so that his word never takes really deep root in us. A third block is our becoming too immersed in both the anxieties and the pleasures of life so that they become our primary reality. In his interpretation of the parable of the sower Jesus shows a realistic grasp of the obstacles within and around us to his presence and to his word, obstacles which he himself has to somehow overcome. However, that realistic picture should not lead us to discouragement. The message of the gospels as a whole is that the Lord's persistence is stronger than those obstacles. When, on one occasion, Jesus' disciples asked him the rather despair-ing question, 'Who can be saved?', Jesus replied, 'For mortals it is impossible, but not for God; for God all things are possible'.

28 July, Saturday, Sixteenth Week in Ordinary Time
Matthew 13:24-30

There is something of a contrast in today's gospel reading between the farmer, who sowed wheat seed in a field, and his servants. When weeds started to appear among the wheat, the instinct of the servants was to dig up the weeds so as to have a field of pure wheat. The farm-er's instinct was different. He was more tolerant of the weeds. He suggested letting both wheat and weeds grow together until the harvest time, and then they can be separated. He was a patient man; he knew he would get his wheat without the weeds eventually. However, in the meantime, he could live with the weeds. He didn't have the zeal of his servants to purify his field immediately. In this parable Jesus was saying something about the kingdom of God and, more particularly, about the sign of that kingdom in our world, the community of his disciples, what we call the Church. Jesus recognises that the Church will be a mixture of the good and the not-so-good up until the end of time, when all that is not of God will disappear. As individual disciples we too will remain a mixture of light and shade until we are fully conformed to the image of God's Son in the next life. We are all the time trying to grow more fully into God's Son. Yet, we have to accept that sin will always be part of our lives, this side of eternity. Like the farmer in the parable, the Lord is patient with us. We need to be patient with ourselves and with each other. This is not complacency; it is simply the realistic recognition that we are all a work in progress. God has begun a good work in our lives, and even if it will never be completed in this life, God will bring that good work to completion in eternity. In the meantime, we try to create a space for God to work in our own lives and in the lives of others.

30 July, Monday, Seventeenth Week in Ordinary Time
Matthew 13:31-35

Sometimes we may feel that our good efforts at something are bearing very little fruit. We can get into a frame of mind that says, 'What good have I been doing with my life?' We can feel that we have precious little to show for our endeavours. Yet, we can be doing a lot of good without realising or recognising it. We can sometimes forget that even a little can go a long way. The little efforts we make, the little good we do, can have an impact for the better beyond our imagining. That seems to be the message of the two parables that Jesus speaks in today's gospel reading. The mustard seed is tiny and yet it grows into a very large shrub. What looks completely insignificant takes on a life of its own and develops in a way that is out of proportion to the small beginning. Sometimes in our own lives, the little we do can go on to become something that we had never envisaged, and might never even get to see. The little bit of yeast that a woman places in a large batch of dough has a huge impact on that large batch. Again, in our own lives, the little good we do can impact on those around us in ways that would surprise us. Jesus says, that is what the kingdom of God is like. What is small and seemingly insignificant can turn out to be powerful and beneficial for many.

31 July, Tuesday, Seventeenth Week in Ordinary Time
Matthew 13:36-43

One of the most striking descriptions about God in the Jewish Scriptures is to be found in today's first reading, 'The Lord, the Lord, a God of tenderness and compassion, slow to anger, rich in kindness and faithfulness'. This is the God whom Jesus revealed all he said and did. Jesus' life was good news for all who knew their need of God's compassion, kindness and faithfulness. In the language of today's gospel reading, this gospel of a gracious God was the 'good seed' that Jesus came to sow in the hearts of all. Yet, the parable of the wheat and the darnel recognises that there were others whose mission in life was to sow a very different kind of seed, a weed that sought to engulf all the good seed that Jesus was sowing. The explanation of the parable in today's gospel reading declares that those responsible for sowing such weeds will encounter the reverse side of God's compassion and kindness. The good God who sent Jesus to sow good seed is affronted by the death-dealing response to Jesus' good, life-giving work, on the part of some. There will be a day of reckoning. In the meantime, our role is to align ourselves with the Lord's good work, opening our hearts and lives to the good seed he is always offering us.

1 August, Wednesday, Seventeenth Week in Ordinary Time

Matthew 13:44-46

Sometimes we can have the experience of stumbling upon something of great value even though we have not been looking for anything. A precious gift comes our way unexpectedly, without our having done anything to make it happen. It might be someone who crosses our path and has a huge impact for good on our lives. It might be an important insight that suddenly comes into our mind when we are sitting back relaxing and thinking about nothing in particular. In a sense, that was the experience of the poor day labourer in the first parable of today's gospel reading. He was being paid to dig up someone's field when suddenly he hit upon buried treasure. He sold the little he had to buy the field and gain that unexpected treasure. There is a different kind of experience where we find something very valuable after a great deal of searching for it. We keep on looking, and, eventually, after a lot of effort we find what we have been looking for. That was the experience of the wealthy merchant in the second parable who kept searching for the finest pearl of all, until, finally, he found it and, then, sold everything to purchase it. Jesus is saying that the kingdom of God is like both of those human experiences. There are times when the Lord suddenly blesses us at a moment in life when we are least expecting it. The Lord is always taking some gracious initiative towards us if we eyes to see and ears to hear; he seeks us out. When it comes to the Lord, there is also a seeking involved on our part. Jesus calls on us to keep on seeking, to keep on asking, to keep on knocking, like the rich merchant in the second parable. When we are graced by the Lord, because of his initiative towards us and our searching for him, then, like the two men in the parables, we must be ready to give up whatever is necessary to hold on to that gift of the Lord, the gift of the kingdom.

2 August, Thursday, Seventeenth Week in Ordinary Time

Matthew 13:47-53

The parable of the dragnet cast into the sea suggests that at the end of time there will be a separation out of the good from the wicked. However, this is God's work and it will happen at the end of time. We often make the mistake of thinking that it is our work and that it should happen in the course of time. We can be prone to deciding who is good and who is bad here and now and behaving in the light of that judgement. Yet, when we make such a judgement, we are prone to getting it wrong. We see the good in ourselves more easily than the good in others and the bad in others more easily than the bad in ourselves. We also fail to appreciate that people can change for the better, with God's help. We are all a work in progress. God may have begun a good work in us but God has yet to bring it to completion. Judgement belongs to God at the end of time, and the judging God is also the creator God who is constantly at work to bring good out of evil and new life out of what has come out wrong. As humans, we should be very slow to take on God's work of separating the good from the evil, because God looks at the heart and humans tend to look at appearances. As Paul says in his first letter to the Corinthians, 'Do not pronounce judgement before the time, before the Lord comes, who will bring to light the things now hidden in darkness.'

3 August, Friday, Seventeenth Week in Ordinary Time

Matthew 13:54-58

Jesus had spent the best part of thirty years in Nazareth. During that time he was known by all as the carpenter, the son of Mary. However, after he left Nazareth, Jesus' life had taken a new direction. He had thrown himself into the work that God had given him to do. He had left Nazareth as a carpenter; in today's gospel he returns to Nazareth as a teacher and a healer. There was in fact much more to this man that his own townspeople had ever suspected while he was living among them. The gospel reading suggests that they could not accept this 'more'; they rejected him because of it. They wanted him to be the person they knew him to be; they would not allow him to move on from being the son of the carpenter. It seems to have been Jesus' very ordinariness that made it difficult for the people of Nazareth to see that there was much more to him that they thought, to see him as he really was, in all his mystery. God was powerfully present to them in and through someone who was, in many respects, as ordinary as they were themselves. God continues to come to us today in and through the ordinary, in and through those who are most familiar to us. It is the ordinary that is filled with God's presence. That burning bush that fascinated Moses is all around us.

4 August, Saturday, Seventeenth Week in Ordinary Time
Matthew 14:1-12

At the beginning of Matthew's Gospel, King Herod the Great is responsible for the murder of innocent children, in an effort to kill the infant king of the Jews, Jesus. In today's gospel reading, Herod the Great's son, Herod Antipas, the tetrarch of Galilee, is responsible for the death of John the Baptist. Like Jesus, John the Baptist interpreted God's will for people's lives; he interpreted God's Law for others, regardless of their background or state in life. God's will had to be proclaimed to all, including the most powerful in the land, people like Herod Antipas and his wife Herodias. Proclaiming God's will to the powerful was risky, if it conflicted with their own will. John the Baptist was imprisoned by Herod Antipas and eventually beheaded because John's proclamation of God's will challenged the lifestyle of Herod and his wife. Jesus would go on to make the same discovery. His fuller proclamation of God's will for our lives was a challenge to the religious and political leaders of his time and, as a result, he was crucified. As well as being a consoling word, the gospel also has a sharp edge to it. It confronts us when we are not living as God intends us to live. When the gospel leaves us feeling uncomfortable, rather than rejecting it, as many of Jesus' and John's contemporaries did, we need to sit with it and allow it to speak to our heart. The path it puts before us may go against the grain at times, but, ultimately, it is the path that leads to life, both in this world and in the next.

6 August, Monday, The Transfiguration of the Lord

Mark 9:2-10

Today's gospel reading describes an extraordinary experience that Peter, James and John had of Jesus on top of a mountain. Jesus had just spoken about himself as the one who must undergo great suffering at the hands of his enemies and be put to death by them. There can be no doubting Jesus' humanity. He entered fully into the human condition, to the point of sharing our darkest experiences. However, on the mountain, Peter, James and John had an experience of the other side to Jesus, his affinity with the heavenly world, his intimacy with God who calls Jesus 'my Son, the Beloved'. His divinity shone through his humanity and it transfigured him. In Jesus, God walked among us, but Jesus' full humanity made it difficult for people to grasp that Jesus was the Son of God as well as the son of humanity. However, on the mount of transfiguration, the disciples were overpowered by God's presence breaking through Jesus' humanity. It was such a wonderful experience that Peter wanted to prolong it. Having caught a glimpse of heaven, as it were, he didn't want to come back down to earth. Yet, the disciples didn't need to remain on the mountain to experience God's presence in Jesus. Jesus remained God-with-us when he came down the mountain, even as he hung from the cross. We believe that Jesus was unique among all human beings because he was God with us in human form. That is why the word that came from God to the disciples on the mountain was, 'Listen to him'. We listen to Jesus in a way that we listen to no one else, because of who Jesus is, the suffering Son of Man who is also the beloved Son of God. We can't all have the experience that Peter, James and John had on the mountain. However, we can all listen to Jesus, allowing the words he spoke to shape our lives, to inform our consciences, to warm our hearts and to guide our steps. Jesus' words found expression in the life he lived. He not only proclaimed God's word; he is that word. His life, death and resurrection is a word that continues to speak to us. God the Father continues to say to all of us, 'Listen to him'.

7 August, Tuesday, Eighteenth Week in Ordinary Time
Matthew 14:22-36

There is quite a contrast between the first and the second part of today's first reading from the prophet Jeremiah. In the first part of the reading, God, speaking through the prophet Jeremiah, declares to the people, 'so great is your guilt, so many your sins'. It is because they have sinned so greatly that God declares, 'your wound is incurable'. It almost sounds as if the people's situation is hopeless; they have turned against God and brought disaster on themselves, and nothing can be done about it. Yet, the second part of the reading has a very different tone. There the Lord declares, 'I will restore the tents of Jacob and take pity on his dwellings … I will make them increase, and not diminish them … You shall be my people and I will be your God'. It seems that God can work in hopeless situations after all; God's creative power can bring good out of the mess that humans make. It is reassuring for all of us to know that human failure and sin does not have the last word. Rather, God's faithfulness and God's creative power will always have the last word. St Paul puts that truth very simply and very well, 'Where sin abounds, grace abounds all the more'. In the gospel reading, Peter began to sink because of his little faith. Yet, his little faith did not have the last word. The Lord's faithfulness to Peter held him and prevented him from sinking beneath the waves. The Lord's power can be made perfect in our weakness.

8 August, Wednesday, Eighteenth Week in Ordinary Time

Matthew 15:21-28

The pagan woman in today's gospel reading has been described as one of the great heroes of the gospel tradition. She displays a mother's identification with her child. Although it is her daughter who is in need, her prayer to Jesus is 'take pity on me ... help me'. Her daughter's distress is her distress; her daughter's need is her need. Twice she appeared to be rebuffed by Jesus. On the first occasion, he responded to her plea with silence. On the second occasion, Jesus declared to her that his mission was to the people of Israel, that the food intended for God's children cannot be thrown to the house dogs, the pagans. Yet, this desperate woman sees an opening in that image of children and house dogs that Jesus uses. She declares that the children and the house dogs can eat together as happens when the house dogs eat the crumbs that fall to the ground from what the children are eating. This witty and ingenious interpretation of Jesus' image finally brings Jesus to grant her request, 'Woman, you have great faith. Let your request be granted'. Jesus may have wanted to limit his mission to the people of Israel during his earthly ministry, but this pagan woman could not wait and, in the end, Jesus could not but grant her request. She displays the kind of faith that moves mountains; her faith certainly moved Jesus. She shows us what persevering with faith against all the odds looks like. Here is a faith that endured in the face of silence and resistance from the Lord. It is perhaps the purest form of faith imaginable. It is the kind of faith that endures the dark night of the soul and waits patiently for the dawn.

9 August, Thursday, Saint Teresa Benedicta of the Cross

Matthew 25:1-13

The gospel reading for the feast of St Teresa Benedicta of the Cross (Edith Stein) is the parable of the wise and foolish virgins from Matthew's Gospel. Of the ten virgins, only five of them had their lamps burning to greet the arrival of the bridegroom at the house of the bride. They were wise enough to have sufficient oil to keep their lamps burning for the long haul, so that, when the bridegroom was unexpectedly delayed, they were not caught out, unlike the five whose oil had run out by then. The image of the wise women calls out to us to keep faithful watch until the end so that our light continues to shine and never dims. Earlier in Matthew's Gospel Jesus declared, 'Let you light shine before others, so that they may see your good works and give glory to your Father in heaven' (*Mt 5:16*). When we are faithful to the good works called for by Jesus, the light of our faith and love will shine for all to see. The challenge is to keep faithful to our good works so that, even though our light may grow dim from time to time, it never goes out, and, when the Lord comes to meet us at the end our lives, we are there to greet him with his light shining through us. Such a person was Edith Stein. She was born a Jew, in 1891 in Poland. She had abandoned her Jewish faith by the time she was thirteen and declared herself an atheist. A brilliant student, she gained her doctorate in philosophy at the age of twenty-three. In the wake of World War I Edith began to feel a growing interest in religion. This culminated one night in 1921 when she happened upon the autobiography of Saint Teresa of Ávila, the sixteenth-century Carmelite nun. With fascination, she read through the night and by morning concluded, 'This is the truth'. She was baptised a Catholic on the following New Year's Day in 1922. She obtained an academic post in the University of Münster in Germany in 1932. However, with the rise of Nazism, she was dismissed from her post because she was considered a Jew. The loss of her job enabled her to pursue her growing attraction to the religious life. She applied to enter the Carmelite convent in Cologne and was formally clothed with the Carmelite habit on 15 April 1934. She took Sister Teresa Benedicta of the Cross as her religious name. Believing that her presence in the convent endangered the sisters, she allowed herself to be smuggled out of the country to a Carmelite convent in Holland. In 1940 the Nazis occupied Holland. She was captured and sent to Auschwitz where she died in a gas chamber on 9 August 1942. The light of her faith and love continues to shine for us today.

10 August, Friday, Saint Lawrence, deacon and martyr
John 12:24-26

Lawrence was a deacon in Rome who was martyred for his faith in Christ in the year 258. There has been continuous devotion to him since shortly after his death. The Emperor Constantine, the first Christian Emperor, publicly honoured his grave with a chapel. The Basilica of Saint Lawrence Outside the Walls in Rome stands over the site today. Today's gospel reading is very suited to the feast of this early Christian martyr. There Jesus refers to himself as the wheat grain which falls to the ground and dies and, in dying, yields a rich harvest. The rich harvest that came from his death and resurrection was the community of believers, the Church. Jesus' self-giving love, even though it led him to death on a cross, was life-giving for himself and for all humanity. He did not try to preserve his life at all costs; he was prepared to empty himself out of love for others and in doing so he gained life for himself and others. Jesus goes on to state that this pattern of life through death applies equally to his followers. If we love our lives above all else, if our primary goal in life is to preserve and protect ourselves, then we risk losing ourselves. We fail to become our true selves, the self that is the image of the Lord. If, like Jesus, we are willing to lose ourselves, to give of ourselves, in the service of the Lord and his people, then we will become alive with the life of God and our presence will be life-giving for others. This is the paradox at the heart of the Christian life. It is in giving that we receive and, as Paul reminds us in the first reading, our giving is always to be cheerful – 'God loves a cheerful giver'.

11 August, Saturday, Eighteenth Week in Ordinary Time
Matthew 17:14-20

In today's gospel reading from the gospel according to Matthew, Jesus rebukes his disciples for their little faith. He doesn't say that they have no faith, but tells them that they have little faith. They had just failed in their efforts to do the work that Jesus had sent them to do, bringing healing to a sick child. Jesus attributes this failure to their little faith. It is a feature of Matthew's Gospel that the disciples are often portrayed as people of little faith. Many of us may find it easy to identify with the disciples. We think of ourselves as people of faith but we sense that our faith is not as strong as it could be. We don't trust the Lord enough. We have that striking promise of Jesus in the gospel reading that if our faith was as small even as a mustard seed we could move mountains, which suggests that the faith of the disciples was even smaller than a mustard seed. Jesus wanted his disciples to grow in their faith; it is what he wants for all of us. In response to that desire of Jesus for a stronger faith within us, we could make our own the prayer of the father of the sick child that we find in Mark's version of this story, 'Lord, I believe; help my unbelief'.

13 August, Monday, Nineteenth Week in Ordinary Time
Matthew 17:22-27

In the time and place of Jesus, people laboured under the burden of taxation. Perhaps that much has not changed! There were various taxes to be paid to the Roman authorities. There was also an annual half-shekel tax to be paid for the upkeep of the Temple in Jerusalem. In today's gospel reading, those who were responsible for collecting this Temple tax were curious to know whether or not Jesus paid it. Peter assures them that he did. However, when Jesus had the opportunity to speak with Peter, he conveyed to him, in the words of the gospel reading, that 'the sons are exempt' from this tax. The 'sons' were the members of the new family that Jesus was gathering about himself.

Yet, even though Jesus no longer saw the Temple tax as obligatory for himself or his disciples, he instructs Peter to go and pay it, 'so as not to offend these people'. Although Jesus was not afraid to offend people when something of consequence was at stake, he didn't go out of his way to offend people when the issue was not so important, as in this instance of the Temple tax. There were issues on which he took a stand and other issues which he let go. We all have to learn to make that distinction. When are we called to stand and fight and when can we just let things be? We look to the Holy Spirit to give us the wisdom to make that judgement.

14 August, Tuesday, Nineteenth Week in Ordinary Time
Matthew 18:1-5, 10, 12-14

Sometimes the kinds of questions people ask reveal their values, their priorities, what they think is important. The question that the disciples put to Jesus in today's gospel reading, 'Who is the greatest in the kingdom of heaven?', suggests a certain interest on their part in status and standing. In response to their question, Jesus both did something and said something. He first of all called a child over and placed the child in front of them; he then informed them that they needed to become like that child just to enter the kingdom of heaven, never mind become the greatest in the kingdom. Jesus was calling on his disciples to become childlike not childish, childlike in the sense of having childlike trust in a loving Father, a trust that awaits everything from God and grabs at nothing, including status and standing. Greatness comes to those who make themselves as dependent on God as children are dependent on adults for their existence and well-being. Jesus' response to the question of his disciples is a kind of a commentary on the first beatitude which he had spoken earlier in Matthew's Gospel, 'Blessed are the poor in spirit, for theirs is the kingdom of heaven'.

15 August, Wednesday, The Assumption of the Blessed Virgin Mary
Luke 1:39-56

The Church has always believed that just as Jesus' earthly body did not remain in the tomb after he rose to new life, but rather was transformed in a glorious way, so too Mary's body underwent the same glorious transformation beyond death. In the words of the Preface of today's Mass, 'Rightly you would not allow her to see the corruption of the tomb'. Mary had a unique relationship with Jesus in life. She carried him in her womb for nine months. Having given birth to Jesus she cared for and looked after him in the way that any mother cares for her child. She was there with the other women and the beloved disciple at the foot of the cross. She was there with the disciples when the Holy Spirit came down upon them all at the first Pentecost. Just as Mary had a unique relationship with Jesus in life, the Church has always believed that she had a unique relationship with him in death and beyond death. For that reason, the glorious woman that features in today's first reading has been interpreted from the early days of the Church as a reference to Mary, 'A woman, adorned with the sun, standing on the moon, and with the twelve stars on her head as a crown'. It is likely that the author of the Book of the Apocalypse from which that reading comes was depicting the whole Church as this woman. Yet, Mary expresses in herself all that is best in the Church.

The Church is the community of the Lord's disciples, the community of believers. Mary is the complete disciple; she is the woman of exemplary faith. Today's gospel reading brings that home to us. There is a striking contrast between the glorious woman of the first reading, and the young woman of Nazareth heading south to the hill country of Judea to visit her older cousin Elizabeth. Yet, the woman in glory in the first reading is the woman of faith in the gospel reading. Just prior to this scene in Luke's Gospel, Mary had given her full consent to God's purpose for her life to the angel Gabriel, 'Let what you have said be done to me'. God's purpose for Mary's life was for her to become the mother of his Son. This was such an extraordinary purpose that Mary could not possibly have fully understood all its implications at the time. Yet, she generously said 'yes' to all that God was asking of her. In her 'yes' she anticipated the opening petitions of the prayer that her adult son would give to his disciples, 'Father, hallowed be thy name; thy kingdom come; thy will be done on earth as in heaven'. It was above all in Mary that God's will was done on earth as it is in heaven. She was the first and greatest believer. In the words of Elizabeth in the gospel reading, 'Blessed is she who believed that the promise made her by the Lord would be fulfilled'. Mary's deep faith immediately expressed itself in love, as she set out on a journey to give support to her older cousin Elizabeth. Paul, in his letter to the Galatians says, 'The only thing that counts is faith, working through love'. All genuine faith in the Lord expresses itself in deeds of love for others. Mary's 'yes' to God was at the same time a 'yes' to those in need. In visiting her cousin Elizabeth, she brought the Lord to her whom she carried in her womb. She portrays our own calling as people of faith to bring the Lord to each other. Mary of the gospels reveals the path we are all called to take as we journey on our pilgrim way towards our sharing in the Lord's risen life.

16 August, Thursday, Nineteenth Week in Ordinary Time
Matthew 18:21-19:1
The parable Jesus speaks in today's gospel reading has two clear messages. The first and most important message relates to God and the second relates to ourselves. The parable declares that God's forgiveness is boundless. The first servant owed ten thousand talents, which is an astronomical sum of money. It is the kind of debt that could never be paid. We might think of the debt that some of the developing countries owe to the World Bank. The king in the parable simply cancelled the debt in response to the pleading of his servant. He allowed mercy to completely override justice. Jesus is giving us an image here of God's

mercy. We always come before God in desperate need of his mercy and God pours out his mercy in abundance upon us in response to our cry. As Pope Francis has said, Jesus reveals the face of God to be Mercy, a mercy that is immeasurable. We constantly live in the grace of God's abundant mercy. The second servant owed this first servant whose debt was cancelled two hundred denarii, about two months wages. This is a manageable sum which could have easily been paid off with a bit of time. However, the first servant would not give his fellow servant the time he needed and had him thrown into prison. He could not pass on even a fraction of the abundant mercy that had been showered on him. As a result, he lost the mercy he had been shown. The parable is saying to us that there is an onus on us to pass on some of the extraordinary mercy we have received from God. When God graces us he looks to us to grace others with what has been so generously given to us.

17 August, Friday, Nineteenth Week in Ordinary Time
Matthew 19:3-12

Jesus' teaching on marriage in today's gospel reading was not the standard understanding of marriage in the Jewish world at that time. The Pharisees, who put a question to Jesus to test him, took it for granted that divorce was permissible in certain circumstances, as was clear from the Book of Deuteronomy. Jewish men were allowed to divorce their wives, although Jewish women could not divorce their husbands. The only question was on what grounds a Jewish man could divorce his wife. This is why the Pharisees asked Jesus if a man could divorce his wife 'on any pretext whatever', as some Jewish teachers held. However, in his response to their question, Jesus showed that he did not accept their premise that divorce was permissible and the only issue was on what grounds. Instead Jesus went back beyond the Book of Deuteronomy to the Book of Genesis to show that God's original intention for marriage was that a man must cling to his wife so that the two become one body for life. Jesus' teaching on life-long fidelity within marriage would have been considered quite radical at the time. In the gospel reading, even Jesus' own disciples declare in response to Jesus' teaching, 'If that is how things are between a husband and wife, it is advisable not to marry'. Jesus believed that a man and woman were capable of a love that lasted until death. The teaching of Jesus, not just in this area of marriage but in other areas as well, must have seemed too demanding, too idealistic, to many of his contemporaries. Yet, Jesus' vision for human living, whether it is married life or single life, always appeals to what is best in us. The way of life he puts before us may be demanding, but he assures us that it is what we were created for and, therefore, it is the path of life.

18 August, Saturday, Nineteenth Week in Ordinary Time
Matthew 19:13-15

In today's gospel reading parents bring children to Jesus for him to lay his hands on them and say a prayer of blessing. Parents instinctively want what is best for their children. They recognise Jesus as someone through whom God is working in a life-giving way, and so they bring their children, their loved ones, to him. In our own times, parents who have an appreciation of Jesus and his message and life will have the same desire to bring their children to him. They recognise Jesus as God's unique gift to us and they want that gift for their children because they want what is best for them. When parents try to bring their children to Jesus they often meet with obstacles of various kinds. In today's gospel reading those obstacles take the form of Jesus' own disciples who tried to prevent parents from bringing their children to Jesus. The disciples are resisting the desire of the parents for their children. In the midst of this struggle, Jesus is not a passive spectator. He insists, against his disciples, that the children be allowed to come to him. The gospel reading assures us that in our own struggle to bring our loved ones to the Lord, and to bring ourselves to him, the Lord is always working with us. The strength of his desire for us to meet with him and, thereby, find life will overcome the various obstacles that are placed in our way. We need to trust that the Lord will find a way of bringing people to him, in spite of the resistances that may be there, of whatever kind.

20 August, Monday, Twentieth Week in Ordinary Time
Matthew 19:16-22

Many young people are receiving their exam results at this time. They are thinking about the options that are open to them on the basis of those results; 'What college should I go to?', 'What course should I do?' It is a time of searching and seeking for them. No doubt many of them will look for guidance and advice so as to make the best decision possible. Today's gospel reading puts before us a young man who is clearly a seeker and a searcher. Indeed, he is struggling with one of the bigger questions of life, 'What good deed must I do to possess eternal life?' Questions don't come much bigger than that. He is asking, 'What does it mean to live a good life?', 'What is the path to true and lasting happiness?' Human beings have always asked this fundamental question. We have probably all asked it of ourselves at some time in our lives. In response to his question, Jesus directs him to his own Jewish tradition, the commandments of the Jewish Law. It is always worth exploring our own religious tradition; there can be a great deal more there than we realise. Yet, this young man knows his religious tradition well, and he is still searching. 'What more do I need to do?' Finally, Jesus points to himself as the goal of the young man's search, 'Come, follow me'. This was a bridge too far for the young man; it would have involved letting go of his many possessions, which he couldn't do. His journey to Jesus ends in sadness; the happiness, the life, he searched for eluded him. Jesus offers himself to all of us as the goal of all our searching, as the answer to our deepest questions. He assures us that in following him, in walking in his way, we will find genuine life, true happiness.

21 August, Tuesday, Twentieth Week in Ordinary Time

Matthew 19:23-30

There are a number of verses in the New Testament that I find myself returning to from time to time because they convey a great deal, at least to me. One of those verses occurs in today's gospel reading, 'For people this is impossible, for God everything is possible'. A somewhat similar saying occurs in Luke's account of the annunciation where, in response to Mary's question, 'How can this be?', Gabriel answers, 'Nothing is impossible with God'. The context of the saying in today's gospel reading is that of the rich young man who came to Jesus looking for the path to eternal life but went away sad because he was possessed by his possessions. How can such a rich man enter into eternal life? It is possible, Jesus declares, but only with God's grace, God's help. In our own lives we can sometimes find ourselves up against impossible odds. We wonder how we will get through some test, how we will keep going. In such circumstances, the saying in this today's gospel reading can be a great encouragement to us, 'For God everything is possible'. Saint Paul knew the truth of that, and he expressed that truth in his inimitable way. In his letter to the Philippian, he declares, 'I can do all things through him who gives me strength'. There are times when we all need to fall back on that conviction.

22 August, Wednesday, Queenship of Mary

Luke 1:26-28

During the Middle Ages, Mary was venerated as Queen of the angels and saints. Pope Pius XII proclaimed the queenship of Mary as a memorial of the universal Church at the close of the Marian Year of 1955. The memorial is placed on this date, 22 August, to stress its connection with the feast of the Assumption, a week earlier. When people of faith gave Mary the title of Queen of Heaven and Earth, it was their way of saying that Mary is worthy of our veneration and that she deserves our honour. We honour and we venerate Mary. We don't worship Mary. Only God can be worshipped, God the Father, God the Son and God the Holy Spirit. We honour Mary as Queen because of who she was in her earthly life, because she was a woman of deep faith. Mary's response to the angel Gabriel conveys the core of her faith, 'Let what you have said be done to me'. The gospel reading suggests that Mary had her reservations about what God appeared to be asking of her, 'How can this come about, since I am a virgin?' The angel Gabriel went on to say to her, 'Nothing is impossible to God'. Mary came to accept that what she herself could not bring about, God would bring about. She then gave herself over to God's purpose for her life, trusting that God could bring his purpose to pass. It could be said that Mary allowed God to be God in her life. This is the essence of faith. The person of faith does not try to manage God or to shape God to his or her purposes. Like Mary, we surrender to God's purpose for our lives and we allow God to be God of our lives. In honouring Mary as Queen, we ask her to intercede for us, to pray for us, so that we can be as open to God's desire for our lives as she was.

23 August, Thursday, Twentieth Week in Ordinary Time
Matthew 22:1-14

In the time of Jesus it would have been considered a great honour to be invited to a wedding banquet, especially if the person doing the inviting was a king and if the invitation was to share table with his son, as in the parable in today's gospel reading. Most people lived simply by today's standards. Invitations to banquets did not come along every day. When they did come along, they presented an opportunity to eat in a way that was not the norm. Most people who received such an invitation would have jumped at it. However, in the parable, Jesus tells the invitation to the wedding banquet of a king's son was turned down by several people, with violence against the king's messengers thrown in. This was foolish behaviour by any standards. Why turn down the gift of a great feast, insulting the host in the process? There was everything to be gained and nothing to be lost by saying 'yes' to the invitation. Jesus may be reminding us that we can all say 'no' to God's invitation, in spite of the fact that God's invitation is always with our best interests in view. God calls us through his Son to nourish us in body, mind and spirit. God's call is always a call to life in its fullness. There is nothing to be lost and everything to be gained by responding positively to this invitation of the Lord. Yet, we can all allow God's invitation to pass us by. Each day is an opportunity to respond with renewed energy to God's invitation to sit at table with his Son, to enter into communion with his Son and to allow his Son to clothe us with himself, with his values and attitudes.

24 August, Friday, Feast of Saint Bartholomew
John 1:45-51

Bartholomew is mentioned in the list of the twelve apostles in all of the gospels. He is traditionally identified with Nathanael in today's gospel reading from John. Nathanael was initially very dismissive of Jesus, wondering if anything good could come from the village of Nazareth. He poured cold water on Philip's witness to his faith, 'We have found the one Moses wrote about in the Law...' Yet there was something about Philip's witness which prompted Nathanael to go with him when Philip said, 'Come and see'. Nathanael's own personal encounter with Jesus led him from his initial dismissive attitude to a sharing in Philip's faith, 'You are the son of God, you are the King of Israel'. This was still only the beginning of Nathanael's journey. Jesus informs him that he will see greater things. Yet, he had already come a long way from his initial scepticism. The story of Nathanael in today's gospel reading reminds us that faith is a journey of coming to see the Lord more clearly and of following the Lord more wholeheartedly. Even if, like Nathanael, we start in a very inauspicious place, a place of doubt and scepticism, the Lord continues to call us, and he calls us in and through each other, as he called Nathanael through Philip. No matter where we are on this faith journey, the Lord continues to say to us, what he said to Nathanael, 'You will see greater things'. We are always on the way until that eternal day when we see the Lord face-to-face.

25 August, Saturday, Twentieth Week in Ordinary Time

Matthew 23:1-12

In today's gospel reading Jesus is critical of the religious leaders who ascribe to themselves titles and behaviours that are more the norm in other forms of leadership at the time, such as political leadership. Jesus portrays them as considering themselves to stand above the people in various ways and as wanting their higher position to be recognised, such as in how people greet them, in where they are positioned at banquets, in the titles that they expect to be addressed by. Jesus was aware that all of this was a very human temptation. Indeed it is a temptation to which religious leaders within the Christian tradition have often succumbed. That is why, having critiqued the style of leadership among the Pharisees, Jesus immediately addresses his own disciples. He is aware that they are as prone to this form of behaviour as any other group. Jesus presents to his disciples a vision of church in which emphasis is placed on the leadership role of God and Jesus and, so, as a result all forms of human leadership are relativised. There is one Father, God, and we are all sons and daughters of God. There is one teacher, Jesus, and we are all students of that teacher. This is a very egalitarian vision of church which cuts across any notion of superiority or inferiority. This is church as family with one heavenly Father and one teacher. Jesus goes on to declare that within this family greatness is defined by service, a service that is self-emptying so that others may live more fully, after the example of the service of Jesus.

27 August, Monday, Twenty-First Week in Ordinary Time
Matthew 23:13-22

In today's gospel reading Jesus condemns the Pharisees because they shut up the kingdom of heaven in people's faces. In other words, they hinder people from entering the kingdom of heaven, presumably by trying to keep people from following Jesus who came to proclaim the nearness of the kingdom of heaven. The gospels suggest that Jesus was critical of those who were an obstacle to people coming to believe in him. He was critical of his own disciples for trying to prevent children drawing near to him, in spite of the wishes of the children's parents for Jesus to bless their children. Rather than shutting up the kingdom of heaven in people's faces, Jesus wants us to open up the kingdom of heaven to each other. We are to bring each other to the Lord, to reveal the Lord to each other, and, in so doing, to support one another on our journey towards the kingdom of heaven. There are many people in the gospels who brought others to Jesus and who can be an inspiration to us. We only have to think of John the Baptist, whose life mission was to lead people to Jesus, to open up the kingdom of heaven to others. We need the support of each other's faith, each other's witness, as we journey on our pilgrim way through life.

28 August, Tuesday, Twenty-First Week in Ordinary Time
Matthew 23:23-26

There is a verse in one of the prophets of the Old Testament, the prophet Micah, which many people feel drawn to. 'What is it that the Lord requires of you but to do justice, to love mercy and to walk humbly with your God?' To do justice is to give people what is their due as human beings and as images of God. To love mercy is to show mercy to others in the sense of forgiving others and serving them in their need. To walk humbly with your God is to be open in faith to God's purpose and desire for your life. These three basic attitudes are a summary of God's will for our lives. It is possible that this text from the prophet Micah lies behind what Jesus calls in today's gospel reading, the weightier matters of the law, 'Justice, mercy and good faith'. Jesus was accusing the religious experts of his day of being too preoccupied with the less important requirements of the law, such as what produce should be tithed, and neglecting these weightier matters of the law. That triad of justice, mercy and faith remains a very succinct statement of what the Lord desires from us in our own day. In a sense, those three elements correspond to the two great commandments that Jesus proclaimed. The first commandment, to love God with all our heart, mind, soul and strength corresponds to faith and the second commandment, to love our neighbour as ourselves corresponds to justice and mercy. These remain the weightier matters of our own Christian tradition. All the other elements of our tradition need to be at the service of these two commandments and these three fundamental values of justice, mercy and faith.

29 August, Wednesday, The Passion of Saint John the Baptist
Mark 6:17-29

It is said of Herod in today's gospel reading that he knew John the Baptist to be a good and holy man. That is a good description of what we call a saint, a good and holy person. Towards the end of June we celebrated the birth of this good and holy man. Today, we remember his death. In spite of the fact that according to our gospel reading Herod knew John to be good and holy and wanted to protect him, he had him beheaded. Having made a rash promise in public to his wife's daughter from a previous marriage, he felt honour-bond to keep his promise. Instead of protecting John the Baptist, he gave priority to protecting his own honour, even though this meant executing someone whom he knew to be good and holy. Herod betrayed his best self, his deepest self. In contrast to Herod, John was faithful and true to what was deepest and best in himself, even though that meant incurring the anger of the powerful. John was faithful to the call of the Lord, even unto death. Herod heard the call of the Lord through John's preaching; the gospel reading says that Herod liked to listen to John. Yet Herod was not faithful to that call; he ended up responding to a different, more superficial call, the call to protect himself, his reputation, his honour. Herod's dilemma is that of every human being, of every believer. The Lord calls from deep within us; we hear that call but we don't always respond to it. We can end up responding to other calls that can be in conflict with the Lord's call. John is an inspiration and an encouragement to us to keep responding generously and courageously to that deeper call in our lives, the Lord's call that sounds from deep with us. It is in responding to that call that we will find life, both now and in eternity.

30 August, Thursday, Twenty-First Week in Ordinary Time
Matthew 24:42-51

In the gospel reading, Jesus calls on his disciples to be ready for the coming of the Son of Man, which will happen at an hour they do not expect. At the end of the first reading we find Paul's prayer for the church in Thessalonica. He prays that the Lord would confirm their hearts in holiness so that they may be blameless in the sight of our God and Father when our Lord Jesus Christ comes with all his saints. The preceding sentence of Paul's prayer reveals his understanding of being 'blameless'. There he prays that the Lord would be generous in increasing their love and would make them love one another and the whole human race, as much as Paul himself loves them. For Paul, it is the person who loves others with the love of the Lord who will stand ready when the Lord comes. Such a love is not just a human achievement. It is fundamentally the fruit of the Holy Spirit, the Spirit of the Lord. It is the work of the Lord in our lives, which is why Paul prays that the Lord would increase the love of the church in Thessalonica. When we read the Lord's call in the gospel reading to stand ready for his coming in the light of the first reading, we come to understand that it is only the Lord himself who can enable us to be ready. We need to open ourselves to the Lord's empowering presence now, if we are to be ready for his coming to us in the future, be it at the hour of our death or the end of this age.

31 August, Friday, Twenty-First Week in Ordinary Time
Matthew 25:1-13

'Be prepared!' is one of the mottos of the scout movement. Before they went hiking, they had to make sure that they had all they needed to meet with any unexpected eventuality that may arise. Five of the bridesmaids in today's gospel reading wouldn't have made good scouts. They weren't prepared for the late arrival of the bridegroom and, as a result, their oil had run out and they couldn't escort the bridegroom with their lighted torches as was expected of them. When the procession set off they were at the shops. By the time they arrived back, the moment had passed, the banquet had started and the big heavy doors of the banqueting room had already been locked and no one was going to open them for them. The parable calls on us to be ready with our lamps brightly burning whenever the Lord, the heavenly bridegroom, comes, whether that is at the end of time or at the end of our lives. Just after a child is baptised, the godfather is invited to light the baptismal candle from the Easter candle and the priest says, 'Parents and godparents, this light is entrusted to you to be kept burning brightly'. As the child becomes an adolescent, at the time of the Sacrament of Confirmation, he or she has to take responsibility to keep the light that has been entrusted to them burning brightly. The parable calls on us to keep this light of Christ, the light of faith, burning brightly, and not allow it to go out completely. Then whenever the Lord comes, be it early or late, we will be ready to welcome him, and the light of our faith will give way to the eternal light of the Lord's presence.

1 September, Saturday, Twenty-First Week in Ordinary Time
Matthew 25:14-30

When we hear the word 'talent' we think instinctively of the gifts and talents we have been given. In the world of Jesus a talent was a sum of money. Indeed, it was the largest unit of currency in existence at the time. In telling his parables Jesus always drew from the world and culture of his time. In the ancient world, servants or slaves could often be entrusted with a great deal of responsibility. It wasn't unusual for a person of wealth who was going on a long journey to give responsible tasks to his servants in his absence. In the story Jesus told, the wealthy man gave quite a lot of his own money, eight talents, to his servants. He wasn't looking for the money back; he simply wanted them to use it well. The first two servants made good use of what was given to them. The third did nothing with what was given to him. According to the parable what held this third servant back was fear. He was afraid of losing what he had been given and thereby incurring the anger of his master. It seems as if he did not trust his master, even though his master trusted him. In his first letter, Saint John says, 'There is no fear in love, but perfect love casts our fear'. Jesus has revealed to us the perfect love of God; he has shown us that God is love and as John says in that letter, 'We love because he first loved us'. We relate to God and his Son not out of fear but out of love. This loving relationship gives us the freedom to take risks with what the Lord has given to us. We witness to the many ways that the Lord has graced us with courage. The Lord doesn't look to us to be successful but he wants us to be generous and daring with what we have been given.

3 September, Monday, Twenty-Second Week in Ordinary Time
Luke 4:16-30

Anger is a normal human emotion. In itself, it is neither good nor bad. What matters is how we express it. We are all aware that anger is an emotion that needs to be managed. We can find ourselves doing things or saying things in anger that we subsequently come to regret. Anger has the potential to be quite damaging and destructive. We find a good example of that destructive power of anger in today's gospel reading. The words that Jesus spoke in the synagogue of his home town Nazareth triggered strong anger in those who were listening to him, 'When they heard this, everyone in the synagogue was enraged'. They gave expression to their anger by taking Jesus to the brow of the hill that Nazareth was built on, intending to throw him down the cliff to his death. This is anger at its most destructive. On this occasion, Luke tells us, Jesus was preserved from their deadly intentions. It is strange that the people of Nazareth should react to Jesus in such a deadly way because what Jesus had to say to them was actually good news. He declared that he was God's anointed one, sent by God to bring the good news of God's favour, God's hospitable love, to everyone, especially to those most in need of it, whether they lived in Israel or outside of it. It seems that the people of Nazareth were not comfortable with such a generous God who favoured the most vulnerable, no matter who they were. The gospel reading invites us to ask the question, 'How do we hear the message of Jesus?' 'Is it good news for us today?' 'Do I experience it as good news in my own personal life?'

4 September, Tuesday, Twenty-Second Week in Ordinary Time

Luke 4:31-37

In the synagogue of Nazareth, Jesus announced that he had come to proclaim the year of the Lord's favour. In today's gospel reading, we find Jesus revealing God's favour to someone who was deeply disturbed and troubled in the synagogue of Capernaum. The power of God's favour at work through Jesus calmed the raging storm within this man. Someone who had initially related to Jesus in a very aggressive way was restored to God's favour because of Jesus' authority and power, the authority and power of the Holy Spirit, the Spirit of God's love. God's favour at work through Jesus overcame the man's hostility, aggression and resistance. As a result of the power of God's favour working through Jesus in this dramatic way we are told that astonishment seized all who witnessed what happened. There are times in all of our lives when we find ourselves disturbed and troubled, when storms rage within us. It is above all then that we need to come before the Lord in prayer and open ourselves to the power of God's favour that he brings to us, a favour that can bring calm where there is turmoil. As we receive the Lord's peace and calm we can then go forth as his peacemakers, bringing the Lord's favour to those who need it, bringing his calming and healing presence to those who are disturbed and broken.

5 September, Wednesday, Twenty-Second Week in Ordinary Time

Luke 4:38-44

In today's gospel reading we hear of people interceding with Jesus on behalf of others. People in the home of Simon Peter asked Jesus to do something for Simon Peter's mother-in-law, who was in bed with a fever. People who had friends suffering from diseases of one kind or another brought them to Jesus, to the house of Simon Peter. These are people who acted as mediators between those in need and the person of Jesus. We are all called to be mediators in that sense, to bring Jesus to others and to bring others to Jesus. One of the ways that we give expression to that role of being a mediator is by interceding with Jesus on behalf of others, just as people interceded with Jesus on behalf of Simon Peter's mother-in-law. The prayer of intercession has always been a central expression of Christian prayer. What we do with our intercessory prayer we are also called to do with our whole lives. We bring others to the Lord and bring the Lord to others by the lives we live. The Lord wants to be present in a life-giving way to others through us. In the first reading, Paul speaks of Epaphras as the missionary who first brought the Lord to the people in Colossae. We are all called to bring the Lord to each other, and we can only do that with the help which the Lord alone can give. That is why we need to pray for ourselves, as well as for others.

6 September, Thursday, Twenty-Second Week in Ordinary Time
Luke 5:1-11
The words of Simon Peter in today's gospel reading, 'We worked hard all night long and caught nothing', would find an echo in many people's hearts. We can all have the experience of investing a lot of time and energy in something or someone and discovering that there is very little to show for all our investment. We live in a very re-sults-orientated world. Targets and outcomes are all important, and if they are not reached then we can be judged a failure by others. The gospel reading today suggests that the Lord does not relate to us on that basis. The Lord spoke a word into Simon Peter's situation of failure, 'Put out into deep water and pay out your nets for a catch'. The Lord saw life in abundance in the deep where Simon and others had only experienced absence. When Simon and his companions re-sponded to the Lord's word, the night of failure gave way to the day of abundance. The Lord's way of seeing is always more hopeful than ours. The Lord's word is always directing us to the presence of new life in places we have come to see as having little to offer. After the abundant catch of fish, Simon Peter came to see himself as having little to offer, 'Leave me, Lord; I am a sinful man'. Yet, Jesus saw him with the same hopeful eyes as he had seen the Sea of Galilee, 'Do not be afraid, from now on it is people you will catch'. The Lord invites us to see as he sees, to see our situation, to see ourselves and others with his hopeful, expectant and generous eyes.

7 September, Friday, Twenty-Second Week in Ordinary Time
Luke 5:33-39
At the end of today's gospel reading, Jesus makes a somewhat hu-morous observation of human life. 'Nobody who has been drinking

old wine wants new. "The old is good", he says'. The world of Jesus was a very traditional one. What was ancient was revered. What had stood the test of time was shown respect. The new was suspect, especially in the domain of religion. The Roman authorities dismissed Christianity initially as a new superstition. It wasn't just one of many superstitions – religions which were not Roman – but it was even more suspect because it was new. We live in a different kind of culture, one defined more by the statement, 'the new is good', rather than 'the old is good'. Innovation is more valued than tradition. Jesus speaks of his ministry in today's gospel reading as 'new wine' which the old wine skins cannot contain. Yet, he did not reject his religious tradition. Indeed, he was steeped in his Jewish religious tradition. He valued and appreciated what was best in it, but he wanted to bring that tradition to completion, to fulfilment. When it comes to matters of faith, we all need to be rooted in a tradition. As followers of Jesus, we are rooted in the Christian tradition, which itself is rooted in the Jewish tradition. Yet, we also need to be open to the new ways that the Lord is working among us, the new ground he is breaking, the new paths he is asking us to take. Saint Augustine once spoke of God as 'beauty, ever ancient, ever new'. Our Christian tradition which seeks to express the beauty of God revealed in Jesus is likewise both ever ancient and ever new.

8 September, Saturday, The Nativity of the Blessed Virgin Mary
Matthew 1:1-16, 18-23

We do not know when Mary was born but the Church has chosen 8 September to celebrate the day of her birth. We celebrate the birth of Mary because of who she was to become, the mother of God's Son. Her birth points ahead to that special child who was to be born from her. Today's gospel reading gives the child that was to be born of her two names, Jesus and Emmanuel. In the Semitic world, names were very important because each name carried a specific meaning. The name Jesus in Hebrew means 'the Lord saves'. As the gospel reading says, 'He is the one who is to save his people from their sins'. The name Emmanuel in Hebrew means, 'God is with us'. These two names reveal a great deal about the child who was born of the woman whose birthday we celebrate today. God was present among us through Mary's son as a merciful God, as a God who works to deliver us from our sins and to reconcile us to himself. Jesus is God with us in a merciful way. Saint Paul gives expression to one aspect of God's mercy in today's first reading. He declares that God co-operates with all those who love him by turning everything to their good. In other words, if we are open in love to the God present in Jesus, this God will turn everything to our good, all the experiences of our lives, including those we consider totally negative. Jesus reveals a God who works in a life-giving way in the midst of all our experiences. It is through Mary that we have come to know this God, which is why it is right and fitting for us to celebrate the day of her birth.

10 September, Monday, Twenty-Third Week in Ordinary Time
Luke 6:6-11

According to today's gospel reading the scribes and Pharisees were 'hoping to find something to use against' Jesus. They were waiting for him to slip up, to act in a way contrary to the Law. This is a very negative way of looking at a person. You watch them to see if they do anything that might show them up in a bad light. It is a case of being on the look-out for some fault or failing. This certainly wasn't Jesus' way of looking at people. He would never be waiting for an opportunity to criticise or condemn someone. He would not watch them, hoping to find something to use against them. On the contrary, his mission in life was not to take people down but to build people up, not to diminish them but to enhance them. This is what we find Jesus doing in today's gospel reading. He healed a man with a disability on the Sabbath, even though he knew that in doing so he would meet with hostility from those who held that he was breaking the Sabbath rest. Yet, Jesus would not be side-tracked from his work of renewing people, recreating them, in body, mind and spirit. This remains his work among us today. His mission remains, in the words of the gospel reading, 'to do good' and 'to save life'. This is the same mission that he has entrusted to each one of us. We are not to be in the business of waiting and hoping that people will fail. The Lord wants to work through us to build up others in body, mind and spirit.

11 September, Tuesday, Twenty-Third Week in Ordinary Time
Luke 6:12-19

There are two locations in today's gospel reading, a mountain and a level place. Jesus went up the mountain to pray. Indeed, Luke tells us that he spent the whole night in prayer to God. He had an important choice to make and he needed to be in prayerful communion with God to make a good choice. He had to choose twelve from among his disciples to be the nucleus of the new community he was forming. Just as the mountain was a place of prayer, the level ground was a place of ministry, both teaching and healing the sick and broken. The gospel reading tells us that people came from a very large area to listen to him and be cured of their diseases. The mountain and the level ground, prayer and ministry to others, formed the pattern of Jesus' life. Our own lives as followers of Jesus will have something of that same pattern. We spend time in prayer and we spend time in the service of others. We need to be in communion with God in prayer and in communion with others in loving service. This two-fold pattern is a feature of each day as well as of our lives as a whole. Each day we spend time in prayer, whether it is the prayer of the Eucharist or other public forms of prayer or more silent and personal prayer. Each day we come from our prayer to each other to bring something of the Lord's love we have experienced in prayer to those we meet.

12 September, Wednesday, Twenty-Third Week in Ordinary Time
Luke 6:20-26

The beatitudes in today's gospel reading sound strange to our ears. Jesus declares blessed and happy the poor, the hungry and those who weep, whereas he declares unfortunate the rich and those who have their fill of everything. Those kind of sentiments seem to go against common sense. They jar with how we normally see life. That is true of a great deal of the teaching of Jesus. It forces us to rethink how we normally view life. Jesus proclaimed a God who wanted to show special favour to the distressed and vulnerable. This is why Jesus addresses this group as blessed, because God is with them and wants to change their situation. Our vulnerability creates an opening for God to work in our lives, whereas when all is well with us we can easily be self-satisfied and dispense with God. We know from our own experience that we often seek God with greater energy when our need is greater, whether it is our individual or communal need. We come before the Lord in our poverty, our hunger and our sadness because it is above all in those times that we realise that we are not self-sufficient. In Luke's Gospel, from which our reading is taken, as Jesus hung from the cross one of the criminals alongside him said, 'Jesus, remember me when you come into your kingdom'. To this poor, hungry, weeping man Jesus said, 'Today, you will be with me in paradise'. It is when we are at our weakest that the Lord's transforming and life-giving presence is at its strongest.

13 September, Thursday, Twenty-Third Week in Ordinary Time
Luke 6:27-38

The teaching of Jesus in today's gospel reading makes us sit up and take notice, because so much of it goes against the grain. It is out of step with what would be considered common sense, day-to-day wisdom. The teaching of Jesus in that reading ends with the exhortation, 'Give, and there will be gifts for you; a full measure …

will be poured into your lap'. In other words, it is in giving that we receive. The common wisdom is that it is in acquiring, in gathering, in taking, that we receive, whereas in giving we lose out. Yet, Jesus' own life bears out the truth of the paradox of his teaching. It was in giving that he received; it was in laying down his life for us that he gained eternal life for himself and for all who believe in him; his giving was life-giving for himself and for others. His way of finding life through death, of receiving through giving, is the way he holds out to all of us, his followers. When we give of ourselves to the Lord, present in others, we discover that we receive from the Lord much more than we give to him. When we die to ourselves so that others may live, we ourselves become more alive; we come to share more fully in the Lord's own risen life. The gospel reading suggests that our self-giving can take many forms. It might mean being compassionate towards others, being slow to judge others, refusing to condemn others, showing love to those who show little love to us, praying for those who treat us badly. This form of self-giving is visible in the life of Jesus. He healed the ear of the person who came to arrest him; he prayed for those who crucified him; he washed the feet of the man who betrayed him. In giving of himself in this way, Jesus was revealing God. When this kind of self-giving is visible in our own lives, we too will be revealing God.

14 September, Friday, The Exaltation of the Holy Cross
John 3:13-17

The words 'triumph' and 'cross' don't normally belong together. Yet, as Christians, we don't find the phrase 'triumph of the cross' in any way strange. When we look on the cross of Jesus with the eyes of faith, we don't simply see the tragic ending of a good man's life. We behold what Paul called the power and wisdom of God, the power of a love greater than any human love, the love spoken about in today's gospel reading. 'God so loved the world that he gave his only Son'.

Our own capacity to love is very influenced by the extent to which our love is returned. It is not so with God. On the cross, Jesus revealed a love so powerful that that it embraced even those who brought about his death. The love that burst forth from the hill of Golgotha 2,000 years ago continues to flow into all of our lives. The Eucharist that we celebrate makes this love present to us in a special way. God so loves the world that he continues to give us his Son in the Eucharist. Not only are we the beneficiaries of the triumph of God's love on Calvary, the triumph of the cross, but our own lives can reveal to others the triumph of the cross. The triumph of the cross shows itself in all kinds of simple ways, in the tolerance and humour we show to each other against all the odds, in the willingness to let go of old hurts, in the bearing of terminal illness with patience and dignity, in the fidelity to significant commitments when they become costly, in the loving service that endures even when it is not appreciated. We pray on this feast that the triumph of the cross would continue to take flesh in all of our lives.

15 September, Saturday, Our Lady of Sorrows

Luke 2:33-35

We are all very interdependent. What affects one person can impact on many others. This is especially true within a family. When one family member suffers in some way, every family member is affected. If we are close to someone in love, the pain and struggle of the loved one becomes our pain and struggle. In today's gospel reading, Simeon announces that Mary's child, whom she has just brought into the Temple, will become a source of division. Some will accept him and 'rise'; others will reject him and 'fall'. His presence will be divisive and those who reject him will bring him much suffering. Mary as the mother of this child cannot escape his dark destiny. A sword will pierce her own soul too. She was the closest human being to Jesus and, inevitably, what happened to him would impact on her. Her sorrow reached its pinnacle as she stood by the cross and watched her son dying a painful death. Perhaps there is no sorrow greater than that of a mother who loses a son or daughter at the prime of their lives. Today's feast of Mary brings her very close to us. It reminds us that she entered into the depths of human pain and suffering. The greatest saint of all time, the one who was closer to Jesus than any other human being, travelled the way of the cross. Our own relationship with Jesus does not preserve us from life's sorrows and pains, no more than it preserved Mary. Yet we can be assured that as she went on to experience her son as Risen Lord and the outpouring of the Spirit at Pentecost, we too will be sustained by the Risen Lord and his Spirit on our own way of the cross.

17 September, Monday, Twenty-Fourth Week in Ordinary Time
Luke 7:1-10

The centurion in today's gospel comes across as an exemplary character. As a man of some means he had servants, one of whom was seriously ill. He clearly had a personal, indeed, loving relationship with this servant; he would do all he could to help his servant. This pagan was also very generous towards the Jewish people among whom he lived. We learn that he built the local synagogue in Capernaum. He evidently had a very positive view of the Jewish religion. He also had a very striking relationship with Jesus. Although the centurion was a respected figure in the community and was a man of authority, he did not consider himself worthy to have Jewish, a Jew, visit his pagan household. Although he was the social superior of others, the centurion considered himself Jesus' inferior, 'I am not worthy...'. He also displayed an extraordinary faith and trust in the power of Jesus' word. He believed that Jesus could heal his servant at a distance by means of his word, without having to come and lay his hands on his servant, the normal mode of healing. This pagan military officer is in many respects a very attractive figure. It is no surprise that Jesus says that he had never come across such faith even in Israel. We can all learn something from this man, from his kindness to others, his respect for the Jewish faith and his faith in the power of Jesus' word. It is perhaps only fitting that a version of the words of such an exemplary character should now form part of the text of our Eucharist, 'Lord, I am not worthy...'.

18 September, Tuesday, Twenty-Fourth Week in Ordinary Time
Luke 7:11-17

It has been remarked that at the beginning of this gospel story a parade of life meets with a parade of death. Jesus, accompanied by his disciples and a great number of other people, approaches the gate of the town of Nain. Coming in the opposite direction is a dead man being carried out for burial, the only son of his widowed mother, surrounded by a considerable number of the people of Nain. When these two very different processions meet, something extraordinary happens. Without waiting to be asked to do anything, Jesus, filled with compassion for the widowed mother, restores life to the young man and gives him back to his mother. The parade of death becomes a parade of joy with people praising God for visiting his people through the person of Jesus. The gospel reading reminds us that Jesus has entered our world as a life-giver. In the words of the great prayer of Zechariah, the father of John the Baptist, Jesus reveals the tender mercy of God by giving light to those who sit in darkness and in the shadow of death. The same Risen Lord stands among us as light in our darkness and as life in our death. Whenever we find ourselves as part of some parade of death, we can be assured that the Lord of life is drawing near to us, even if he has not been called upon. He comes to bring us life so that we in turn can be life-givers in our world. The Lord who visits us at the head of a parade of life, sends us out as his messengers of life to enhance and protect life in all its forms.

19 September, Wednesday, Twenty-Fourth Week in Ordinary Time
Luke 7:31-35

Jesus uses a very striking image in this gospel reading to describe the reaction of the people of his generation to his ministry and that of John the Baptist. They are like children who refuse to dance when other children in the playground play the pipes; they are also like children refuse to cry when other children in the playground sing dirges. Jesus identifies himself with the children who play the pipes and John with the children who sing dirges. It is striking that Jesus speaks of himself in terms of children who play pipes for other children to dance. It is interesting to think of Jesus as a piper who plays a tune that invites people to dance to it. In a sense, that is what we are about as followers of Jesus. We are people who dance to Jesus' tune. We often use that phrase of dancing to someone's tune in our day-to-day conversation. The gospel reading suggests that, as followers of Jesus, we are people who try to attune ourselves to his rhythm, to his music, and then, having done so, to try and move in time with his music. In other words we are to allow the music that Jesus plays by his life, death and resurrection, the song that he sings, to shape our lives. That particular image suggests that attentive and ongoing listening is very important in our relationship with the Lord, because we can only move to music that we listen attentively to, and that, in some sense, has become part of us. Mary was an attentive listener to the Lord's word, and she, more than anyone, is the person whose life is in tune with the music of Jesus. Her own song, the Magnificat, is very much in keeping with the song of Jesus, the message and the life of Jesus. She is our model and our inspiration as we try to live in tune with Jesus' song.

20 September, Thursday, Twenty-Fourth Week in Ordinary Time
Luke 7:36-50

There are three characters in the story we have just heard, Simon who hosted the meal, Jesus his guest and a woman whom no one expected to turn up. We discover as we read through the story that Simon the host failed to show Jesus the usual signs of hospitality that would have been expected in that culture, a basin of water for the guest to wash his feet, a welcome kiss, an anointing of the head with oil. It was the uninvited guest, the woman whom Simon considered a sinner, who showed Jesus all these signs of hospitality in the most extravagant way imaginable. She behaved as the host should have behaved. She showed Jesus a love that the host had failed to show him. The little parable about the two debtors that Jesus speaks in the middle of the story explains why she showed Jesus more love than Simon had showed. She loved more because she had been forgiven more. Prior to this meal she had experienced the forgiveness of Jesus, the forgiveness of God in Jesus, and that had a transforming effect on her. Her experience of this gift of divine love made her a loving person. Simon, in contrast, had not experienced God's forgiving love through Jesus, probably because he had no sense of his need for it. Hence, he comes across as cold, distant, unloving. The story suggests that we are all equally in need of the Lord's forgiveness and to the extent that we recognise our need of the Lord's forgiveness and are open to receive it we will become loving people.

21 September, Friday, Saint Matthew, apostle and evangelist
Matthew 9:9-13
We have all had some experience of doctors. Sooner or later we all need them, because we all fall ill at some time or another. Doctors will never be short of work; their profession is recession proof. In the gospel reading today, Jesus uses a popular saying which, in a sense, states the obvious. He declares, 'It is not the healthy who need the doctor but the sick'. Jesus compares himself to the doctor whose interest is more in the sick than in the healthy. Jesus is declaring there that the real focus of his ministry is the broken rather than those who are whole. Who are the broken? They are all of us in one way or an-

other. We all struggle with brokenness in one shape or form. Yet, there is a fundamental difference between the average doctor and Jesus. When we are sick, we take the initiative to seek out the doctor; the doctor does not come after us. Jesus, however, takes the initiative in our regard; he comes after us. He took the initiative to call Matthew, the tax collector, the public sinner. He declares that he came to call, not on the virtuous, but sinners. The Lord seeks us out in our brokenness. He is seeking us out long before we ever think of seeking him out. Our calling is to respond to the Lord's initiative towards us, as Matthew did in the gospel reading. The Lord always takes the first step; he enters our lives, as he entered the life of Matthew. Our role is to respond to the Lord's initiative towards us, as generously as Matthew did.

22 September, Saturday, Twenty-Fourth Week in Ordinary Time
Luke 8:4-15

In the parable that Jesus preaches, when the sower sows the seed not all of it takes root and produces a crop. Indeed a great deal of it goes to waste. Only some found the right soil and went on to provide a harvest. The seed is vulnerable; there can be all kinds of forces working against it. The environment is not always supportive of the seed. The same could be said of our life of faith. The seed of faith that is sown in our hearts at baptism is vulnerable. The environment in which we live is not always supportive of our faith. Trials can come our way and shake our faith. The worries and riches and pleasures of life can choke it. We need to nurture the seed of faith that we have received. We have a part to play in providing the good soil that the seed needs. One element of such good soil is prayer, both our own personal prayer and the prayer of the community of believers. The reading equates the good soil with those who hear the word with a noble and generous heart and take it to themselves. That form of prayer, in particular, creates an environment that allows the seed of faith to grow. It is the prayer of real listening to the word of the Lord, the kind of listening that bears fruit in how we live and relate to others.

24 September, Monday, Twenty-Fifth Week in Ordinary Time
Luke 8:16-18

In today's gospel reading, Jesus tells us that a lamp is meant to be put on a lamp stand so that people may see the light when they come in; a lamp is not intended to be covered with a bowl. Jesus is suggesting that if the lamp of faith is lit in a human life, it is not meant to be hidden but to keep on shining and spread light. That lamp of faith was lit in our own lives at baptism. When we come of age we have the responsibility of keeping the light of faith, the light of the Lord, burning brightly so that it shines through a life that is shaped by our faith. On another occasion Jesus said, 'Let your light shine before others, so that they may see your good works and give glory to your Father in heaven'. The light that shone upon us at baptism is to shape how we live, our works. Today's gospel reading reminds me of a reflection by Marianne Williamson, 'We are all meant to shine, as children do. We are born to manifest the glory of God that is within us. It's not just in some of us: it's in everyone. And as we let our light shine, we unconsciously give other people permission to do the same. As we are liberated from our own fear, our presence automatically liberates others.' The conclusion of today's gospel reading reminds us that the more we give in terms of letting the light of our faith shine before others, the more we will receive from the Lord and the brighter the light of our faith will become, 'For anyone who has will be given more'.

25 September, Tuesday, Twenty-Fifth Week in Ordinary Time
Luke 8:19-21

The sense we get from today's gospel reading is that Jesus is distancing himself from his family of origin. His mother and brothers were outside the house in which he was present; they had been looking for him and, now, they wanted to see him. However, when word of their presence gets to Jesus, he does not go out to them in response to their desire. Rather, he redefines who his family now are. His new family are those who hear the word of God and keep it. Jesus had just spoken the parable of the sower, in which the seed that fell on good soil was identified as those who, 'When they hear the word (of God), hold it fast in an honest and good heart, and bear fruit with patient endurance'. It is such people who now constitute Jesus' true family. His mother and the other members of his blood family can become part of this new family to the extent that they too hear the word of God and keep it. In practice, that would mean for them to allow Jesus the freedom to do the work that God is asking him to do. We too are members of the new family Jesus came to form in so far as we allow God's word, as spoken by Jesus, to shape our lives. This is the work and journey of a lifetime. As long as we are faithful to this journey, in spite of our weaknesses, we too will be considered brothers and sisters of Jesus, sons and daughters of God.

26 September, Wednesday, Twenty-Fifth Week in Ordinary Time
Luke 9:1-6

When Jesus sent out the twelve in today's gospel reading it may strike us as strange that he told them to take nothing for the journey. I suspect that none of us would set out on a journey without taking with us what we think we need for the journey. Most of us feel the need to be prepared for every eventuality. We like to be independent, self-sufficient, in control of our journey. In the gospel reading, however, Jesus sends out his disciples in a very vulnerable state. They are to depend on others, rather than on themselves, trusting that they will be given hospitality when it is needed. They are, in a sense, to let go of the reins of control and hand control over to the Lord who will look after them in and through others. Although our own circumstances are very different from that of the twelve, there is a message here for all of us.

It is, perhaps, in those situations, on those journeys when we have to surrender control, that the Lord can provide for us in the most surprising ways. At the end of the day, we are not self-sufficient; we depend on the Lord for everything.

27 September, Thursday, Twenty-Fifth Week in Ordinary Time

Luke 9:7-9

In today's gospel reading, we hear that people had various views about who Jesus was. The three views that are mentioned all have one thing in common. Jesus is considered a prophet of the past come back to life, whether that be John the Baptist who had been recently executed, or Elijah or some other ancient prophet. This must have been how many people saw Jesus, as a prophet in the line of the prophets of old. It is how Muslims, and many Jews, continue to see Jesus today. He is a great prophet. Luke, from whose gospel the reading is taken, would acknowledge that there is some truth in this understanding of Jesus. Jesus stands in the tradition of those prophets who proclaimed God's word to God's people. Yet, for Luke and for the early Church as a whole, there is more to Jesus than just one more prophet from God. The question of Herod Antipas in today's gospel reading, 'Who is this that I hear such reports about?' is a valid question. Shortly after this gospel passage, Luke gives us his account of the Transfiguration of Jesus, in the course of which, God says of Jesus, 'This is my Son, my Chosen'. This had never been said of any prophet. Jesus had a more intimate relationship with God than any of the prophets before him. God was more fully and powerfully present in Jesus than in any of the previous prophets. It is because we believe that Jesus is God's Son that we seek to listen even more attentively to his word and allow that word to shape our lives.

28 September, Friday, Twenty-Fifth Week in Ordinary Time
Luke 9:18-22

Jesus' question in today's gospel reading, 'Who do you say I am?', would have been answered in various ways by Jesus' contemporaries. Some of the answers given by people would not have been too complimentary. The answer Peter gives, 'You are the Christ of God', is very insightful. Peter was declaring that Jesus was the Messiah sent from God. Jesus was indeed God's anointed one, sent to usher in the longed for Messianic age. However, there were many different understandings of 'Messiah' in the time of Jesus. A common understanding was that the Messiah would be a glorious king who would militarily defeat Israel's enemies. Jesus was not going to be this kind of Messiah. That is why, in response to Peter's answer, Jesus declares that as Messiah, he is also the suffering Son of Man who would be rejected by the powerful within Israel and be put to death on a Roman cross. Here was a Messiah who would plumb the depths of human suffering. Yes, he would be glorious but only after he had trodden the path of suffering and an ignominious death. This was not the kind of Messiah people were expecting. Yet, in allowing his anointed one to suffer and die, God was showing us his solidarity with us in our own suffering. Jesus reveals God to be with us in our brokenness and suffering. God is not absent from the darkest experiences of our lives, but is at the very heart of them as our light and our strength.

29 September, Saturday, Saints Michael, Gabriel and Raphael
John 1:47-51

Three archangels are named in Scripture. Michael is the defender of the Church against Satan in the Book of Revelation; Gabriel is God's messenger to Mary, the mother of Jesus, in the Gospel of Luke; and Raphael heals the blindness of Tobit in the Book of Tobit. Each of these angelic figures in the Scriptures brings new life to others, whether in the form of proclaiming good news of great joy or healing or protecting from evil. They are messengers of the living God, the living God who wishes us to have life to the full. They point ahead to Jesus, the greatest messenger of God. The angels always point us to Jesus. If we stop at the angels and go no further, we have lost our bearings. In the gospel reading, Jesus speaks of himself as the Son of Man, on whom the angels of God are ascending and descending. This is a reference to the dream of Jacob, in the Book of Genesis. Jacob dreamt of a ladder reaching between heaven and earth with the angels of God ascending and descending on it. He realised upon waking that the place where he stood was the meeting place of heaven and earth. The image of the angels ascending and descending on the Son of Man suggests that Jesus is the meeting point of heaven and earth. This could not be said of any angel. Jesus is both of the earth and of heaven, fully human and fully divine. He is God in human form. The invitation that Philip gave to Nathanael in the gospel reading, 'Come and see', is given to each one of us by Jesus himself. He calls out to each of us to come to him, to journey towards him, and to see him as he really is, the one through whom God is fully present to us. As we come to him and see him, we are then sent out to witness to him with our lives.

1 October, Monday, Twenty-Sixth Week in Ordinary Time
Luke 9:46-50

Jesus' statement at the end of today's gospel reading is very generous in its embrace: 'Anyone who is not against you is for you'. Jesus was reminding John, one of the disciples, that even if someone was doing good without acknowledging the name of Jesus, there is still something to rejoice in. Good is being done and God's purpose for the world is being served. Jesus was prompting his disciples to recognise that God's gracious activity was not confined to their own circle. God can be working powerfully through those who do not see themselves as part of the family of the disciples. The sphere of God's activity is not confined to the community of those who explicitly acknowledge Jesus as Lord. The signs of the Spirit are to be found outside the Church as well as within it. We should rejoice in whatever good people do, whether or not they think of themselves as part of the family of Jesus' disciples. The grace of Jesus is effective outside the circle of disciples. God's power cannot be limited to the community of disciples. In the gospel reading, John saw those who were doing good work but were not part of the circle of disciples as competitors. Jesus was inviting John to see them as co-workers. As believers in the Lord we need to work with all people of goodwill for the healing of the broken and the freeing of the oppressed. As the fourth gospel reminds us, the Holy Spirit, like the wind, 'Blows where it chooses'.

2 October, Tuesday, The Guardian Angels
Matthew 18:1-5, 10
Devotion to the guardian angels has been part of popular piety within the Church from the earliest times. Such devotion already had a place in Judaism before the time of Jesus. Saint Basil the Great, one of the great theologians of the fourth century, taught that each and every member of the faithful has a guardian angel to protect, guide and guard them through life. There has been a great interest in angels in recent times, and religious bookshops are not short of popular books on angels. The danger is that the angels can come to be seen in isolation, rather than in terms of their relationship to God and to his Son, Jesus, and to God's people, the Church. In today's first reading, God sends an angel to guide his people and bring them to their destination. The angel is one of the ways that God is present to his people, both in the past and here and now. In the gospel reading, Jesus speaks about the angels of children who stand before the presence of God in heaven, pleading their cause before God. Angels are both close to God's people, as suggested by the first reading, and close to God, as suggested by Jesus in the gospel reading. They relate to God's people

as a whole, as suggested by the first reading, but also to each of us individually, as is clear from the gospel reading. The Catechism of the Catholic Church says, 'The whole life of the Church benefits from the mysterious and powerful help of angels.' It continues, 'From infancy to death, human life is surrounded by their watchful care and intercession ... Already here on earth the Christian shares by faith in the company of angels and people united in God'. Today's memorial is an opportunity to remind ourselves of these spiritual friends that God has given to us to support us on our shared journey of faith in this life.

3 October, Wednesday, Twenty-Sixth Week in Ordinary Time
Luke 9:57-62

In today's gospel reading, three people show their willingness to become followers of Jesus, physically walking with him wherever he leads. However, the first one seems to lack an awareness of what is involved. The other two claim they have some important duties to attend to first at home. You would have thought that burying one's father was indeed an important duty. However, the question implies that the man's father is still alive and he is asking to wait at home until his father dies so that he can bury him, whenever that might happen. Jesus' call to this man was too urgent for such an indefinite wait. Jesus does not prevent the other person from saying goodbye to his family but warns him that following him requires a clear focus, without constantly looking back over one's shoulder to what has been left behind. This is one of probably several gospel texts that can seem very challenging to our ears. Jesus seems to be so demanding. Yet, following him, becoming and remaining his disciple, whatever form it takes, in whatever age, is demanding. It is never going to be an easy or a soft option. Jesus does demand a level of allegiance to himself that is greater than the allegiance owed to family, even though it is not in any sense incompatible with our family allegiances. There may come a time when our fidelity to the values of the gospel will put us at odds with those closest to us. Today's gospel reading brings home to us that walking in the way of the Lord is a serious business.

4 October, Thursday, Twenty-Sixth Week in Ordinary Time
Luke 10:1-12

In the instructions that Jesus gives to the seventy-two in today's gospel reading, he tells them that regardless of the reception they receive from a particular town, they are to announce, 'The kingdom of God is very near to you'. If they are made welcome in a town, they are to make that announcement, but even if they are not made welcome, they are still to make that announcement. Jesus is saying that regardless of whether the gospel is well received or badly received, the kingdom of God remains very near to us. In other words, people may differ, but God remains the same. God remains powerfully present, his reign of love is close at hand, regardless of how the message of Jesus is received. It can be encouraging to remind ourselves of that, especially at times when the hunger for the Lord and for his word does not seem to be as deep or as prevalent as it once was. It is always good to remind ourselves that God was as much present on Good Friday as he was on Easter Sunday. God is powerfully at work when the gospel is being rejected as much as when it is being received. What matters is that the gospel is proclaimed.

5 October, Friday, Twenty-Sixth Week in Ordinary Time
Luke 10:13-16

In today's gospel reading, Jesus seems very frustrated with some of the towns of Galilee, Chorazin, Bethsaida and, even, Capernaum where Jesus engaged in a great deal of his ministry. He is exasperated that the response of many in these towns to him has been so ungenerous. They witnessed his deeds of power and, yet, were unmoved by what they saw. They heard his preaching and teaching and, yet, were unresponsive to what they heard. We might be tempted to ask, 'How could people be so resistant to all that Jesus said and did?' Yet, we are of the same flesh and blood as the people of those towns named by Jesus. We too can be unresponsive to the Lord who continues to speak and work among us. At the end of the gospel reading, Jesus identifies himself very closely with his disciples, 'Whoever listens to you, listens to me'. We are being reminded that the Lord continues to come to us in and through his followers, the community of his disciples, which we call the Church, just as he came in person to the people of Chorazin, Bethsaida and Capernaum. Yet, like them, we can be blind and deaf to his coming to us, his daily coming. The Lord may be as frustrated with us at times as he was with them. We need to keep our ears and our eyes open to the many ways the Lord speaks to us and moves among us, and then respond to his presence with that generosity of heart which many of his contemporaries lacked.

6 October, Saturday, Twenty-Sixth Week in Ordinary Time
Luke 10:17-24

We live in an age that values achievement and, when we achieve something worthwhile, we understandably experience a deep satisfaction and joy. At the beginning of today's gospel reading, the disciples were full of joy at having achieved something worthwhile. Jesus had sent them out on mission and their mission had been successful, 'Even the devils submit to us when we use your name'. Jesus acknowledges their achievement, 'I watched Satan fall like lightning from heaven' and he recognises the joy that it brings his disciples. Yet, at this moment of successful mission, Jesus reminds them of something even more important that is a source of an even deeper joy. 'Rejoice rather that your names are written in heaven.' It is their relationship with God and the eternal destiny that it promises which is to be the source of their joy. Their work will not always be successful, but their relationship with God will endure, if they want it to. Jesus is reminding us all that our work will pass, our various successes will pass, but God's relationship with us and ours with him will not pass away. Jesus goes on in that gospel reading to state that our relationship with God is nothing less than a sharing in Jesus' own intimate relationship with God. The Father and Son know and love each other intimately, and Jesus seeks to draw us into that intimate relationship with his Father. That is why he can declare to all of us that which he declares to his disciples at the end of the gospel reading, 'Happy are the eyes that see what you see'. It is this intimate relationship with God that is primary and the cause of our joy, not the success or otherwise of our work. It is from this relationship that our sharing in the Lord's work flows.

8 October, Monday, Twenty-Seventh Week in Ordinary Time
Luke 10:25-37
The question asked by the lawyer in the gospel reading, 'What must I do to inherit eternal life?', is a really important question. He knew the answer to his own question and, at the prompting of Jesus, he gave the answer from his own religious tradition. What he had to do to inherit eternal life was to love. To love God first with all his being, and then, inseparable from that first love, to love his neighbour as if the neighbour were his own self. That could have been the end of the conversation, but the lawyer had another question, 'Who is my neighbour?' If his first question was a really important one, his second question was a little problematic. In asking, 'Who is my neighbour?', he was implying that some people were not his neighbour. The parable Jesus told in response to his second question showed that every human being in need is a neighbour. The injured man in the story was presumably a Jew. Yet, the one who helped him was a Samaritan, the traditional enemy of the Jew. For the Samaritan, this Jew lying by the roadside was not an enemy but a neighbour because his need was desperate. The Samaritan loved this Jewish man into life by his self-giving actions. The Samaritan didn't ask the lawyer's question –

'Is this my neighbour?' – he simply got to work; he showed himself a neighbour to this broken man. At the end of the story Jesus tells the lawyer, 'Go and do likewise'. Here was the answer to the lawyer's question, 'What must I do?' Jesus is saying to him and to all of us, 'Go and be a neighbour to those who cross your path in life, whoever they are, whatever their race, religion or creed'. Those who are truly a neighbour don't ask, 'Who is my neighbour?'

9 October, Tuesday, Twenty-Seventh Week in Ordinary Time
Luke 10:38-42

There is a reading from the Book of Ecclesiastes that is often chosen for a funeral Mass. One of the lines in the reading speaks of a 'time to keep silence, and a time to speak'. One way of hearing today's gospel reading is that when Jesus entered the house of Martha and Mary it was a time to keep silence. Jesus, the Word of God, had something important to say. It was Mary who discerned the time correctly. She sat at the Lord's feet in silence and listened to him speaking. She showed Jesus the kind of hospitality he was seeking on this occasion, the hospitality of listening. Martha, in contrast, was unnecessarily anxious about providing a meal for Jesus. In frustration at not being helped by her sister, she rebuked Jesus for not caring sufficiently for her predicament. In response to Martha's accusing question, Jesus called her twice by her name, 'Martha, Martha', and suggested to her that on this occasion she had something to learn from her sister, rather than something to rebuke her for. We all need to discern the right time to be silent and the right time to speak. We can fuss over someone too much when a listening ear is called for. We can offer them the hospitality we think they need rather than the hospitality they want. The same is true of our relationship with the Lord. There are times when the Lord calls us to be silent in his presence. Our inclination to anxious activity can lead us to miss those times. Sometimes we too need to choose the better part, to listen to the Lord in prayer when that is what he is calling us to do.

10 October, Wednesday, Twenty-Seventh Week in Ordinary Time
Luke 11:1-4

In yesterday's gospel reading, Mary was commended for her prayerful listening to the word of the Lord. Jesus himself was a person of prayer, while leading a very active life. The gospels suggest that he often went away to a lonely place to pray. His own prayerfulness inspired his disciples with a desire to become people of prayer, like himself, 'Lord, teach us to pray'. The disciples seemed to recognise that if they were to pray they would need the Lord's help. Prayer is not just a human activity; it is the Lord's activity in us, through the Spirit. The disciples' request is, in itself, a valuable prayer, 'Lord teach us to pray', or to express that prayer in different words, 'Lord, help me to pray; Lord, pray within me'. The 'Our Father' has been rightly called the 'Lord's prayer' because it is a prayer that the Lord himself has given us. The prayer begins with a focus on God and on God's purposes for our lives and the world, and it then shifts to a focus on our primary needs as human beings and the Lord's disciples. There is a pattern there that is valid for all of our prayer. We attend first to God and to whatever God desires and then to our needs before God.

11 October, Thursday, Twenty-Seventh Week in Ordinary Time
Luke 11:5-13

This gospel reading opens with a story that is drawn from village life in Galilee. It concludes with a reference to family life within the village. A villager who finds he has nothing to offer an unexpected guest should be able to rely on a friend within the village to help him out in his need. A son who asks his father for food, whether it is bread, fish or an egg, can expect to be given what he asks for. In between these two little scenarios, Jesus gives an instruction based on both images, 'Ask, and it will be given to you...'. Jesus recognised that all of human life had the potential to speak to us about God. All of human experience spoke to Jesus of God's relationship with us and of our relationship with God. He appreciated what we might call today the sacramental quality of all of life. If someone in a small village can rely on a good friend to help him out in an emergency and if a son can rely on his father to feed him, how much more can we rely on God. Even the best of human loves are but a pale reflection of God's love. It is because of who God is that we can ask him with confidence for our needs, that we can search for God in the expectation of finding and that we can knock on God's door in the expectation of having it opened. What are we to ask for, what are we to seek, above all else? At the very end of the gospel reading, Jesus suggests that what we need to ask for and seek above all is the Holy Spirit. It is in and through the Spirit that we know ourselves to be enfolded by God's love and are empowered to share God's love with others.

12 October, Friday, Twenty-Seventh Week in Ordinary Time
Luke 11:15-26

We all know from our own experience how easy it is to misjudge people. We see someone doing something or not doing something and we draw certain conclusions. We subsequently discover that the conclusions we have drawn were very wide of the mark. Jesus was also misjudged. Some people came to certain conclusions about him which were very far from the truth. We find a particularly dramatic example of that in today's gospel reading. Some came to the conclusion that the power that was at work in Jesus was not the power of God but the power of Satan. It is hard to imagine a greater misjudgement than to call good evil. Some people were completely closed to all the good that was being done through Jesus. In contrast, Jesus was always open to the good that was present in the lives of others, even when they themselves were not very aware of it. When Peter said to Jesus by the Sea of Galilee, 'Depart from me, for I am a sinful man', Jesus replied,

'Do not be afraid, from now on it is people you will catch'. Jesus was alert to the traces of the Spirit in the lives of others. As his followers, we are called to have the same sensitivity to the traces of the Spirit in the lives of those around us. We are to be more attuned to the presence of goodness in others than to the presence of sin in them.

13 October, Saturday, Twenty-Seventh Week in Ordinary Time
Luke 11:27-28

In the prayer of Mary in Luke's Gospel, which we call the Magnificat, Mary announced that all generations would call her blessed. In today's gospel, we hear of one woman who declares Mary blessed, announcing to Jesus, 'Blessed the womb that bore you and the breasts you sucked!' This is one of several beatitudes in the gospels and one of only two directed at Mary in particular. Jesus responds to the woman's beatitude with his own beatitude, one which embraces his mother, but a much wider group as well, 'Blessed rather are those who hear the word of God and keep it'. Mary is the great example of someone who heard the word of God and kept it. Earlier in Luke's Gospel, at the hour of the annunciation, Mary surrendered herself to the word of Gabriel, the word of God, 'Let it be with me according to your word'. At the time of the visitation, Elizabeth pronounced her own beatitude over Mary that reflected Mary's response to God's word, 'Blessed is she who believed that there would be a fulfilment of what was spoken to her by the Lord'. Elisabeth declared Mary blessed not primarily because she is the physical mother of Jesus, but because of her faith, because she responded to God's word and lived by that word, kept that word, allowed that word to shape her life. Like Mary, we are all called to hear the word of God as proclaimed by Jesus and then to keep that word, to live by it. Insofar as we allow our lives to be shaped by God's word, we too will be declared blessed by Jesus, as Mary was.

15 October, Monday, Twenty-Eighth Week in Ordinary Time
Luke 11:29-32

In today's gospel reading, Jesus is exasperated with his contemporaries because they fail to take him seriously. They look for a sign from him, while being indifferent to all that he is offering them through his words and deeds. Jesus reminds his hearers that, in the Scriptures, the people of Nineveh took the prophet Jonah seriously and the Queen of the South took Solomon seriously. Yet, Jesus' own contemporaries do not take him seriously, even though, as Jesus says, 'There is something greater than Solomon here ... there is something greater than Jonah here'. Jesus is indeed greater than Jonah and all the other prophets of Israel; he is greater than Solomon and all the other wise people that appeared in Israel since Solomon. Jesus is the Son of God; he is God in human form. There is such a richness and depth to Jesus' identity that we never fully grasp him in this life. There is always more to Jesus than we can conceive. There is always something greater to him that we have not yet come to appreciate. In his letter to the Ephesians, Paul speaks about the love of Christ that surpasses knowledge, and yet he prays that we would come to know this love of Christ. This knowledge Paul prays for us to have is not just knowledge of the mind, but knowledge of the heart. We are always on a journey towards this knowing the love of Christ because it is always greater than we imagine.

16 October, Tuesday, Twenty-Eighth Week in Ordinary Time
Luke 11:37-41

The gospels, especially the Gospel of Luke, suggest that Jesus was often invited to people's table. He shared the table of his friends, like Mary and Martha. He shared the table of tax collectors, like Zacchaeus, much to the disgust of many. He also shared the table of those at the other end of the spectrum to tax collectors, the Pharisees who wanted to live their lives according to God's Law. This is the scenario in today's gospel reading. When Jesus was at the table of tax collectors and sinners, they found his presence a comfort. When Jesus was at the table of Pharisees, they often found his presence unsettling. In the gospel reading, Jesus does not follow the washing rituals that were so important to the Pharisees. Furthermore, he accuses his host and fellow guests of being more concerned with external cleanliness, the ritual cleansing of cups and plates, than with inner, moral cleanliness, which finds expression in almsgiving. Jesus suggests that his host and fellow guests had a somewhat skewed hierarchy of values. They gave too much attention to what was unimportant and too little attention to what was really important. This is a human failing and we are all prone to it in all sorts of ways. We all need to keep going back to the words and deeds of Jesus in order to keep rediscovering what is really important in God's eyes and what is less so.

17 October, Wednesday, Twenty-Eighth Week in Ordinary Time
Luke 11:42-46

Most of us find ourselves burdened from time to time. There is an inevitable burden that comes with living. Sometimes that burden can seem to weigh very heavily on us; at other times it is much lighter. However, we know that people can also burden us unnecessarily. The Lord calls on us to help carry each other's burdens, but the opposite can happen. In today's gospel reading, Jesus accuses the lawyers, the experts in the Jewish Law, of loading burdens on people that are unendurable, without moving a finger to lift them. They interpreted the Jewish Law in such a way that it had become a burden for people. Rather than a path to life, the Law had become another burden on an already burdened people. Jesus did not come to further burden those who were already burdened. Rather he called out to them, 'Come to me all you who are weary and are carrying heavy burdens, and I will give you rest.' He came to draw us into a loving relationship with God and thereby to empower us to live as God is calling us to live. The call of the gospel does make demands of us, but they are the demands of love. They are the demands of a loving Lord who wants us to have life and have it to the full and who gives us the gift of the Holy Spirit to enable us to respond to the challenging but life-giving call of the gospel.

18 October, Thursday, Saint Luke, evangelist

Luke 10:1-9

The Gospel of Luke, whose feast we celebrate today, could be termed the gospel of mercy. Luke portrays Jesus as the face of God's mercy, which is one of Pope Francis' favourite ways of referring to Jesus. Some of the most memorable passages of mercy are only to be found in Luke's Gospel, such as the story of the sinful woman anointing the feet of Jesus, the parable of the prodigal son, the parable of the Pharisee and the tax collector, the meeting of Jesus and Zacchaeus, the dialogue between the good thief and Jesus on the cross. It is above all in Luke that Jesus is portrayed as revealing the hospitable love of God to the broken in spirit or body. A symbol that has traditionally been associated with each of the four gospels, the symbol of Luke's Gospel is the ox. This is an animal that is capable of carrying heavy burdens. In Luke's Gospel, Jesus takes upon himself the burdens of others, especially the burden of sin which weighs heavily on a person's spirit. There is a saying of Jesus in Luke which is unique to this gospel and which sums up Luke's portrait of Jesus, 'The Son of Man came to seek out and to save the lost'. Today's gospel reading is also unique to Luke. It is only this gospel who gives us this passage of Jesus sending out seventy-two as labourers in God's harvest to proclaim in word and deed the message of the kingdom, the message of God's merciful and hospitable love. We all belong among that large group of seventy-two. If Jesus is the face of God's merciful love, he sends us all out to reveal something of that same face of God's mercy to all those we encounter in life.

19 October, Friday, Twenty-Eighth Week in Ordinary Time

Luke 12:1-7

In this gospel reading, Jesus draws a contrast between two different kinds of fear, one being a misplaced fear and the other a reasonable fear. His followers are not to fear those who can only kill the body, their opponents who seek their bodily harm. However, they are to have a salutary fear of God because it is not just our bodily well-being that lies in God's hands but our ultimate wellbeing, our salvation. Yet, Jesus immediately places alongside this salutary fear of God the need for a profound trust in God. If not even one sparrow is forgotten in God's sight, how much more will we, who are worth more than hundreds of sparrows, be lovingly remembered by God. Just as God is attentive to the details of his non-human creation, the tiniest bird of all, the sparrow, so God is attentive to the details of our lives. As Jesus says, 'Every hair on your head has been counted'. Jesus invites us to trust in God's loving provision for us. There has been a breakdown in trust at all kinds of levels in society and in the Church. The betrayal of trust has made us all less trusting of others. Yet, in reality, we cannot live our lives without some level of trust in others. In the gospel reading, Jesus declares that God is always worthy of our trust. Jesus entrusted himself into the hands of his loving Father both in life and in death; this gave him a wonderful freedom. He invites us to have the same trust in God our loving Father as he had.

20 October, Saturday, Twenty-Eighth Week in Ordinary Time

Luke 12:9-12

In today's gospel reading, Jesus speaks in the awareness that it will often be difficult for his followers to publicly acknowledge him. It will be tempting to hide their faith in Jesus, because to do otherwise may entail being dragged before synagogues and magistrates and authorities. Knowing that this scenario awaits them, Jesus speaks a word of encouragement to his disciples. He assures them that if they have the courage to publicly acknowledge him in the presence of others, then in the life of the kingdom he, Jesus, will publicly acknowledge them in the presence of the angels. He also assures them that in courageously bearing witness to him before others, they won't be left to their own resources. Rather, the Holy Spirit will be given to them and will teach them what they are to say in such hostile situations. These words of Jesus remain an encouragement to us today. We can be tempted to keep our faith very quiet, to keep a low profile when it comes to our relationship with the Lord. There is a subtle pressure in our society to push faith to the margins. We can be made to feel a little odd if we show ourselves to be people of faith in the Lord and his Church. Yet, the Lord needs us to publicly acknowledge him, just as he needed his first disciples to do the same. He asks us to be courageous in witnessing to our faith; he promises to publicly acknowledge us in eternity, if we publicly acknowledge him now. He also assures us of the help and inspiration of the Holy Spirit in our efforts to live our faith publicly.

22 October, Monday, Twenty-Ninth Week in Ordinary Time
Luke 12:13-21

The parable Jesus tells in today's gospel reading is the story of a man who sought to make his life secure by holding on to and enhancing what he owns. At the beginning of the story he is already a rich man; he has more than he needs. When he has an even bigger harvest than expected, his only problem is how to store this unexpected bonus. The answer he comes up with is to tear down his perfectly good barns and to build bigger ones. His preoccupation with storing his surplus blinds him to other more important considerations, such as, 'What might God be asking me to do with my surplus?' 'How can I serve others with this surplus?' He was looking for security in the wrong place. He thought that a greater abundance of possessions would make his life more secure. However, death came to him in the midst of his abundance; his life could not be secured in the way he thought. Jesus is saying to us that what makes our life really secure is making ourselves rich in the sight of God. We become rich in the sight of God by recognising that all we have is ultimately a gift from God to be shared with others. God graces us so that we in turn can grace others. If we make ourselves rich in the sight of God by living generously out of the abundance that God has given us, then our lives will be truly secure with a security that endures beyond this earthly life into eternity.

23 October, Tuesday, Twenty-Ninth Week in Ordinary Time
Luke 12:35-38

In the parable that Jesus speaks in today's gospel reading, we have the very unusual image of the master of a household putting on an apron, sitting his slaves down at table and then waiting on them. The kind of picture Jesus was painting there had no place in the culture in which he and his disciples lived. Yet, the picture in the parable that Jesus speaks there does put us in mind of the scene in John's Gospel where Jesus puts a towel around himself and washes the feet of his disciples. The Lord, it seems, wants to serve us; the Lord wants to be our servant. Normally, the role of lord and the role of servant are at opposite ends of a spectrum, but in Jesus they are combined. In the parable Jesus tells in today's gospel reading, the master's service is in response to his servants' faithfulness and vigilance. The lord who serves us looks to us to be faithful and vigilant, so that we are ready to open the door as soon as he comes and knocks. We are reminded of that saying of the Risen Lord in the Book of Revelation, 'Behold, I stand at the door and knock'. The Lord is always knocking at the door of our lives; he comes and knocks every day. If we respond to his daily coming, today's gospel reading assures us that he will be our servant in ways that will surprise us.

24 October, Wednesday, Twenty-Ninth Week in Ordinary Time
Luke 12:39-48

In the second image in today's gospel reading, Jesus speaks of the faithful and wise steward who remains loyal to the task given to him by his master and is steadfastly working away at it when the master returns after being away on a journey. We are all called to be faithful and wise stewards in that same sense. We are to remain faithful to our calling, to our task of living the gospel day in and day out. Faithfulness was what characterised the ministry of Jesus. He was faithful to the work that God gave him to do, even though it meant his crucifixion. He was faithful to the disciples he had chosen, even though they let him down and abandoned him when he most needed them. According to Luke in his gospel, he was faithful even to his enemies, healing the ear of one of those who came to arrest him and praying on the cross for those responsible for his crucifixion. In a variety of ways, Jesus showed himself to be the Faithful One. His faithfulness can inspire and empower something of the same level of faithfulness in us. Like Paul, we want to be able to say at the end of our lives, 'I have fought the good fight, I have finished the race, I have kept the faith'.

25 October, Thursday, Twenty-Ninth Week in Ordinary Time
Luke 12:49-53

At the beginning of today's gospel reading, Jesus speaks in the language of metaphor. He uses two different metaphors (or images). He first declares that he has come to bring fire to the earth. Earlier in Luke's Gospel, John the Baptist had announced that Jesus would baptise with the Holy Spirit and fire. The fire that Jesus came to bring to the earth is the fire of the Holy Spirit, the same Spirit that would come down on his disciples in the form of tongues of fire at Pentecost. The language of fire for the Spirit suggests that the Spirit has a twofold role in our lives. Like fire, the Spirit brings warmth and light, the warmth and light of God's love. Saint Paul in his letter to the Romans says that, 'God's love has been poured into our hearts through the Holy Spirit'. Like fire, the Holy Spirit can also mould and purify. The Holy Spirit at work in our lives purifies us of sin so as to mould us more fully into the image and likeness of Jesus. Using a second metaphor, Jesus says that there is a painful and distressing baptism he must receive before he can bring this fire of the Spirit to the earth. Jesus is referring here to his forthcoming passion and death into which he is soon to be plunged. The love that God pours into our hearts through the Spirit is the self-emptying love revealed by Jesus on the cross. It is the love of the servant who is prepared to die so that others may have life. The Holy Spirit at work in our lives will always inspire us and empower us to love in the same self-giving and self-emptying way that Jesus loved.

26 October, Friday, Twenty-Ninth Week in Ordinary Time
Luke 12:54-59

In the gospel reading, Jesus suggests that it can often be better to settle a dispute with an opponent out of court than to end up in court and lose your case. Perhaps Jesus was aware that the court system of the time favoured those with status and money, and most of those he was speaking to were not in that category. Jesus is calling for an urgency in the settling of disputes; it is not always good to wait for the case to be brought to court. Why does Jesus draw attention to this aspect of human interaction? He is suggesting that the same kind of urgency is needed in the way people interact with himself. Many of Jesus' contemporaries were not taking him seriously. Jesus was saying that the time of his presence was a crucial time; it was a time to take seriously what he was saying and doing and to respond appropriately. Earlier in the gospel reading, he used another image, this time drawn from nature, to make the same point. His contemporaries know how to interpret the significance of the signs in nature for forecasting the weather, but they do not seem to know how to interpret the significance of Jesus' presence among them. The Lord is present to each one of us just as much as he was present to the people of Galilee. We too need a sense of urgency in responding to the Lord's presence, the Lord's call. We too need to be alert to the significance of the signs of his presence among us; we need to read the signs of his presence to us and act accordingly.

27 October, Saturday, Twenty-Ninth Week in Ordinary Time
Luke 13:1-9

In his letter to the Galatians, Paul speaks of patience as one expression of the fruit of the Spirit. We live in a somewhat impatient age; speed is highly valued. There can be pressure on us all to travel at a fast pace. There can be a tendency to want immediately what people were prepared to wait for patiently in the past. Patience can be a more difficult virtue to cultivate in an age like our own than it might have been in the past. Yet, we all know from experience that some things cannot be rushed. People move at different paces at all kinds of levels and we need to be patient with each other. We know that growth in nature can be forced under certain conditions, but, nonetheless, nature too has its own pace, just like people. In the parable that Jesus told in today's gospel, a tree that refused to bear fruit for three years met with two very different responses. The response of the vineyard owner was an impatient response, 'Cut it down'. The response of the gardener showed great patience, 'Leave it one more year'. It is likely that Jesus saw more of himself in the gardener than in the vineyard owner. Jesus could be impatient with the self-satisfied, but he was always patient with those who were struggling, like the tree in the parable. He is patient with us in our weakness; he gives us time. He hopes that we will make the most of the time and the opportunity which his patience gives us.

29 October, Monday, Thirtieth Week in Ordinary Time

Luke 13:10-17

There are several stories about women in the Gospel of Luke that are not to be found in any of the other gospels, and the gospel reading today is one of those stories. Jesus touches the life of a woman who had been bent over for eighteen years and he enables her to stand up straight again. There is an image here of the whole of Jesus' ministry. He works to release people from whatever burden is oppressing them, and he enables them to stand straight again. When Jesus released this woman from the burden that had weighed upon her for so many years, her immediate response was to glorify God. The Lord is constantly at work in our own lives, calling out to us when we are burdened to come to him. He came to help us carry our burdens so that we can experience his liberating love and glorify God for it, as the woman did. There was really something to rejoice over in what Jesus did in the synagogue on that Sabbath day. At the end of that reading, Luke tells us that all the people were overjoyed. This is the joy of the Christian life, the joy that is generated by the Lord's liberating and life-giving presence among us and within us. Yet, there was someone who tried to spoil this moment of liberation and joy. The synagogue official was indignant. Indignation is at the other end of the spectrum to joy. Why was he so angry? In his eyes, Jesus was breaking the law. The official was so zealous for God's law that he failed to see God at work outside the law. God is always so much bigger than law, including religious law. The gospel reading reminds us that we need a heart that is open to the surprising movements of the Spirit of God in others and in our world. Otherwise, we risk losing out on the joy of the gospel.

30 October, Tuesday, Thirtieth Week in Ordinary Time

Luke 13:18-21

In using the image of the mustard seed in the soil, and the image of the leaven in three measures of flour for the kingdom of God, Jesus is suggesting that the kingdom of God, the goodness of God, can often be present in small and insignificant ways in people's lives. Those looking at soil might never suspect that a mustard seed is hidden there; those looking at three measures of flour might never suspect that leaven is hidden there. Yet, the mustard seed in the soil can transform the garden and the leaven in the flour can transform the dough. We can miss the little signs of God's presence, of God's goodness in ourselves and in others. Deep within our nature God has planted the seed of God's life that can grow in surprising ways; deep within our hearts God has placed the yeast of grace that has the potential to transform us into the image of Jesus. We need to keep reminding ourselves of this good news, especially in times of failure, when we may not be living as the Lord is calling us to live. Even at those times when we look unpromising to ourselves and others, we still carry deep inside us a divine treasure whose power at work within us, as Paul reminds us, can do immeasurably more than all we might imagine.

31 October, Wednesday, Thirtieth Week in Ordinary Time
Luke 13:22-30

People in the gospel story often ask questions of Jesus. We find one such question in today's gospel reading. Someone asks Jesus, 'Sir, will only a few be saved?' Will the great banquet of eternal life be shared by only a few or by many? Jesus does not answer the question directly. In response to the question, he says something about God and something about ourselves. He declares that the hospitality of God is ample and generous. At the feast in the kingdom of God, people will be present from north, south, east and west. This is not a select gathering; it is not a meal for the chosen few. People from every corner of the earth will be there. Jesus' answer to the question, 'Will only a few be saved?' is 'no'. However, Jesus also insists that the wonderful hospitality of God is not to be taken for granted; it should not breed complacency. We have to strive to enter by the narrow door, which will require effort on our part. Furthermore, we can't just ramble up to God at a time that suits us, like the man in the parable who arrived at a house expecting to be let in when the owner and his family were all in bed with the door locked for the night. We need a greater sense of urgency than that. The effort we need to make, and the sense of urgency we need to have, however, does not make us anxious or fearful, because we know that God's table is large and God's heart is very hospitable, and the Lord is there to help us through the door if we turn to him in our poverty.

1 November, Thursday, Feast of All Saints

Matthew 5:1-12

It could be said that the feast of all saints is the feast of goodness. There is a line in Paul's letter to the Philippians to which I am often drawn. 'I am confident of this,' he says, 'that the one who began a good work among you will bring it to completion by the day of Jesus Christ'. God's good work began in the womb. There was a new beginning of that good work on the day of our baptism. That good work will only be brought to completion in eternity. Today we celebrate the feast of those people in whose lives God's good work was well on the way to completion before the end of their earthly lives. None of us will have become all that God desires us to be before our death. That is where the Church's teaching on Purgatory comes in. We tend to think of Purgatory, and indeed Heaven and Hell, as a place. However, beyond this earthly life, the categories of time and space no longer apply. Purgatory is a state rather than a place or a length of time. A state of purification, or transformation, awaits us beyond death, in order for us be fully conformed to the image and likeness of Jesus. This purifying, transforming work is not a punishment but the work of a loving God who brings to completion the good work that he has begun in us, so that we can become all that God intended us to be.

The saints are those who were completely open to God's transforming work in this life and who by the end of their earthly lives are as close to becoming the person God desires them to be as is possible this side of eternity. Some of these saints have been officially canonised by the Church. Many have not. There are many hidden saints among us today. Their influence for good in the Church and the world will never be appreciated this side of eternity. Today's first reading speaks of a huge number, impossible to count, of people from every nation, race, tribe and language standing in front of the throne and in front of the Lamb. Some of that huge number are likely to be here among us, as well as in heaven before God and his Son. We are all called to be among that huge number. The saints are not some elite. They are the baptised who have allowed the Lord to have his way in their lives. The beatitudes, which form today's gospel reading, are Jesus' self-portrait as well as his portrait of the saint, his faithful disciple. The qualities articulated in the various beatitudes find full expression in his life. Jesus calls on us to learn from him so that his qualities become ours and we grow more and more into his likeness. This growth towards sanctity is ultimately the work of the Spirit in our lives, with which we are called to cooperate. As we increasingly become the person of the beatitudes, the wonderful promises that Jesus makes at the end of each beatitude will begin to come to pass for us even in this earthly life.

2 November, Friday, Commemoration of All the Faithful Departed
Matthew 11:25-30

The feast of all souls is a day when we remember all our loved ones who have died. We all have people we want to remember and pray for today. Our praying for the dead is one of the ways that we give expression to our continuing communion with our loved ones who have died. We believe in the communion of saints, that deep spiritual bond between those who have reached the end of their earthly pilgrimage and those, like ourselves, who are still on that pilgrimage. Our deceased loved ones continue to relate to us and we continue to them, in a new and different way. Because of Jesus' death and resurrection, we believe that beyond death, our loved ones are being drawn into the risen life of Jesus. In the language of today's gospel reading, the Son who knows the Father intimately is now fully revealing the Father to them, and in coming to share in Jesus' own intimate relationship with God his Father, they are finding rest from all that burdened them in this life. For them, life has changed not ended, and our relationship with them has changed not ended. Their closer relationship with the Lord brings them closer to us in the Lord. Every year, the Church gives us this day, 2 November, to express our relationship with those we were close to in this life who have died. We pause this day to give thanks for their lives, to pray for them, and to ask them to pray for us.

3 November, Saturday, Thirtieth Week in Ordinary Time

Luke 14:1, 7-11

Jesus often reflects on some aspect of human experience to say something about our relationship with God. He recognised that all of human life, including the less noble elements, could speak to us of God. The aspect of human experience that Jesus notices and then highlights in today's gospel reading is the very human tendency to promote ourselves over others. What Jesus specifically notices at the meal to which he had been invited is the concern of his fellow-guests to pick out the places of honour at the banquet table. In the culture of Jesus' day, receiving honour from others was a high priority for people. In many respects that is still true today. However, Jesus goes on to declare that what really matters is the honour we receive from God and not the honour we receive from others. Who are those whom God will honour? According to Jesus in the gospel reading, it is the people who humble themselves who will be exalted or honoured by God. To humble ourselves is not to make little of ourselves. Rather, it is to serve others rather than ourselves, to empty ourselves in the service of others. Jesus is the supreme example of the one who humbled himself and was exalted by God. Jesus knew that if he emptied himself and humbled himself in the service of others, God would exalt him in God's time. We too can live with the same confident assurance.

5 November, Monday, Thirty First Week in Ordinary Time
Luke 14:12-14

The opening words of Jesus in today's gospel reading can seem a little strange to us, 'When you give a lunch or a dinner, do not invite your friends'. We know from the gospels that Jesus' friends invited him to their table and he accepted their invitation. He shared the table of his friends Mary, Martha and Lazarus. The last meal Jesus ate before he died, the last supper, was shared with his friends, those who had been closest to him during his ministry. Jesus certainly recognised the value of a meal among friends. However, in today's gospel reading, as a guest of a leading Pharisee with other Pharisees present at table, Jesus wanted to highlight another value. Jesus noticed that his host and fellow guests had the habit of inviting to their table only those who could give them something in return, such as their friends, family and rich neighbours. He calls on them to invite into their lives those who appear to have nothing to give in return. He is highlighting the value of a truly selfless form of giving. Some forms of giving can be ultimately self-serving. We can give with a view to getting. Not all giving is an expression of authentic love. Saint Paul, in his first letter to the Corinthians, declares that we can give away all our possessions and still not have love. Genuine love never asks the question, 'What is in it for me?' This is the love that Jesus revealed in his life and, above all, in his death; it is the love of God. In his letter to the Romans, Paul says that this is the kind of love that God wishes to pour into our hearts through the Holy Spirit.

5 November, Monday, All the Saints of Ireland

Luke 6:20-26

There is a very strange paradox at the heart of today's gospel reading for the feast of all the saints of Ireland. Jesus begins by declaring happy those who are afflicted in any way, the poor, the hungry, those who are weeping. That seems to fly in the face of the normal human way of looking at things. When we are afflicted in any of these ways, we generally consider ourselves to be very unfortunate. When we look back on such an experience we say to ourselves, 'That was a bad time in my life. Hopefully, things will improve'. Yet, from Jesus' perspective our affliction, our vulnerability, creates a space for God to act and to reverse our situation. The ultimate expression of this is the death and resurrection of Jesus. When Jesus was crucified, when he was at his most afflicted and most vulnerable, God raised him to new life. Our greatest struggles can open us to the God of life, and can create a space for God to act in a life-giving way. Paul knew this from his own experience; he spoke of God's power being made perfect in weakness. Jesus is not canonising poverty or misery. Elsewhere in Luke's Gospel, he insists that the rich should provide for the poor. He expected the promises he makes to the afflicted in these beatitudes to begin to come to pass in this earthly life. However, in today's gospel he insists that God certainly will provide for us in our poverty, in our affliction, in our weakness and vulnerability, if we are open to his presence. Many of our Irish saints whose feast we celebrate today experienced great affliction in their struggle to remain faithful to the gospel. Yet, they also knew the Lord's strength in their weakness, and the promises Jesus makes in the beatitudes of today's gospel reading are now coming to pass for them.

6 November, Tuesday, Thirty-First Week in Ordinary Time
Luke 14:15-24

In the gospels, especially in Luke's Gospel, Jesus is very often found at table. In today's gospel reading he is guest at a meal hosted by a leading Pharisee at which other Pharisees and experts in the Jewish law were present. One of the guests utters a beatitude, 'Happy the one who will be at the table in the kingdom of God'. In reply, Jesus speaks a parable. Whereas the beatitude refers to a great feast in the future, Jesus' parable is about a feast to which invitations have already gone out in the present. Jesus focuses people's attention from the future to the present. The invitations have already gone out. What is to be our response in the present? In the parable, people who had initially said 'yes' to the invitation turn it down just as the meal was ready to be served, 'Come along, everything is ready now'. They all get distracted by various worldly attachments, which are all good in themselves but are not the primary good. As a result of their refusal, a surprising invitation goes out to the kinds of people who would never get invited to anything. They have no strong attachments and are delighted to respond. The parable is a reminder to us to be attentive to the Lord's invitation in the present moment and not to allow the good things of this world to so absorb us that we are no longer free to respond to his invitation as it comes to us in the here and now of our daily lives.

7 November, Wednesday, Thirty-First Week in Ordinary Time
Luke 14:25-33

In the gospel reading today, Jesus tells two parables, the parable of the builder and the parable of the king marching to war. In both parables two men rush into some important enterprise without reflecting sufficiently on what they were about to undertake. Their action was not matched by a corresponding reflection and, so, they failed to complete what they began. Jesus seems to be suggesting that following him, becoming his disciple, requires us to be reflective as well as active, prayerfully reflective. We need to keep stepping back before setting out, or, in the language of the parables, we need to keep sitting down to prayerfully consider before launching forth. Following the Lord is not a casual affair, no more than building a tower should be for the builder or going to war should be for a king. We don't remain the Lord's disciple, we don't persevere on that road, without prayerful consideration. Such prayerful consideration can take many forms; it might mean asking the Lord for the wisdom and courage we need to take the right path, his path. It might mean prayerfully entrusting ourselves to the Lord with all our heart, in the conviction that we cannot follow him perseveringly without the resources he alone can provide.

8 November, Thursday, Thirty-First Week in Ordinary Time
Luke 14:25-33

At the beginning of today's gospel reading, Jesus is criticised by the experts in the Jewish Law for sharing table with sinners, those who were adjudged not to keep the Jewish Law, the Law of God. In reply to that criticism, Jesus speaks the two parables we have just heard, one which features a man and the other a woman. The actions of the two characters in the two stories seem a bit extravagant. Why would a shepherd abandon ninety-nine sheep, leaving them at risk, to go in search of one sheep that has strayed? Having found that sheep and carried him home on his shoulders, does it seem a little over the top to invite friends and neighbours to join in a celebratory meal? The same questions could be asked of the woman. Why spend the day searching for a lost coin that is of little value, and then entertain friends and neighbours to celebrate with her when she found it? The cost of entertaining was probably more than the value of the coin. If the actions of these characters seem a bit extravagant, it is because, in telling these stories, Jesus is really talking about the ways of God, which are extravagant by human standards. Jesus is saying that God's love for us is so strong, God's desire to be in communion with us is so great, that God seeks us out with great energy whenever we stray from him and end up lost. Then when we allow ourselves to be found by God, God's joy knows no bounds. This is the God Jesus revealed in his style of eating, his way of life, and that he continues to reveal to us today.

9 November, Friday, Dedication of the Lateran Basilica
John 2:13-22

In the early fourth century, the first Christian emperor, Constantine, had a church built on land that once belonged to the Laterani family. That church of Constantine was the precursor of the present basilica. This basilica is now the cathedral church of the Diocese of Rome. It is the church of the Pope in his capacity as Bishop of Rome. For that reason, it has the title, 'Mother and head of all the churches of the world'. Every church building tells a story about the faith community who gather in the building. In that sense, today's feast is less about a church building and more about the people we call church. Paul's words to the Corinthians, in today's second reading, are addressed to every parish community: 'You are God's building', you are 'God's temple'. If for John, in the gospel reading, Jesus is the temple of God, where God is dwelling, for Paul, the local faith community is the temple of God, where God's Spirit is dwelling. The local parish church is most itself when it is filled with the people who are the Church, the baptised and believing community. Paul, in that second reading, reminds us that the foundation of the believing community is Jesus Christ. As individual believers and as a community of faith we are called to build our lives on the person of Jesus, by keeping his words and by remaining open to his Spirit. That is our shared baptismal calling. In attending to that calling we give meaning to the building in which we gather.

10 November, Saturday, Thirty-First Week in Ordinary Time
Luke 16:9-15

There is a statement in one of the letters attributed to Paul which declares that money is the root of all evil. In today's gospel reading, however, Jesus's concern is not about money in itself but rather about the use that money is put to. He declares, 'Use money, tainted as it is, to win you friends, and thus make sure that when it fails you, they will welcome you into the tents of eternity.' He uses the language of trust in relation to money. It is something that we are trusted with to use well, and if we show ourselves to be worthy of that trust, by using it well, then the day will come when we will be entrusted with genuine riches, the riches of eternal life. Jesus seems to be saying that, more important even than what we have, it is what we do with what we have that matters. Whatever resources that come our way, we are called upon to use them in the service of others. The gospel challenges us every day to use what we possess to benefit others, and what we possess includes not only our material possessions, but our gifts, our talents, our experience and our time. We all have something that can benefit someone else, if we are willing to give it away and to share it.

12 November, Monday, Thirty-Second Week in Ordinary Time
Luke 17:1-6

Many of us may be able to reflect on our lives and identify those who helped to nurture our faith. Our parents may come to mind, as well as teachers or what could be termed faith friends. We give thanks for all those people who helped to bring us closer to the Lord. At the beginning of today's gospel reading, Jesus draws attention to the negative effect that people can also have on the faith of others. He issues a strong warning to those who lead members of the community of faith astray by placing an obstacle in the way of their faith. We have had to live with scandals of various kinds within the Church in recent times.

Such scandals have been a feature of the Church's history since its earliest days, taking different forms at different times. No one can deny that the more recent scandals have undermined and weakened the faith of many. It is possible for any one of us to lead others astray, to undermine their faith in the Lord. This realisation may be behind the request of the disciples to Jesus towards the end of the gospel reading, 'Increase our faith'. It is a prayer we can all make our own. If we are to nurture the faith of others, rather become an obstacle to their faith, we need the Lord to keep increasing our own faith. Yet, Jesus' response to the prayer of the disciples suggests that we should never underestimate the power of even our little faith, faith the size of a mustard seed. If we keep seeking the Lord, even out of our little faith, then he will work powerfully through that little faith to build up the faith of others.

13 November, Tuesday, Thirty-Second Week in Ordinary Time
Luke 17:7-10

In the gospel reading, Jesus draws on an aspect of human interaction that we are not as familiar with today, at least in this part of the world, the master-slave relationship. Jesus recognised all of human life as having the potential to speak to us about our relationship with God. When a slave had done all that was expected of him, he would not expect thanks from his master, because he was only doing his duty. People were thanked for acting over and beyond what was expected of them. Jesus does not explicitly draw out a lesson from this little image or parable. We have to reflect on the image ourselves and listen to what it might be saying to us about our relationship with God. Jesus seems to be saying that when we live the life that he calls us to live, and empowers us to live through his Spirit, we should not expect God to thank us for it as if we were doing God a favour. To serve others in response to the call of Jesus is a privilege. It requires no further reward. Our service of others is a response to the more wonderful service that God has given to us through his Son. At the end of the day, it is we who need to thank God and not God who needs to thank us.

14 November, Wednesday, Thirty-Second Week in Ordinary Time
Luke 17:11-19

In today's gospel reading, ten lepers approached Jesus crying out to him, 'Jesus, Master! Take pity on us!' Jesus responded to their desperate plight and healed them of their leprosy. However, only one, a Samaritan, came back to praise God and to thank Jesus. The unexpected gift of good health distracted the other nine so that they forgot about Jesus and failed in the normal human courtesy of returning to thank him for their cure. Only one of the ten, a Samaritan, turned towards God present in Jesus in sickness and in health; the other nine turned towards him only in sickness and forgot about him in health. Sometimes God's greatest gifts to us can separate us from God. We can be so focused on the gift that we forget the source of the gift. It is only to the Samaritan that Jesus says, 'Your faith has saved you'. Whereas all ten received the gift of physical health, he alone received the gift of salvation, which is the fruit of faith, a relationship with God that is alive and vital in health as well as in sickness. It is the outsider, the despised Samaritan, who teaches us the importance of valuing God at all times in and through all his gifts.

15 November, Thursday, Thirty-Second Week in Ordinary Time
Luke 17:20-25

In the gospel reading, the Pharisees ask Jesus when the kingdom of God was to come, and Jesus replies that it is already here, 'You must know, the kingdom of God is among you'. The kingdom of God was already present in and through the ministry of Jesus, in his preaching and teaching, in his healing of the sick, in his seeking the lost and in his including the excluded. Jesus goes on to acknowledge that the kingdom of God has not yet fully arrived. That will only happen when, as he says, the day of the Son of Man comes, when the Lord comes again in glory at the end of time. However, in many respects this future is already present, even if not fully present; the coming rule of God is already at work in the here and now through Jesus, our Risen Lord. Jesus could teach us to pray, 'Father, thy kingdom come', while also declaring, 'The kingdom of God is at hand'. We all might be tempted to ask the question the Pharisees ask in the gospel reading, 'When will the kingdom of God come?' We are very aware that the world in which we live, with its various earthly kingdoms, is a long way from being the kingdom of God; we easily recognise that God's will is not being done on earth as it is in heaven. Yet, Jesus' response to the Pharisees' question invites us to be attentive to the signs of God's kingdom that are already among us. Wherever God's love, that filled the life of Jesus, finds some expression in any human life, there the kingdom of God is present. It is above all when we are tempted to become discouraged at the state of our world that we need to become more attuned to those signs of God's kingdom that are all around us.

16 November, Friday, Thirty-Second Week in Ordinary Time
Luke 17:26-37

Today's gospel reading speaks about the activities of eating and drinking, taking wives and husbands, buying and selling, planting and building. These will always be some of the main activities of any human life. Jesus reminds his listeners that, in the time of Noah, people were all engaged in these activities when, suddenly, disaster struck, the flood came and all these vitally important human activities seemed less important. On this basis Jesus warns his contemporaries not to become so absorbed by these very human and necessary activities that when he, the Son of Man, comes at the end of time, they will be unprepared for his coming and caught off guard. Jesus is reminding us that we need to keep a proper sense of perspective. The activities of life can be so absorbing and so wonderful in many ways that they can become an end in themselves. There is a deeper dimension to these activities which we can miss. The Lord who comes at the end of time is present to us in and through all of our daily activities. The Lord is present in all things. We need that contemplative approach to life which allows us to recognise the Lord present to us in all our activities. The Word became flesh and dwelt among us. We encounter the Lord in and through the flesh of life. If we are open to his presence at the heart of life, then his coming to us at the end of time or at the end of our own earthly time will not take us by surprise.

17 November, Saturday, Thirty-Second Week in Ordinary Time
Luke 18:1-8

The situation that Jesus depicts in today's parable is one that will always have a contemporary ring to it. A woman without status looks for justice from a powerful figure whose responsibility it is to see that justice is done, and, yet, for long periods her legitimate pleas for justice go unheard. A vulnerable individual finds herself up against a powerful institution and, even though she has right on her side, she is ignored. Such a scenario can be found in every age. Yet, this story ends up having an unexpected ending. The powerless woman turns out to be powerful after all; the powerful judge becomes powerless before the woman's persistent plea. In his comment on the parable, Jesus emphasises that God is not like the judge in the story. The judge neither feared God nor respected people. God, in contrast, is a God of justice who, at the end of the day, will ensure that those who are deprived of justice will receive it. If the widow never lost heart even though she was up against an unjust judge, then surely we need not lose heart before the God, whom Jesus reveals. Surely we can be faithful and persevering in our pleas, our prayers, to the Father of Jesus who is also our Father. Yet, the question Jesus asks at the end of the gospel reading raises the possibility that we may not be as faithful and persevering as the widow was, 'When the Son of Man comes, will he find any faith on earth?' Jesus implies that faith, if it is to endure, must find expression in continual and persevering prayer.

19 November, Monday, Thirty-Third Week in Ordinary Time
Luke 18:35-43

We find a character in today's gospel reading who cries out to Jesus for mercy, 'Son of David, have mercy on me'. He had become blind and he wanted to see again and he looked to Jesus as the one who could restore his sight. The mercy that Jesus showed to others could take many forms, restoring the sight of the blind being one expression of his mercy. Most of us may have the gift of physical sight, even if many of us have to wear glasses, but we cannot but be aware of areas of blindness in our own lives. We often see only what we want to see or what our culture has conditioned us to see. We too can make our own the prayer of the man sitting by the road into Jericho, 'Lord, have mercy on me. Let me see again'. The man's cry for mercy was belittled by the crowd who were going ahead of Jesus. They tried to silence him; they made light of his desire to live a fuller life, to be a recipient of the Lord's mercy. When we try to open ourselves more fully to the Lord's work of mercy in our lives, we too can find ourselves somewhat isolated in our efforts. Yet, the Lord takes our desire seriously even if others do not, just as he insisted that the blind man be brought to him despite the objection of the crowd. When the man cried out, 'Jesus stopped'. Jesus stops for us all. He can heal our blindness if we truly seek him out. His mercy is there for the asking. The blind man shows us not only how to seek the Lord's mercy but how to respond after receiving it. 'He followed him, praising God'.

20 November, Tuesday, Thirty-Third Week in Ordinary Time
Luke 19:1-10

Zacchaeus had a lot going for him. He was wealthy; he had a respon-sible job, a chief tax collector. He probably had a fine house by the standards of the time. Yet, there was a kind of restlessness about him. He was searching for something more. He had heard about Jesus and when Jesus came to his home city of Jericho he literally went out on a limb to see him, climbing a sycamore tree. This would have been considered a very undignified way for someone of his standing to behave. He was used to being dismissed by others as a 'sinner'. Yet, there was a great deal more to him than that. He may not have been a saint but he wasn't satisfied with where he was in his life. As he went searching for Jesus, he discovered that Jesus was searching for him. Once Zacchaeus put himself in the way of meeting Jesus by climbing that tree, Jesus addressed him by name, invited himself to Zacchaeus' house and declared that he had come to seek out and to save the lost – people like Zacchaeus. There is something of Zacchaeus in all of us. We are seekers; we are aware of some kind restlessness of spirit within us. Only the Lord can respond to that restlessness fully and today's gospel reading reminds us that he seeks us out even before we begin to seek for him. He is always coming towards us, calling us by name, asking to be admitted to our table, into our hearts. His love for us is prior to our love for him and it remains constant even when our love for him grows cold.

21 November, Wednesday, Presentation of the Blessed Virgin Mary
Matthew 12:46-50

When we hear the word 'presentation' in a religious context, we tend to think of the presentation of Jesus in the Temple of Jerusalem, the fourth joyful mystery of the Rosary. The Church celebrates the feast of the presentation of Jesus on 2 February. The Church also celebrates the memorial of the presentation of Mary, on this day, 21 November. This memorial has been kept in the Church since at least the eight century. It commemorates the consecration of Mary's life to God. In the first reading today, God calls on the city of Jerusalem, the daughter of Zion, to sing and rejoice because he is coming to dwell in the midst of them. These are words that could easily be addressed to Mary. She too can sing and rejoice because the Lord came to dwell in the midst of her, in her womb. Indeed, according to Luke's Gospel, she did sing and rejoice in response to this good news, in her prayer that has come to be known as the Magnificat. We too can sing and rejoice that the Lord has come to dwell within Mary, because through the Lord's dwelling within her, he has come to dwell in the midst of us all. It is through Mary that God became Emmanuel, God with us. The Lord was able to dwell within Mary because, in the words of the gospel reading, she was someone who did the will of God the Father in heaven. She was completely given over to doing God's will, to allowing God to do his will in and through her. This is the aspect of Mary's life we are celebrating today, her giving over of herself to God and to God's purposes. Through Mary, God has come to dwell among us in the person of Jesus, now Risen Lord. Mary shows us how to respond to that wonderful initiative of God towards us. Like her, we are to give ourselves over to doing God our Father's will, as that will has been revealed to us by Jesus.

22 November, Thursday, Thirty-Third Week in Ordinary Time
Luke 19:41-44

At the beginning of his ministry, Jesus announced that God was powerfully reigning in and through his ministry, 'The kingdom of God is at hand'. God's life-giving power was at work through Jesus for the healing of the sick, for the forgiving of sinners, for the inclusion of the excluded and for the accepting of the rejected. Yet, today's gospel reading reminds us that there were limits to this power of God working through Jesus. Jesus weeps over the city of Jerusalem because its people, especially its leaders, did not recognise the opportunity God was offering everyone in and through the person of Jesus. For all his power, Jesus was powerless before their refusal to recognise that his coming was a visit from God. The power of Jesus was the power of love, the power of a divine love which is stronger than sin and death. All love, even divine love, must be freely received because it is in the nature of love to be a free gift. Jesus' tears speak volumes about the capacity of human freedom to reject the gift of God's unconditional love offered to us through his Son. The Lord's tears could be shed for any of us because we can all fail to recognise the opportunity when God offers it. Yet, the good news, the gospel, is that our failure need never have the last word because God's love revealed in Jesus is stronger than our failure and it endures in the face of it.

23 November, Friday, Thirty-Third Week in Ordinary Time

Luke 19:45-48

In today's gospel reading, Jesus, quoting one of the prophets, speaks of the Temple in Jerusalem as a 'house of prayer'. Prayer was to be the primary activity of the Temple. However, in Jesus' day, certain economic activities had become so important that they had gotten in the way of the Temple being a house of prayer for everyone, including non-Jews. Jesus is suggesting that the Temple had lost its way; it was no longer serving God's purpose but was at the service of various human purposes. We can all lose our way. We can all end up serving our own purpose rather than God's purpose. This can happen not only with individuals but with institutions, even institutions as sacred as the Temple in Jerusalem. Every so often we need to hear a prophetic voice calling us back to God's way. For us as Christians, the most authoritative prophetic voice is the voice of Jesus which we hear above all in the gospels. We need to keep returning to his voice, to his living word, as it comes to us through the Scriptures, so that we can live our lives in keeping with God's purpose. Every parish church, like the Temple in Jerusalem, is a house of prayer. It is above all in that setting that we can prayerfully listen to the word of the Lord addressed to each of us individually and to all of us as members of God's people, the Church.

24 November, Saturday, Thirty-Third Week in Ordinary Time
Luke 20:27-40

The Sadducees were a group within Judaism who did not believe in a life beyond death. The situation they present to Jesus was intended to make fun of the notion of rising to new life. In response to the Sadducees' caricature of the life beyond this earthly life, Jesus declares that life in the other world, what we call heaven, will be something so totally new that no earthly experience, such as multiple marriages, can compare with it. As Saint Paul declares, 'No eye has seen, nor ear heard, nor the human heart conceived, what God has prepared for those who love him.' In the gospel reading, Jesus speaks of God as the God of the living. Even though Abraham, Isaac and Jacob have died, God remains their God; God remains alive to them and they remain alive to God. The bond of love and faithfulness that God has with these three great patriarchs has not been broken by death. Jesus implies that God's love for us, God's faithfulness to us, also endures beyond this life. God continues to hold us in the embrace of his faithful love beyond death. Jesus believes in a God who keeps his promises to his faithful ones, even beyond this earthly life. All true human love is life-giving and God's love is supremely life-giving. God's love always works to bring new life out of our death. Elsewhere in the gospels, Jesus uses the image of the banquet for life in God's kingdom. It is an image which suggests that this life is one where all our deepest hungers and thirsts will be fully satisfied, especially our hunger and thirst for a love that is stronger than sin and death.

26 November, Monday, Thirty-Fourth Week in Ordinary Time
Luke 21:1-4

It is striking how many terms and phrases from the gospels and from the Scriptures as a whole have made their way into the English language. When a person is described as a good Samaritan, for example, we know exactly what is meant. Based on today's gospel reading, we sometimes hear reference to the widow's mite. We understand that to mean something small but truly valuable. The widow in today's gospel reading gave very little, but in relation to what she possessed she gave an enormous amount. Jesus declares that she put in all she had to live on. In giving a little, she, in reality, gave her all. That could not be said of the rich people who put much more into the temple treasury than she did. They gave out of their abundance; she gave out of her poverty. Most people looking at what was happening would have said that those who gave the most were the most generous but Jesus knew that the poor widow was the most generous. If all we have to give is a little and yet we give that little than we are being truly generous. That is the case not just in the matter of giving money. Our physical condition can mean that our ability to give of ourselves can be very limited but we can still be extraordinarily generous. In giving a little we can be giving our all. Sometimes we can be hard on ourselves and say, 'I am not doing as much as I used to do or I am not giving as much as I used to give'. Yet the little we give now can mean more in the Lord's eyes than the great deal we used to give because that little may be our all. No one would have taken any notice of the widow if Jesus had not drawn attention to her. It is often the way that great generosity goes largely unnoticed because it is so ordinary, so seemingly small. The gospel reading suggests that the Lord notices.

27 November, Tuesday, Thirty-Fourth Week in Ordinary Time
Luke 21:5-11

In the time of Jesus, the Temple in Jerusalem that was built by King Herod the Great was considered one of the seven wonders of the world. In the gospel reading today, the disciples of Jesus, looking across at it from the Mount of Olives, talk among themselves about what a wonderful building the Temple is. Jesus, however, foresees a time when the Temple will no longer be present. As he says, 'Everything will be destroyed'. His words came to pass forty years later when the Romans destroyed Jerusalem and its Temple, in putting down the Jewish revolt against Rome. The statement 'everything will be destroyed' must have been difficult for the disciples to hear. It is difficult for us to hear today. We can be tempted to ask, 'Where is the good news in that statement?' 'How does it qualify as gospel?' In his first letter to the Corinthians, Paul expresses what Jesus states in a slightly different way, 'The present form of this world is passing away'. On that basis, Paul calls on the church in Corinth not to become overly absorbed in the things of this world. Rather, Paul would say, we are to absorb ourselves in the one who will never pass away, the Lord. If our relationship with the Lord, the one who never passes away, is central to our lives, then our relationship with the present form of the world which is destined to pass away will find its proper level. The Lord comes first for us; everything else is secondary, including the wonderful buildings that have been built in his honour. Even when these were to pass away, the Lord will endure, and that is good news.

28 November, Wednesday, Thirty-Fourth Week in Ordinary Time
Luke 21:12-19

Today's gospel reading is set shortly before Jesus enters into his passion. In this setting, Jesus speaks to his disciples about their own passion. He tells them that they will be seized and persecuted, handed over to the authorities and imprisoned, all because they bear the name of Jesus. Those words of Jesus have come to pass throughout the history of the Church. Indeed, people are being persecuted for their faith in Jesus today in huge numbers. Although we are not being persecuted for our faith here at home, it is more difficult to be a believer in today's world than in the more recent past. The social support is much less strong. In a sense, every Christian generation has its problems and difficulties. In the gospel reading, Jesus assures us that he himself will be with us when we find ourselves facing opposition and hostility and are tempted to discouragement. 'I myself will give you an eloquence and a wisdom that none of your opponents will be able to resist.' At such times we are not left to our own strength. Moreover, because the Lord is with us to support us, the trials and tribulations that come our way because of our faith are an opportunity for us to bear witness to our faith. Jesus declares, 'That will be your opportunity to bear witness'. We witness not in our own strength but in the strength the Lord gives us. Jesus goes on in that gospel reading to make a wonderful promise to all who are faithful to him during difficult times, 'Your endurance will win you your lives'.

29 November, Thursday, Thirty Fourth Week in Ordinary Time
Luke 21:20-28

Today we have another of those rather dark gospel readings that are typical of the concluding days of the liturgical year. Jesus depicts the disturbing scenario of the destruction of the city of Jerusalem with traumatic consequences for its inhabitants. We can think of cities that are being destroyed today, cities in parts of the Middle East. We are very aware of the suffering of their inhabitants at this time. We can be tempted to ask, 'Is there life beyond all this destruction?' In the gospel reading, the answer of Jesus to this question is a resounding 'yes'. He speaks of the coming of the Son of Man in the midst of so much destruction and upheaval. He will come with power and great glory announcing that liberation is at hand. Death and destruction does not have the last word in the Lord's purpose. He enters into the heart of every darkness with great power, always with a view to our ultimate liberation from all that diminishes and damages us. He has come so that we may have life and have it to the full. He sheds tears when we choose paths that bring destruction and death to those he loves. He is passionately committed to our present and ultimate well-being. He is constantly coming to bring this to pass, to bring to earth the kingdom of heaven. If this is to happen, he needs us all to welcome his coming into our own lives and to allow him to work through us in all his liberating power.

30 November, Friday, Saint Andrew, apostle

Matthew 4:18-22

Andrew is always listed second in the list of the twelve apostles, after his brother, Simon Peter. On this feast of Saint Andrew we hear the story of the call of Andrew along with his brother Simon Peter and another set of brothers, James and John. There is a great simplicity about the passage. Jesus saw the two brothers, Simon and Andrew, making a cast with their net in the Sea of Galilee, going about their daily work, and he called out to them, 'Follow me and I will make you fishers of people'. Immediately the two brothers left their nets and followed Jesus. The evangelist has perhaps streamlined an experience in the lives of these two brothers that, in reality, may have been a lot more complex. You would expect that there must have been some hesitation on their part before the call of Jesus, because it meant leaving what they were familiar with and good at, and heading out into the unknown. Becoming fishers of people, catching people, is a lot more challenging than catching fish. Gathering people into the net of God's kingdom, proclaimed by Jesus, is much more complicated than gathering fish into fishing nets. Yet, if there was hesitation in Andrew and Simon, they obviously overcame it; they threw in their lot with Jesus. They responded to his invitation, his call, and they went on to become great preachers of the gospel. The way the Lord works in our own lives is perhaps not all that different to the way he worked in the lives of Andrew and Simon. He often calls us out to us in the midst of our daily tasks. He frequently calls us beyond where we are, beyond the familiar, inviting us to take on some new task in the service of the coming of God's kingdom. That call can come to us in small and subtle ways. We may find ourselves resisting it, but if we attend to it and allow it to resonate within us, and if we then respond to it, we will often discover that the Lord works through us for good in ways that surprise us. The Lord can work powerfully through our willingness and generosity of spirit.

1 December, Saturday, Thirty Fourth Week in Ordinary Time
Luke 21:34-36

The call of Jesus in today's gospel reading is to 'watch' and to 'stay awake'. It is clear that Jesus is speaking of a spiritual state of watchfulness or wakefulness because he identifies staying away with 'praying at all times'. We might well ask, 'How can we pray at all times?' Surely the most we can expect of ourselves is to pray from time to time, maybe at set periods of the day. However, that call of Jesus is echoed by Saint Paul in what was almost certainly his earliest letter to have survived, dated to about twenty years after Jesus' death and resurrection. In his first letter to the Thessalonians, he calls on the Church to 'pray without ceasing'. Paul was well aware that believers could not spend all their time at prayer. Indeed, in the previous chapter of that letter, he called on believers to, 'Work with your hands, as we directed you'. The call of Jesus to pray at all times and of Paul to pray without ceasing must relate to an attitude of prayer that we bring to everything that we do. As we are engaged in our daily tasks we remain spiritually awake to the Lord who is present to us at all times. This could be termed a contemplative attitude to all of life. We live and move and have our being in the awareness of the Lord who is beside us and before us and behind us. If we are to develop this contemplative attitude, there needs to be some moments in our lives when we step back from all we do to give ourselves over completely to prayerful engagement with the Lord.

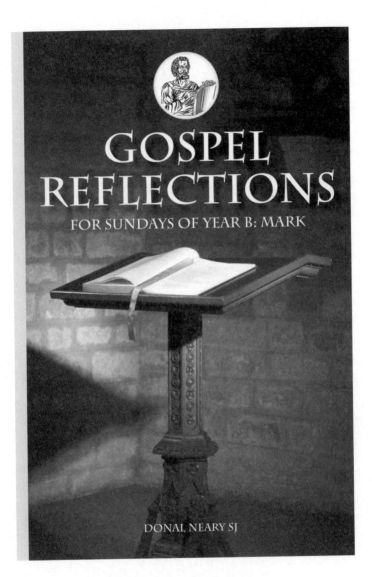

GOSPEL REFLECTIONS

FOR SUNDAYS OF YEAR B: MARK

DONAL NEARY SJ

www.messenger.ie

Email: sales@messenger.ie

Phone 353 1 6767491

The Prayer Book 2018

SACRED SPACE

THE IRISH JESUITS ✳ Sacred Space

from the website www.sacredspace.ie

www.messenger.ie

Email: sales@messenger.ie

Phone 353 1 6767491